A HOUSE
BUILT BY SLAVES

A HOUSE BUILT BY SLAVES

*African American Visitors
to the Lincoln White House*

Jonathan W. White

ROWMAN & LITTLEFIELD
Lanham • Boulder • New York • London

Published by Rowman & Littlefield
An imprint of The Rowman & Littlefield Publishing Group, Inc.
4501 Forbes Boulevard, Suite 200, Lanham, Maryland 20706
www.rowman.com

86-90 Paul Street, London EC2A 4NE

Distributed by NATIONAL BOOK NETWORK

British Library Cataloguing in Publication Information Available

Library of Congress Cataloging-in-Publication Data

Names: White, Jonathan W., 1979- author.
Title: A house built by slaves : African American visitors to the Lincoln White House / Jonathan W. White.
Other titles: African American visitors to the Lincoln White House
Description: Lanham : Rowman & Littlefield, [2022] | Includes bibliographical references and index. | Summary: "Jonathan White illuminates why Lincoln's then-unprecedented welcome of African
Americans to the White House transformed the trajectory of race relations in the United States. Drawing from an array of primary sources, White reveals how the Great Emancipator used the White House as the stage to empower Black voices in our country's most divisive era"— Provided by publisher.
Identifiers: LCCN 2021051090 (print) | LCCN 2021051091 (ebook) | ISBN 9781538161807 (cloth) | ISBN 9781538161814 (ebook) Subjects: LCSH: Lincoln, Abraham, 1809-1865—Relations with African Americans. | Lincoln, Abraham, 1809-1865—Views on slavery. | White House (Washington, D.C.)—History—19th century. |Hospitality—Washington (D.C.)—History—19th century. | United States—Race relations—Political aspects. | African Americans—Colonization—Africa. | African Americans—Social conditions—19th century. | Washington (D.C.)—History—Civil War, 1861-1865.
Classification: LCC E457.2 .W612 2022 (print) | LCC E457.2 (ebook) | DDC 973.7092—dc23/eng/20211020
LC record available at https://lccn.loc.gov/2021051090
LC ebook record available at https://lccn.loc.gov/2021051091

For Lewis Lehrman,
whose generosity has been instrumental in my career.

In all my interviews with Mr. Lincoln I was impressed with his entire freedom from popular prejudice against the colored race. He was the first great man that I talked with in the United States freely, who in no single instance reminded me of the difference between himself and myself, of the difference of color, and I thought that all the more remarkable because he came from a State where there were black laws. I account partially for his kindness to me because of the similarity with which I had fought my way up, we both starting at the lowest round of the ladder.

—Frederick Douglass

CONTENTS

ILLUSTRATIONS

PREFACE

"There Was No Color Line There"

In January 2021, the San Francisco Unified School District voted to rename Abraham Lincoln High School because of the former president's policies toward Native Americans and African Americans. According to Jeremiah Jeffries, chairman of the renaming committee and a first-grade teacher, "Lincoln, like the presidents before him and most after, did not show through policy or rhetoric that black lives ever mattered to them outside of human capital and as casualties of wealth building." Only a month earlier, a statue of Lincoln outside of San Francisco City Hall had been vandalized with red paint, presumably to symbolize the guilt the former president bears for his role in the nation's racial history.[1]

Statues of Lincoln had, in fact, come under fire in a number of cities in 2020 (as far away as London). In June, Delegate Eleanor Holmes Norton announced that she would introduce legislation in the US House of Representatives to remove the famous Freedmen's Memorial in Lincoln Park in Washington, DC, which Frederick Douglass had dedicated in 1876. Although the legislation died in committee, the statue had to be surrounded by fences and barricades during the long, hot summer of 2020 to protect it from being torn down by protestors. After the National Park Service removed the fences in October, two people drove an automobile into the statue's base on November 26. The car flipped over and the driver and passenger had to be rescued by police. In Boston, a replica of the "Emancipation Group" that had stood since 1879 was removed from its pedestal on December 29.

The statues in Boston and Washington were controversial because they depicted Lincoln towering above a former slave named Archer Alexander. To be sure, Frederick Douglass expressed misgivings about the statue's pose around the time of its unveiling.[2] Yet for many African Americans at the time, the statue represented the black community's appreciation for what Lincoln had accomplished during the Civil War. Moreover, as Douglass captured in the closing lines of his dedicatory remarks, they hoped it would be a permanent symbol of the connection between black freedom and Lincoln's legacy. "We have done good work for our race today," he said at the dedication in April 1876. "In doing honor to the memory of our friend and liberator, we are doing the highest honors to ourselves and those who come after us. We have been fastening ourselves to a name and fame imperishable and immortal." Douglass hoped that when future generations of white Americans disparaged their black neighbors, "we may calmly point to the monument we have this day erected to the memory of Abraham Lincoln."[3]

Of course, some black leaders—including Douglass—had been critical of Lincoln since the time of his presidency. Those critiques only increased during the twentieth century and into the twenty-first. W. E. B. Du Bois famously wrote in 1922, "Abraham Lincoln was a Southern poor white, of illegitimate birth, poorly educated and unusually ugly, awkward, ill-dressed. He liked smutty stories and was a politician down to his toes." In 1968, Lerone Bennett, editor of *Ebony* magazine, provocatively asked, "Was Abe Lincoln a white supremacist?" His answer was an unequivocal *yes*! For Bennett, Lincoln was "an opportunist," a "firm believer in white supremacy," and "no social revolutionary." Moreover, according to Bennett, Lincoln moved toward emancipation only "from necessity, not conviction."[4]

Bennett's views have gained currency in mainstream popular culture, as can be seen in the lyrics of popular hip-hop songs from the last thirty years. In 1991, Tupac Shakur echoed Bennett's rejection of Lincoln as a great emancipator, writing, "Honor a man that refused to respect us / Emancipation Proclamation? Please! / Lincoln just said that to save the nation." Several hip-hop artists have offered profanity-laced assessments of Lincoln. One rapper claimed, "the jig's up, the Constitution and Emancipation Proclamation's just a fuckin' piece of paper." Capturing the increasing prevalence of the self-emancipation thesis in American historical understanding, Nasir Jones recently rhymed, "Abe Lincoln did not free the enslaved, progress was made 'cause we forced the proclamation, fuck your proclamation."[5]

In August 2019, Nikole Hannah-Jones criticized Lincoln in her Pulitzer Prize-winning lead essay in the *New York Times*'s controversial 1619 Project. One of the primary pieces of evidence Hannah-Jones marshaled was a meeting Lincoln had at the White House with five black men in August 1862. The president condescendingly lectured his guests on why they should lead black Americans out of the country through a process known as colonization. Hannah-Jones holds this meeting out as exemplary of Lincoln's attitude toward African Americans. The implication is that Lincoln clearly treated black people as second-class citizens.[6] And yet, as this book will reveal, this infamous meeting is the exception that proves the rule. When Lincoln met with African Americans—whether enslaved or free—he treated them with dignity and respect. As Frederick Douglass was so proud to say, Lincoln welcomed him at the White House "just as you have seen one gentleman receive another!"

Lincoln's White House became a site of significant transformations in the history of race in America. Perhaps most importantly, it was the place where he signed the Emancipation Proclamation on January 1, 1863. Lincoln famously said that day, "If my name ever goes into history it will be for this act, and my whole soul is in it." On another occasion, he called the proclamation "the central act of my administration, and the greatest event of the nineteenth century." Even one of Lincoln's harshest black critics, H. Ford Douglas, had to acknowledge that "by one simple act of Justice to the slave" Lincoln "links his memory with immortality."[7]

A huge celebration took place on January 1 outside of the Executive Mansion. "Men squealed, women fainted, dogs barked, white and colored people shook hands, songs were sung, and by this time cannons began to fire," recalled Henry McNeal Turner, an African Methodist Episcopal minister who was present at the White House lawn. "Great processions of colored and white men marched to and fro and passed in front of the White House and congratulated President Lincoln on his proclamation. The President came to the window and made responsive bows, and thousands told him, if he would come out of that palace, they would hug him to death." It was a festive atmosphere that Turner believed would never "be seen again in this life."[8]

Following emancipation, African Americans in Washington, DC, and the surrounding vicinity gathered at the White House grounds for social, political, and religious purposes. President Lincoln's sons, Willie and Tad, also regularly played with black children at their home. "There was no color line there," recalled a White House waiter's son who had met Lincoln. "The bootblacks and other colored boys who peeped through the fence were invited in." And though not given full equality, there were "always plenty of little Negroes" at the White House Easter egg roll to eat the eggs that cracked.[9]

The White House became a symbol with tremendous meaning for African Americans. One black visitor to the nation's capital in October 1863 was captivated by what he saw. In a letter to the New York *Anglo-African*, he concluded, "you turn your eyes toward the WHITE HOUSE, and you know that there resides the man, who, under God, has been permitted to break up to a great extent, this horrid iniquity—to emancipate millions of men, and the mind instinctively says: GOD BLESS ABRAHAM LINCOLN." A white onlooker similarly observed "the wild fervor and strange enthusiasm which our colored friends always manifest over the name of Abraham Lincoln. . . . In the great crowds which gather from time to time in front of the White House in honor of the President, none shout so loudly and so wildly, and swing their hats with such utter abandon, while their eyes are beaming with the intensest joy, as do these simple-minded and grateful people."[10]

From his office window, Lincoln could observe the ways American race relations were evolving during the war. One Sunday in 1864, the president's private secretary, William O. Stoddard, saw a regiment of US Colored Troops marching down Pennsylvania Avenue. He stood by the White House gate "to have a good look at them." Soon Secretary of State William H. Seward joined him, smoking a cigar. "They were really a fine looking body of men, and marched well for such new recruits," recalled Stoddard. "It was indeed a curious and deeply interesting sight, seen for the first time." Seward watched the men intently. After the regiment passed, Stoddard asked him, "Well, Mr. Seward, what do you think of our black troops?" Seward took the cigar from his mouth and, without looking up, replied, "It grows, it grows." Stoddard returned to his office in the White House, which looked out onto Pennsylvania Avenue. After a short while, the regiment marched past again. Standing by the window, Stoddard heard Lincoln's "heavy step behind me." Stoddard turned to him and asked, "Well, Mr. President, what do you think of that?" Lincoln thought for a moment and then replied in a low voice, "It'll do, it'll do!"[11]

The admiration was mutual. On another occasion when Lincoln had the opportunity to review several regiments of black soldiers in April 1864, he acknowledged them with "dignified kindness and courtesy," while they in turn became overjoyed when they saw him. "They swing their caps, clap their hands and shout their joy," reported one journalist. "Long, loud and jubilant are the rejoicings of these redeemed sons of Africa." Another witness to the scene wrote that the soldiers saluted "gracefully with their colors and [gave] loud hurrahs for the Great Emancipator of their race."[12] In March 1865, when Lincoln reviewed black soldiers of the Army of the James, a newspaperman reported, "The troops received the President with repeated cheers; and when it is recollected that they were shouting in honor of the man who had probably done more than any other to break their chains and make them freemen, it is easy to believe that their enthusiasm was sincere."[13]

Some black men and women did more than just march past the White House—they chose to enter through its doors to have an intimate, personal conversation with the commander in chief.[14] Much to their surprise—and to the surprise of the white press—Lincoln treated these visitors as equals, just as he would any other guest in his home. African Americans began claiming this sort of accessibility to the president as early as April 1862, and these claims only increased as the war progressed. In an unprecedented way, a president of the United States treated black men and women as equal participants in an important part of American civic life—the right to be constituents with a voice that could be heard by the highest political officer in the nation. In the process, the Executive Mansion became a space where black people could make a claim to the rights of US citizenship. Lincoln's welcoming of African Americans into the White House for political discussions and social functions, therefore, was a tremendous step forward in American race relations, countering what Chief Justice Roger Taney had written in the *Dred Scott* decision just a few years earlier—that Africans Americans were "beings of an inferior order, and altogether unfit to associate with the white race, either in social or political relations; and so far inferior, that they had no rights which the white man was bound to respect."[15]

Lincoln knew that there could be a steep political cost to pay for welcoming black visitors into his home and office, but he did it anyway. Newspapers throughout the North reported on his meetings with African Americans, and many expressed outrage at the kind reception he gave them. The Cincinnati *Enquirer*, a Democratic newspaper, lamented that with "negro officers in the army, negro lawyers in the Supreme Court, and negroes at the White House receptions, who can doubt that the negro race is 'looking up,' or rather looking down on the white race from the elevated place it has attained under this Administration."[16] From the Democratic perspective, the expansion of social rights for African Americans had an inverse relationship with the rights of white citizens. And they saw Lincoln's meetings with black men and women as akin to his other policies that they believed were unconstitutional. In a litany that brought up many aspects of Lincoln's wartime agenda, the *Holmes County Farmer* of Millersburg, Ohio, explicitly linked the expansion of rights for African Americans to his alleged tyrannical actions against white Democrats. "He suspended the writ of habeas corpus—set aside the Constitution—made a law of his own to free the niggers—rides in a carriage guarded by soldiers—admits nigger guests to the White House—sends ministers to Hayti and Liberia—buys all the niggers in the District of Columbia—muzzles the Press—[and] puts down Free Speech." Then, in language meant to spoof a black preacher, the paper continued, "And, my breetheren, you know our father has done more for the noble African than any man on earth-ah."[17]

It is little wonder that Democrats who read these things in the papers feared the consequences of granting political rights to free blacks and ex-slaves. They believed that Lincoln's racially egalitarian decisions would mean the active diminishing of rights for whites. A Pennsylvania newspaper sneered at Lincoln for his kind public treatment of African Americans. "When did we ever have a President that made so much of the negro, or was ever willing to take him into his private and social circles as Abraham Lincoln does?" asked the editors of the Bloomsburg *Star of the North* in December 1864. "Mr. Lincoln is emphatically the black man's President and the white man's curse. What act has the President ever done in his official capacity, trace it out to its legitimate ends, that has been beneficial to the country, or to the white man? *Not one, and we defy contradiction!*"[18] Ironically, Frederick Douglass would use this very same phrase—calling Lincoln "emphatically the black man's president"—in a eulogy praising Lincoln in June 1865. To add to the irony, Douglass used that phrase in the lead-up to his telling an audience about his personal meetings with Lincoln.

This book tells the stories of the black visitors who came to the Lincoln White House during the Civil War. Some came by the invitation of the president; others walked through the White House gates uninvited and unannounced. The remarkable drama that unfolds is one of President Lincoln welcoming these visitors with open arms and an outstretched hand. Indeed, many of the visitors explicitly remarked on how he treated them with dignity and respect; many were touched by how Lincoln shook their hands and made no acknowledgment of their race or skin color. And Lincoln's hospitality toward African Americans came to be well known at the time. Union nurse Mary Livermore observed, "To the lowly, to the humble, the timid colored man or woman, he bent in special kindliness."[19] Writing in 1866, a white Washingtonian noted that the "good and just heart of Abraham Lincoln prompted him to receive representatives of every class then fighting for the Union, nor was he above shaking black hands, for hands of that color then carried the stars and stripes, or used musket or sabre in its defense. This, too, when cowardly white men remained at home, folding their white hands peacefully."[20]

In most of the narratives that follow, Lincoln shook hands with his black guests. In almost every instance he appears to have initiated the human contact. Shaking hands, for Lincoln, could be an understandably tiresome chore. When he shook hands, one observer noted, "he does it with a hearty will, in which his entire body joins" so that "he is more weary after receiving a hundred people than some public men we could all name after being shaken by a thousand."[21]

And yet he warmly, kindly, eagerly, and repeatedly grasped the hands of his black guests. This small gesture should not be discounted, for it carried not only great personal meaning for the visitors, but also important symbolic meaning for all Americans who read of the encounters.

Most white politicians would not have been so genuinely welcoming to African Americans. Even white reformers and abolitionists were prone to show disdain for black visitors. When Paschal B. Randolph and another black leader entered the office of Francis G. Shaw—president of the National Freedmen's Relief Association and the father of the recently deceased Col. Robert Gould Shaw of the famous Fifty-Fourth Massachusetts Infantry—to volunteer their services to assist former slaves, Shaw looked up from his desk "and seeing our color, and before we had time to open our lips, rudely waved his hand; and ordered us to leave the room and stay in the hall till he got ready." When Randolph tried to speak, Shaw repeated his order two more times "in the most offensive manner." Randolph indignantly left the building, "positively assured that our color alone was the pretext for the insult."[22] This experience must have come as something of a shock to Randolph, for earlier in the war he had already had a much different experience when meeting with Lincoln. As historian James O. Horton and sociologist Lois E. Horton write, "Blacks often worked with white reformers . . . who displayed racially prejudiced views and treated blacks with paternalistic disrespect," including some who "refused to shake the hand of a black man." Radicals and reformers continued to offer snubs like this in the postwar period. During his run for the presidency in 1872, Horace Greeley ostentatiously showed disdain for a black delegation in Erie, Pennsylvania, when they sought to shake his hand.[23]

Not so with Lincoln.

When Lincoln shook his black visitors' hands they talked about it in letters, memoirs, and speeches. In the postwar years, some elderly ex-slaves also claimed to have shaken hands with him.[24] Clearly the gesture meant something significant to them. For some, Lincoln's hands seemed to possess a sort of talismanic power. A gesture by Mary Lincoln's seamstress, former slave Elizabeth Keckly, captures the special meaning of Lincoln's right hand for many African Americans. In 1864, Keckly asked Mrs. Lincoln for the glove that Lincoln would wear on his "honest hand" when he shook the hands of thousands of people following his second inauguration in March 1865. When Mrs. Lincoln agreed to give it to her, Keckly replied, "I shall cherish it as a precious memento of the second inauguration of the man who has done so much for my race. He has been a Jehovah to my people—has lifted them out of bondage, and directed their footsteps from darkness to light." Keckly received the glove shortly after the inaugural festivities and treasured it as one of her most prized possessions. In 1868 she donated a number of "sacred relics" to Wilberforce University, a black institution of higher learning near Xenia, Ohio. Keckly informed African Methodist Episcopal (AME) Bishop Daniel A. Payne, the president of Wilberforce, that she had received many offers from people who wanted to purchase these items, but she deemed them "too *sacred* to sell." Instead, she chose to donate them "for the cause of educating the four millions of slaves liberated by our President, whose private character I revere." Initially, Keckly planned to donate the glove that Lincoln wore "on his precious hand at that last inaugural reception," but she soon decided that she could not part with such "a precious *souvenir* of our beloved President."[25]

Following the assassination, Frederick Douglass also received a gift from Mrs. Lincoln related to Lincoln's hand. When, in 1865, Mary Lincoln gave Douglass Lincoln's "favorite walking stick," the black abolitionist replied: "I assure you that this inestimable memento of his excellency will be retained in my possession while I live, an object of sacred interest; a token not merely of the kind consideration in which I have reason to know that the president was pleased to hold me personally, but as an indication of his humane interest in the welfare of my whole race." Two of Lincoln's other canes went to Rev. Henry Highland Garnet and Lincoln's valet William Slade. According to Slade's daughter, the president regularly discussed his speeches and political decisions with Slade, and by the time the Emancipation Proclamation was released Slade "already knew every word of it."[26] For these black leaders, these relics, which had been held closely by Lincoln's right hand, carried special meaning. It was a special hand, as Sojourner Truth stated, because it was "the same hand that signed the death-warrant of *Slavery*." Even fifty years later, the black poet James Weldon Johnson would celebrate the golden anniversary of the Emancipation Proclamation by noting, "Since God, through Lincoln's ready hand, / Struck off our bonds and made us men."[27]

Historians have underestimated the racial egalitarianism that emerged in the Lincoln White House during the Civil War. James O. Horton and Lois E. Horton treat Lincoln's meeting with Frederick Douglass in August 1863 as though it were an anomaly, writing, "Lincoln had dealt with other blacks during his time in the White House, but never on such an equal footing as with Douglass."[28] Similarly, Kate Masur argues that Lincoln did not defend the right of African Americans to visit the White House on "social" occasions. She writes, "The president had proven willing to meet with African Americans on political business, but he evidently did not take a strong stand for admitting them on more 'social' occasions, such as public receptions, New Year's Day levees, or the second inaugural ball." She discounts the story of Frederick Douglass attending the reception at the White House following Lincoln's second inauguration in March 1865, writing, "This incident is often cited as evidence of Lincoln and Douglass's friendly rapport, but it also suggests that Douglass was able to attend the party not because African Americans were welcome, but because he had a special relationship with the president. Indeed, Lincoln's staff and perhaps Lincoln himself seem to have observed a distinction between admitting African Americans on political business and admitting them on more social occasions."[29]

As we will see, however, Lincoln warmly welcomed black visitors into his home and office, regardless of their race, color, or previous condition of servitude. With one glaring exception—the infamous August 1862 meeting in which he discussed colonization—Lincoln never lectured his guests. He almost always listened patiently to what they had to say, and he usually responded with kind and thoughtful words of his own. They learned from him, and he learned from them. On several occasions he appears to have changed his mind about major domestic policies because of these interactions. Moreover, much may depend on how one defines "social" and "political." Many of the chapters that follow tell stories that have "political" significance but that were also "social" in nature. Lincoln welcomed guests who wished to bring him gifts, or who simply wished to thank him for what he had done "for the colored race" during his time in office. In at least one instance, he and Mary Lincoln spent the evening conversing with a black guest while drinking tea. These were both social and political visits. And, as we shall see, Lincoln welcomed African American men and women to public receptions and New Year's Day levees as well.

For African Americans to be welcomed in these ways into the home of any white person—whether the president or not—would have been simply unthinkable to most mid-nineteenth-century white people. More common was what Henry McNeal Turner experienced when he visited a white Union officer at a boardinghouse a few blocks from the White House in early 1863. The landlady, indignant upon finding a black man in her home, exclaimed that she "was willing white men should come in her parlor, but niggers should go to the kitchen." Turner defiantly retorted that "his was a better house [than hers], and he would leave."[30] As we will see, Turner never would have suffered such an indignity at Lincoln's White House. In fact, Lincoln appears to have welcomed Turner as a political confidante in September 1862.

Finally, and most importantly, Lincoln's welcoming of African Americans to the White House was an act of political courage and great political risk. He did not shy away from having public meetings with black visitors even in the run-up to the highly contentious presidential election in 1864. In late September 1864, the Philadelphia *Age*, a Democratic organ, complained, "With negro picnics in the White House grounds, and negro cronies in the White House itself, displaying their teeth at the Presidential wit, white people will have to wait a long time for their turn." The editors continued that "Mr. Lincoln was like the conscientious actor, who, when he played Othello, insisted on *blacking himself all over*."[31]

Lincoln knew that newspaper coverage like this could cost him votes, but that did not stop him from welcoming African Americans into his home and office. Indeed, Frederick Douglass, probably more than any other person, understood the significance of Lincoln's open-door policy. "He knew that he could do nothing which would call down upon him more fiercely the ribaldry of the vulgar than by showing any respect to a colored man," said Douglass shortly after Lincoln's death. And yet that is precisely what Lincoln did. Douglass continued: "Some men there are who can face death and dangers, but have not the moral courage to contradict a prejudice or face ridicule. In daring to admit, nay in daring to invite a Negro to an audience at the White house, Mr. Lincoln did that which he knew would be offensive to the crowd and excite their ribaldry. It was saying to the country, I am President of the black people as well as the white, and I mean to respect their rights and feelings as men and as citizens."[32]

~

The title of this book comes from a line in First Lady Michelle Obama's address at the Democratic National Convention in 2016. "That is the story of this country," she said, "the story that has brought me to this stage tonight, the story of generations of people who felt the lash of bondage, the shame of servitude, the sting of segregation, but who kept on striving and hoping and doing what needed to be done so that today I wake up every morning in a house that was built by slaves."[33] Slaves did, indeed, play a central role in the construction of the Executive Mansion. And from Thomas Jefferson to Zachary Taylor, Southern presidents brought enslaved people with them to work in the White House.[34] James K. Polk notoriously bought and sold at least nineteen slaves while serving as president.[35] Other than as stonemasons, laborers, craftsmen, cooks, and domestic servants, African Americans were rarely welcome within the great building's walls in America's formative years. In the late 1850s, James Buchanan even changed White House policy so as to hire only new staff who had been "trained in the British system of domestic service" because he believed that they would respect his privacy and offer better service than Americans. The White House, therefore, became even whiter.[36]

Indeed, prior to Lincoln's presidency, there were few precedents for the sorts of meetings that would take place between 1862 and 1865. (In January 1799, Joseph Bunel, a diplomat from San Domingo, dined with John Adams and Secretary of State Timothy Pickering—the first time a person of African descent dined with a sitting president. This meeting took place in Philadelphia, however, as it was more than a year before Adams moved to the White House.)[37] In the first decade of the nineteenth century, a "destitute black man" came to the Executive Mansion to say he "had lost his only coat to one of the servants, who had falsely accused him of taking it from the President's House." Thomas Jefferson "heard him out, then called for the coat, took a quick look, and gave it back to the poor man." It looked like the coats that were worn by servants, he said, but was not trimmed in the same way.[38] In 1812, James Madison met with Paul Cuffe, a wealthy black merchant and ship builder, who came to the White House to recover cargo that had been illegally seized by customs officials. Cuffe allegedly addressed the president quite informally, saying, "James, I have been put to much trouble, and have been abused. . . . I have come here for thy protection."[39] Following Andrew Jackson's inauguration in 1829, black faces could be seen among the throngs of people who poured into the White House, but the president had already abandoned his residence by that point and nobody in that raucous crowd got to meet him.[40] Three decades elapsed between Paul Cuffe's visit with Madison and 1844, when the black minister Daniel A. Payne briefly met John Tyler at the White House when he delivered the funeral sermon for a black servant who had been killed in the *Princeton* disaster.[41] More than fifteen more years passed before another African American would be welcomed into the White House, but this one would be as an entertainer, not a guest. In June 1860, President James Buchanan's niece, Harriet Lane, invited an eleven-year-old slave to perform for the president and other guests. "Blind Tom" was a musical prodigy who, sadly, was publicized by his enslavers "more as a sideshow freak than as the gifted artist he was," writes one historian.[42] There may be more than these few instances between 1800, when John Adams moved into the White House, and 1862, when Daniel Payne returned to meet with Lincoln, but the reality is that African Americans were more likely to be bought and sold by a sitting president than to be welcomed as his guests.

By 1861, the thought of a black man at the White House was little more than a joke. During the secession crisis, an article circulated in Northern newspapers about a US senator who "met an old and well-known negro lumbering toward the White House. The old negro accosted him in his usual manner. 'Good mor'n, massa.' 'Good morning, Pete,' was the response; 'where are you going in such haste?' 'Well, massa, I'ze 'gwine to de White House to get a government 'pintment.' 'Indeed! what appointment?' 'I'ze gwine to get de 'pintment to *pick de stars out of de flag of de Union.*'"[43] The editors who ran this story in 1861 never could have imagined how quickly things would begin to change within a mere fifteen months. But perhaps they should have. Shortly before Lincoln's inauguration, a young woman in Tennessee bitterly suggested that the name of the Executive Mansion should be changed to "Black House" and that it should be repainted black, "emblematic of the negro equality principles of which Lincoln is the representative."[44]

In telling the following stories I have, as much as possible, given the accounts in the words of the participants themselves. My goal is to reproduce the voices of Lincoln's guests, as well as of some of their critics in the white press, enabling readers to see the White House as they saw it, and the president as they encountered him. Before we turn to these stories, however, it is worth briefly surveying Lincoln's interactions with African Americans in the pre-presidential years.

1

"A CONTINUAL TORMENT TO ME"

If slavery is not wrong, nothing is wrong. I can not remember when I did not so think, and feel.

—Abraham Lincoln to Albert G. Hodges, April 4, 1864

In the summer of 1841, a young Abraham Lincoln traveled down the Ohio River on a steamboat from Louisville to St. Louis. One night on board the ship he and his friend Joshua F. Speed observed a dozen Kentucky slaves "shackled together with irons" being transported to the Deep South to be sold. The men were "strung together" on a single chain, Lincoln wrote in a letter to Speed's sister, Mary, "precisely like so many fish upon a trot-line." Lincoln ruminated on the fact that in this sad condition they were "going into perpetual slavery where the lash of the master" would be "ruthless and unrelenting." Moreover, Lincoln noted, these poor men "were being separated forever from the scenes of their childhood, their friends, their fathers and mothers, and brothers and sisters, and many of them, from their wives and children." Having lost a mother, sister, infant brother, and sweetheart to death, Lincoln knew something about the pain of such loss.

Yet Lincoln was struck that these slaves appeared to be "the most cheerful and apparantly [*sic*] happy creatures on board." This perplexed him, considering their unhappy state of affairs. "One, whose offence for which he had been sold was an over-fondness for his wife, played the fiddle almost continually; and the others danced, sung, cracked jokes, and played various games with cards from day to day," Lincoln wrote in wonder. (Lincoln could have only known the slave's offense from having conversed with him or the slave trader. Knowing the disdain that Lincoln had for slave traders, it is quite possible he had a conversation with the slave.) "How true it is that 'God tempers the wind to the shorn lamb,' or in other words, that He renders the worst of human conditions tolerable, while He permits the best, to be nothing better than tolerable," Lincoln concluded.[1]

Lincoln's reaction to this scene seems callous, almost bizarre. Historian Allen C. Guelzo, for example, cites Lincoln's letter to Mary Speed as evidence of his "indifference to black slavery" as a young man, writing that this letter might be evidence "that Lincoln regarded blacks as being sufficiently inferior to whites as a race that slavery simply didn't mean the same thing to them."[2] This interpretation is plausible; however, it seems more likely that Lincoln's commentary on the suffering of the slaves has more to do with his own life circumstances than with anything else. Lincoln was not thinking about black people as a separate, inferior race. On the contrary, in this particular moment he was completely self-absorbed, thinking only about his own personal problems. In 1841, Lincoln's courtship with Mary Todd had been a disaster, and he was utterly preoccupied with his own personal hardships and emotional suffering. Earlier in the year he had written about "the deplorable state of my mind at this time," and referred to himself as "the most miserable man living." He went on: "If what I feel were equally distributed to the whole human family, there would not be one cheerful face on the earth. Whether I shall ever be better I can not tell; I awfully forebode I shall not. To remain as I am is impossible; I must die or be better, it appears to me."[3] It was within this context that Lincoln expressed surprise at the "cheerful" demeanor of these slaves. How could *they* appear happy when *he*—someone who was attaining some position in the world as a lawyer and politician (albeit still a poor one)—could not? He was incredulous when he observed their reaction to their unfortunate life circumstances because he could not figure out how to master his own sense of anguish.

Despite his peculiar initial reaction—which seemed to make light of the slaves' suffering—the injustice of the scene never left him. Fourteen years later, Lincoln reminded his old friend Joshua Speed of that trip. "That sight was a continual torment to me," he wrote in 1855, "and I see something like it every time I touch the Ohio, or any other slave-border." Moreover, Lincoln told Speed that seeing such injustice had "the power of making me miserable."[4] What a change in Lincoln's description of his own state of mind. No longer was it his own personal woes that caused his misery; now it was his reflection on the unjust calamities endured by others.

Lincoln had, in fact, encountered the horrors of slavery prior to this moment. According to one source, an elderly slave woman was present to assist at Lincoln's birth because his father, Thomas, was away serving on jury duty.[5] When Abe was only two years old the Lincoln family moved to a farm near Knob Creek in Hardin County, Kentucky. Their cabin fronted a portion of the Cumberland Road that ran between Louisville and Nashville, over which slave coffles regularly traveled. One contemporary stated that it was "a very common sight in the early history of the road" to see slaves "arranged in couples and fastened to a long, thick rope or cable, like horses." Lincoln almost certainly saw such scenes pass right by his front door between 1811 and 1816.[6]

In 1816, when Lincoln was eight years old, his family moved to Indiana. Lincoln later explained that his father made this move to a free state "partly on account of slavery."[7] According to historian Benjamin Quarles, Lincoln's "first recorded experience with a Negro" took place during this move when a black servant named Minerva gave the young boy a drink of milk during the ninety-one-mile journey from Kentucky to Indiana.[8]

In the Hoosier State, Lincoln grew into a young man. In 1828, a local shopkeeper named James Gentry asked Lincoln—now nineteen years old—to assist in taking a flatboat full of produce and other goods down to New Orleans. Gentry's son, Allen, would be in charge of the vessel, and Lincoln would get paid eight dollars per month plus the cost of his return ticket home by steamboat. The boys got underway in December 1828, first heading down the Ohio River and then down the Mississippi. From Rockport, Illinois, to New Orleans would be a distance of more than twelve hundred miles.

When Lincoln and Allen reached Baton Rouge, they faced a harrowing experience. One night, seven local slaves noticed the two boys securing their boat by the riverbank for the evening. The slaves determined to kill Lincoln and Allen, steal as much cargo as they could hide in their cabins, and then sink the boat, thus destroying the evidence. But when the slaves attacked, Lincoln and Allen fought back fiercely (it should be noted that Lincoln was a strong and skilled wrestler). The enslaved men had hickory clubs, while Lincoln and Allen simply pretended to have guns. "Lincoln get the guns and Shoot," shouted Allen. At that the slaves fled, but not before leaving Lincoln badly wounded with at least one scar on the right side of his face. How ironic that Louisiana slaves came so close to killing the man some of them later likely hailed as the Great Emancipator.

Eventually Lincoln and Allen made it to the Crescent City. They sold their wares and boat and then spent several days walking around the city. The slave markets in New Orleans were bustling. By the early nineteenth century farmers in the Upper South and Mid-Atlantic had depleted their soil and had less use for slaves, so they sold their surplus "stock" to professional slave traders who took them southward—some in slave coffles on a thousand-mile march by foot and others by boat along the Atlantic Coast. Newspapers in New Orleans almost daily announced the arrival of ships loaded with human cargo, and classified advertisements enticed buyers to purchase "young Virginia slaves of both sexes to be sold cheap for cash." A few months after Lincoln and Allen Gentry arrived in the city, two ships arrived from Baltimore, the *Lafayette* carrying 211 slaves, and the *Henry Clay* with another 144, sixty-one of whom were twelve years old or younger.

One visitor described this unseemly aspect of the city in his travel diary: "I observed in walking through the streets several large rooms fitted out as slave markets, and generally filled with unhappy blacks, dressed up for the occasion. The men and women are ranged on opposite sides of the apartment, where they may traffic for human beings with the same indifference as purchasing a horse. New Orleans I conclude is a good market for this kind of human stock." The sights, sounds, and smells of the slave trade were ubiquitous. Allen later recalled, "We stood and watched the slaves sold in New Orleans and Abraham was very angry."[9]

In 1831, Lincoln took another flatboat trip to New Orleans. In the Crescent City, he and his cousin John Hanks allegedly visited "an old fortune teller, a Voudou negress," who became "very much excited" and said to Lincoln, "You will be President, and all the negroes will be free." Again in New Orleans, Lincoln saw the slave trade firsthand. Lincoln's cousin John Hanks later claimed, "we Saw Negroes Chained—maltreated—whipt & scourged. Lincoln Saw it— his heart bled—Said nothing much—was silent from feeling—was Sad—looked bad—felt bad—was thoughtful & abstracted—I Can say Knowingly that it was on this trip that he formed his opinions of Slavery: it ran its iron in him then & there—May 1831. I have heard him say—often & often."[10]

Lincoln's law partner, William H. Herndon, later described this scene in greater detail in his 1888 biography of Lincoln:

> One morning in their rambles over the city the trio passed a slave auction. A vigorous and comely mulatto girl was being sold. She underwent a thorough examination at the hands of the bidders; they pinched her flesh and made her trot up and down the room like a horse, to show how she moved, and in order, as the auctioneer said, that 'bidders might satisfy themselves' whether the article they were offering to buy was sound or not. The whole thing was so revolting

that Lincoln moved away from the scene with a deep feeling of 'unconquerable hate.' Bidding his companions follow him he said, 'By God, boys, let's get away from this. If ever I get a chance to hit that thing [meaning slavery], I'll hit it hard.'

Herndon concluded, "This incident was furnished me in 1865, by John Hanks. I have also heard Mr. Lincoln refer to it himself." (Incidentally, Herndon could not confirm the fortune-teller story, writing that he thought he had heard the story at some point but he was not certain.)[11]

Historians and biographers have cast doubt upon this story, in large part because Hanks apparently did not complete the trip to New Orleans. According to an autobiographical sketch written by Lincoln in 1860, Hanks had only gone as far as St. Louis (although one piece of evidence suggests that Hanks may have heard the story from Lincoln's stepbrother, John D. Johnston, who did go all of the way to New Orleans).[12] But that ought not to discount the story entirely, especially since Herndon claimed to have heard it firsthand from Lincoln. (No historian or biographer, to my knowledge, has pointed out how bizarre it is that Lincoln mentioned who was with him on this obscure trip when he composed a short presidential campaign biography three decades after the event took place. It is unclear why Lincoln would have included such an unimportant life detail. It is also possible that Lincoln got this detail wrong and that Hanks had actually completed the journey.) In fact, before Herndon published his biography of Lincoln he reported Hanks's account in a letter:

> At that time and place Lincoln was made an anti-slavery man. He saw a slave, a beautiful mulatto girl, sold at auction. She was *felt over, pinched, trotted* around to show to bidders that said article was sound, etc. Lincoln walked away from the sad, inhuman scene with a deep feeling of *unsmotherable* hate. He said to John Hanks this: 'By God! If I ever get a chance to hit that institution, I'll hit it hard, John.' . . . John Hanks, who was two or three times examined by me, told me the above facts about the negro girl and Lincoln's declaration. There is no doubt about this.[13]

Whether or not Lincoln said he would hit slavery hard when he saw it first-hand in New Orleans, these riverboat trips undoubtedly had profound effects on him. According to one acquaintance, Lincoln once said, "I saw it all myself when I was only a little older than you are now, and the horrid pictures are in my mind yet." And in 1852, Lincoln told several attorneys that he became "disgusted" when he "saw young women, as white as any that walk these streets to-day, sold on the auction-block simply because they had some Negro blood in their veins."[14]

CHAPTER 1

Lincoln also encountered forms of slavery and the slave trade back home in Illinois. The state constitution of 1818 prohibited slavery from "hereafter" being "introduced into this state." However, those who owned slaves prior to statehood could keep them. The 1830 census counted nineteen African Americans in Springfield, nine of whom were listed as slaves. Ten years later, Springfield still had six slaves, some of whom were men and women Lincoln knew. Indeed, Lincoln had close personal relationships with at least three slave owners in Springfield, as well as with other white neighbors who had black indentured servants.[15]

State lawmakers in the antebellum period also enacted Black Codes that deprived African Americans of political rights. One of these laws established a form of virtual slavery within the free state's borders. In 1853 the legislature passed a law barring "any negro, or mulatto, bond or free" from entering the state and remaining for ten days "with the evident intention of residing in the same." Any black person found guilty of violating this act would be adjudged guilty of a high misdemeanor and fined fifty dollars. If he or she could not pay the fine, a justice of the peace was to "advertise said negro or mulatto" and "at public auction, proceed to sell the said negro or mulatto to any person or persons who will pay said fine and costs, for the shortest time." The purchaser then had "the right to compel said negro or mulatto to work for and serve out said time, and he shall furnish said negro or mulatto with comfortable food, clothing and lodging during said servitude." If the black person did not depart the state within ten days of these proceedings, the fine would increase by fifty dollars for each subsequent offense.[16] Black men and women, in other words, could be forced into unfree labor in the free state of Illinois.

Some white people in Illinois also believed that they could buy and sell their "servants" just as they could any other property. In 1841, Lincoln took the case of a young black woman named Nance who had been orphaned as a young girl and sold at auction in 1827 for $150. When Nance protested that she was free, she was chained and imprisoned. Nance sued for her freedom the following year, but an Illinois court ruled, "A servant is a possession and CAN BE SOLD." In 1836, Nance's owner, Nathan Cromwell, decided to travel to Texas. Before leaving, he sold Nance for $400 to another man in Springfield named David Bailey. After several years of litigation, Lincoln argued *Bailey v. Cromwell* before the Illinois Supreme Court. Lincoln maintained that slavery was illegal in Illinois and that Nance should be free. The court accepted Lincoln's argument, ruling that in Illinois the presumption was that "every person is free, without regard to color," and that it was illegal to sell a free person.

Thus, Nance "was free, and not the subject of sale." Her case helped bring about the abolition of slavery and the slave trade in Illinois.[17]

As a lawyer, Lincoln took at least twenty-five cases involving African American litigants. In some cases he defended black clients. In one case in 1854, he even raised funds through a private subscription to help liberate a free black man from St. Louis who had been arrested in New Orleans for being out after dark without "free papers." The man was on the verge of being sold into slavery because he was unable to pay his fines to get out of prison.[18] However, in one infamous case Lincoln argued on behalf of a Kentucky slave owner who had brought slaves into Illinois. The *Matson Slave* case has proved a stumbling block for scholars who wish to depict Lincoln as antislavery from the beginning of his political career, although some have ventured plausible explanations for why he might have taken the case. For instance, Lincoln might have been following the advice of George Sharswood, the eminent nineteenth-century legal commentator, that lawyers ought "not to pass moral judgments on potential clients, but to rely on the legal process itself to determine the merits of the claim" because a lawyer "who refuses his professional assistance because in his judgment the case is unjust and indefensible, usurps the function of both judge and jury."[19]

In 1842, Lincoln married Mary Todd, the daughter of a prominent Kentucky family. It is quite possible that a black indentured servant named Hepsey was present at the wedding ceremony in Springfield. When Lincoln visited his in-laws in Lexington, he encountered black servants and slaves in the Todd home, and almost certainly witnessed slave coffles file past the Todd house on West Main Street, as well as slave auctions at the public square. One witness to such scenes there stated that "incorrigible or delinquent negroes are flogged unmercifully. I saw this punishment inflicted on two of these wretches. Their screams soon collected a numerous crowd—I could not help saying to myself, 'These cries are the knell of Kentucky liberty.'"[20]

At home in Illinois, Lincoln lived in what today would be considered an integrated neighborhood. When he moved to Springfield in 1837, twenty-six African Americans lived in the city—1.7 percent of the city's total population. When he left for Washington in 1861, the number had risen to 234—approximately 2.5 percent of its population. Lincoln interacted with these residents on a daily basis. They were friends and neighbors, servants and slaves, ministers and activists, and customers and legal clients. At the time of his election to the presidency, almost thirty black men, women, and children—which amounted to approximately 10 percent of Springfield's black population—lived within a three-block radius of his house at the corner of 8th and Jackson Streets. At least two black women—"Aunt" Ruth Stanton and Maria Vance—worked in Lincoln's home. And William de Fleurville (sometimes spelled Florville), a Haitian immigrant, had been one of his closest friends since 1831. Affectionately known as "Billy the Barber," Fleurville and Lincoln spent many hours in conversation at Billy's barbershop, and Lincoln also advised him in legal matters and investments, even paying Fleurville's property taxes for several of his properties. By some accounts, Billy's barbershop was Lincoln's "second home" before his marriage to Mary Todd in 1842. Lincoln also represented Fleurville in at least three legal cases. Years later, the *Illinois State Journal* wrote, "Only two men in Springfield understood Lincoln, his law partner, William H. Herndon, and his barber, William de Fleurville."[21]

As a young politician in Illinois, Lincoln took several courageous stands against slavery. When the state legislature adopted anti-abolitionist resolutions in 1837, he and one other Whig, Dan Stone, filed a protest. (Lincoln wrote the protest and circulated it among fellow Whigs; Stone, who was not standing for reelection, was the only one willing to sign on.) The legislature's resolutions had said, among other things, "that the right of property in slaves, is sacred to the slave-holding States by the Federal Constitution, and that they cannot be deprived of that right without their consent." In their protest, Lincoln and Stone agreed with the majority that Congress could not abolish slavery in the Southern states. They also took a dim view of abolitionist societies. But their reason for this view was distinctively different. The original resolutions had stated "that we highly disapprove of the formation of abolition societies, and of the doctrines promulgated by them." Lincoln and Stone, however, argued "that the promulgation of abolition doctrines tends rather to increase than to abate its evils." In other words, slavery was an evil and abolitionist tactics were backfiring. Moreover, they argued that "the institution of slavery is founded on both injustice and bad policy." Finally, Lincoln and Stone maintained that Congress had the constitutional authority to abolish slavery in the national capital.

Lincoln and Stone were part of a very small minority to vote against the original resolutions, and they were the only legislators to file a protest. In some ways, it was easy for Stone to join the protest because he would soon be leaving the legislature to become a state judge. Lincoln, however, would continue to sit in that body and be held accountable by the voters. It took incredible courage for Lincoln to take this stand—virtually alone—in 1837 in Illinois, where the governor spoke for most of his constituents when he called abolition societies—not slavery—"wicked and sinful." But Lincoln was firm in his beliefs. As a candidate for president in 1860, he recalled this moment and said that his 1837 protest "defined" his "position on the slavery question; and so far as it goes, it was then the same that it is now."[22]

In the late 1830s and early 1840s, Lincoln was not above race baiting when delivering political stump speeches, and he publicly opposed extending the right of suffrage to black men. Throughout his life he was also known for telling jokes and stories that included the word "nigger" or had racist overtones. But he never shied away from publicly stating his opposition to slavery. When, in 1837, a neighbor asked him if he was an abolitionist, Lincoln replied, "I am mighty near one." In 1845 when out on the campaign trail, two Free Soilers were "so well pleased with what he said on the subject [of slavery] that we advised that our anti-slavery friend[s] throughout the district should cast their vote for Mr. Lincoln: which was genirally done."[23] The following year Lincoln was elected to serve in Congress, where he would begin to build a national reputation as a vocal opponent of slavery.

Lincoln arrived in Washington, DC, a freshman congressman in December 1847. At that time the nation was involved in the Mexican-American War, something Lincoln saw as an unconstitutional Democratic plot to expand slavery to new Western territories. He took up residence at Ann G. Sprigg's boardinghouse, a Federal-style townhouse that sat on First Street, near A Street in Southeast Washington (now the site of the Library of Congress). Mrs. Sprigg's boardinghouse was known as the "Abolition House" because most of the boarders were antislavery advocates—men like Rep. Joshua R. Giddings of Ohio. Sitting around the dinner table, the boarders frequently discussed the slavery issue, with the discussions sometimes getting heated since one of the members was Patrick Tompkins of Mississippi. But soon the slave trade would come to outrage the boarders at Mrs. Sprigg's in a very personal way.

Mrs. Sprigg was not a slave owner, but she hired three slaves and five free black servants to work for her, including an enslaved man named Henry Wilson and his wife, Sylvia, who had previously been a servant for President William Henry Harrison. Although Wilson had worked out a deal with his owner to purchase his freedom for $300—and he only had $60 left to pay—the "old Jezebel" sold him to a local slave trader for $550. Late at night on Friday, January 14, 1848, a group of three armed men broke into Wilson's home and "violently seized" him "and in the presence of his wife gagged him, placed him in irons, and with loaded pistols forced him into one of the slave prisons of this city." They then transported him to a Richmond slave jail for further shipment to New Orleans.

This sort of kidnapping was all too common in the North, and a city like Washington was an easy staging point for sending human cargo to the Deep

South. One Virginian said the city was "a depot for a systematic slave market—an assemblage of prisons where the unfortunate beings, reluctant, no doubt, to be torn from their connexions, and the affections of their lives, [are] incarcerated and chained down, and thence driven in fetters like beasts, to be paid for like cattle." Lincoln later recollected that "in view from the windows of the capitol" there was "a sort of negro-livery stable, where droves of negroes were collected, temporarily kept, and finally taken to Southern markets, precisely like droves of horses."

The slave pens in Washington were dark, cold, and terrifying. From the outside they looked like a typical "quiet private residence." But the inside told another story. Solomon Northup, the most famous victim of kidnapping in antebellum America, described his cell in a Washington, DC, slave pen as a twelve-foot square with "walls of solid masonry" and a "heavy plank" floor. "There was one small window, crossed with great iron bars, with an outside shutter, securely fastened." No furniture or blankets were in the room other than a wooden bench and "an old-fashioned, dirty box stove." An iron door led into a very dark, windowless cell. In the rear of the house was a yard, about thirty feet long, surrounded by a ten- or twelve-foot-high brick wall. One side of the wall had a roof that formed "a kind of open shed" under which "slaves, if so disposed, might sleep at night, or in inclement weather seek shelter from the storm." Northup remarked that it "was like a farmer's barnyard in most respects, save it was so constructed that the outside world could never see the human cattle that were herded there."

On Monday, January 17, Lincoln's housemate Joshua Giddings introduced a resolution in the House of Representatives decrying this unfortunate incident. After recounting the facts of the case—and noting that Henry Wilson "had become well and favorably known to members of this House"—he called on Congress to appoint a select committee to investigate the incident. Moreover, since such "outrages . . . have been of common occurrence in this district, and are sanctioned by the laws of Congress, and are extremely painful to many of the members of this House, as well as in themselves inhuman," Giddings called on the House to inquire into whether Congress should ban the slave trade in Washington or "remove the seat of government to some free State."

In making this resolution, Giddings may have overreached. Had he simply called for an investigation of the kidnapping, his resolution almost certainly would have passed. But in calling for a ban on the domestic slave trade in Washington or the removal of the national capital to a free state, Giddings lost all possible Southern support. Not even Representative Tompkins, the boarder from Mississippi who knew the lamented waiter, voted in favor of the resolution.

Fortunately, Giddings and another congressional boarder from Mrs. Sprigg's house were able to track down Wilson in Richmond before he was sent to New Orleans. At first the slave trader refused to relinquish his captive for less than $700, but when Giddings threatened legal action, the kidnapper relented and returned him for the purchase price of $550. Giddings took a subscription and in "some twenty or thirty minutes" raised the necessary funds to purchase Wilson back, plus the $60 Wilson needed to purchase his freedom. It was an unusually happy coda to what could have been an even greater tragedy.[24]

This small event in Lincoln's life was emblematic of a larger trend in the antebellum slave trade. Political developments, technological advancements, and market forces conspired to make the kidnapping of free blacks in the North a profitable enterprise for avaricious and unscrupulous slave traders between 1790 and 1865. The invention of the cotton gin in 1794, the opening up of the Louisiana Territory to cotton cultivation, and the closing of the trans-Atlantic slave trade in 1808, all contributed to an increase in the demand for slave labor in the states and territories of the Deep South. At the same time, most whites were apathetic toward the problem of kidnapping. As a result, hundreds—probably thousands—of free black men, women, and children were kidnapped and sent south in the decades before the Civil War.[25]

The kidnapping of Mrs. Sprigg's waiter also highlighted the international embarrassment of the slave trade in DC. Foreign dignitaries coming to the capital would pass by a slave market on their way between the White House and the Capitol. And at the train station they would see dozens of slaves preparing to be sent away, in the words of Joshua R. Giddings, "to drag out a miserable existence" in the cotton fields of the Deep South. One day at the station in 1848, Giddings observed some fifty African Americans, with "wives bidding adieu to their husbands; mothers in an agony of despair . . . [and] little boys and girls weeping amid the general distress, scarcely knowing the cause of their grief." Antislavery men knew that it would be politically impossible to abolish slavery in the District of Columbia. But abolishing the slave trade might be accomplished, for Washington was not as large a slave market as some Southern cities (although its proximity to the Chesapeake Bay did facilitate transportation of human cargoes farther south).

For decades, antislavery advocates had unsuccessfully pushed for the abolition of slavery and the slave trade in the District. Finally in December 1848, there seemed to be a glimmer of hope. Rep. Daniel Gott of New York introduced a resolution instructing the Committee on the District of Columbia "to report a bill, as soon as practicable, prohibiting the slave trade in the said District." The resolution passed in the House 98 to 88 on December 23. Southerners mobilized their opposition, however, and the House reversed itself by a 119 to 81 vote on January 10, 1849.[26]

Lincoln voted in favor of Gott's resolution both times it came on the floor. He also prepared his own resolution, which he introduced as an amendment to Gott's resolution, on January 10. Lincoln crafted a moderate proposal full of compromises—granting some concessions to antislavery advocates and others to slave owners. In taking this approach, Lincoln's goal was to advance human liberty, even if only in small, incremental steps. Lincoln's messmate, Joshua R. Giddings, wrote in his diary that the congressmen living at Mrs. Sprigg's had discussed and approved of Lincoln's proposal. "I believe it as good a bill as we could get at this time," wrote Giddings, "and am willing to pay for slaves in order to save them from the Southern market, as I suppose every man in the District would sell his slaves if he saw that slavery was to be abolished."[27]

Titled "A bill for an act to abolish slavery in the District of Columbia, by the consent of the free white people of said District, and with compensation to owners," Lincoln's proposal would have almost entirely ended the domestic slave trade within the nation's capital. The first section declared that persons outside of DC could no longer be enslaved within the District, while section 2 held that slaves in DC could never be held in bondage outside of the District. (Lincoln made an exception for government officials who traveled with servants.) Section 3 provided for gradual emancipation for all children born to enslaved women on or after January 1, 1850. Section 4 protected the rights of whites to own human chattels but also gave them the option to "receive from the treasury of the United States the full value of his or her slave . . . upon which such slave shall be forthwith and forever free." Section 5 required the municipal authorities in the District "to provide active and efficient means" to recapture fugitive slaves. Finally, the bill stated that "involuntary servitude for the punishment of crime" would still be permitted by the law, and that the law would only go into effect once it had been approved by the voters of Washington, who were all white and male.

After reading the bill on the floor of the House on January 10, Lincoln declared that he had shown it to "about fifteen of the leading citizens of the District of Columbia" all of whom "desired that some proposition like this should pass." When several incredulous members shouted, "Who are they?" and "Give us their names!" Lincoln did not answer. Three days later, on January 13, the young congressman gave notice that he had intended to introduce the bill, but he "learned that many leading southern members of Congress" had gone to see those "who favored my Bill, and had drawn them over to their way of thinking. Finding that I was abandoned by my former backers and having little personal influence, I *dropped* the matter knowing that it was useless to prosecute the business at that time."[28]

The Washington correspondent for the *New-York Tribune* praised Lincoln's effort, writing, "He is a strong but judicious enemy to Slavery, and his efforts are usually very practical, if not always successful." While Lincoln's measure failed, the professional slave trade in DC would be short lived. Congress abolished it one year later as part of the Compromise of 1850. Slavery itself would not be abolished in DC, however, until Lincoln signed such an act into law as president on April 16, 1862. Ironically, during the debate over DC emancipation in 1862, a conservative Unionist reintroduced Lincoln's bill in the Senate as a means to bring about gradual emancipation in Washington, but the Senate rejected the measure by a 27 to 10 vote, with one senator calling the bill "crude" and "imperfect."[29]

When his one term in the House of Representatives ended in 1849, Lincoln left politics until 1854, when Congress passed the Kansas-Nebraska Act—a law that opened up large swaths of federal territory to slavery. Angered by the law, Lincoln devoted himself to stopping the spread of human bondage. The *Dred Scott* case (1857) then brought him even more prominently into the political fray. In response to that decision—in which the Supreme Court held that African Americans were not citizens of the United States and could not sue in the federal courts—Lincoln made the case that black men and women were fully human, and therefore deserving of at least some of the rights of citizenship. To be sure, Lincoln infamously—and unfortunately—declared at the Lincoln-Douglas debate at Charleston, Illinois, in 1858, that "I am not, nor ever have been, in favor of bringing about in any way the social and political equality of the white and black races." Nor did he claim to advocate granting black men and women the right to vote, hold office, or sit on juries. Still, he continued, "I say upon this occasion I do not perceive that because the white man is to have the superior position the negro should be denied everything."[30] The rights he did believe African Americans should possess were the natural rights to pursue life, liberty, and happiness.

It is easy to bludgeon Lincoln for statements like these. Abolitionists then, and many commentators since, have suggested that Lincoln did not really oppose slavery, or that he was weak when it came to promoting political rights and social equality for African Americans. The black abolitionist H. Ford Douglas was furious when Lincoln refused to sign a petition calling for the repeal of Illinois's infamous Black Law, which forbade black testimony against whites in court. (Douglas had personally met with Lincoln during the 1858 US senate race and asked him to sign it.) In a public speech during the presidential election campaign of 1860, Douglas seemed to have more anger for Lincoln than for the race-baiting and proslavery candidates of the Democratic Party. He chafed at Lincoln's "pro-slavery character and principles" and said that Lincoln was "on the same side of this Slave Power."[31]

This criticism was unfair for it completely discounted Lincoln's powerful attacks against slavery after 1854. It also ignored what Stephen Douglas said at Charleston. Consider his words:

> I say that this government was established on the white basis. It was made by white men, for the benefit of white men and their posterity forever, and never should be administered by any except white men. (Cheers.) I declare that a negro ought not to be a citizen, whether his parents were imported into this country as slaves or not, or whether or not he was born here. It does not depend upon the place a negro's parents were born, or whether they were slaves or not, but upon the fact that he is a negro, belonging to a race incapable of self-government, and for that reason ought not to be on an equality with white men. (Immense applause.)

As Lucas Morel has written, "If Lincoln played the race card, then Douglas played the whole deck."[32]

Lincoln was a careful politician. He knew his audience at Charleston was heavily Democratic and in favor of white supremacy. When he denied supporting political rights for African Americans, he was ceding ground he could not hold in order to gain points he believed he could win. (This was a tactic Lincoln often utilized as a trial lawyer when making his case before a jury.[33]) Lincoln knew that most white Northerners would not be willing to entertain the thought of black voters, jurors, militiamen, witnesses in court, or spouses. He considered issues like interracial marriage "false issues" that Democrats raised "to force the controversy." Only an extremely small portion of white American society, after all, was pushing for full social equality for African Americans. So he felt no need to defend it publicly. "The real issue in this controversy," Lincoln argued, was the immorality of slavery.[34] Lincoln's primary political goal was to persuade voters that slavery was evil. Only then would he be able to work effectively toward its permanent extinction. Political rights and social equality for African Americans could only come *after* slavery was destroyed. That is why he knew he could not sign H. Ford Douglas's petition when he was running for statewide office in 1858. (Ironically, Lincoln privately said that he had no objection to interracial marriage. "I shall never marry a Negress, but I have no objection to anyone else doing so," he once quipped. "If a white man wants to marry a Negro woman, let him do it—if the Negro woman can stand it.")

While Lincoln's public approach to matters of race appears quite moderate—if not conservative—from a twenty-first-century perspective, it was enlightened for its time. He challenged his friends and neighbors to recognize that African Americans were part of "the people" who established the United States. In a speech delivered at Springfield, Illinois, on June 26, 1857, Lincoln maintained that black men and women were entitled to the natural rights enumerated in the Declaration of Independence. In what must have been a jarring example, he argued that even a black woman deserved these rights as much as any white man. "In some respects she certainly is not my equal," Lincoln conceded to his auditors, "but in her natural right to eat the bread she earns with her own hands without asking leave of any one else, she is my equal, and the equal of all others." Throughout the speech, Lincoln underscored that African Americans were part of the "human family"—a proposition that, astoundingly, was not fully accepted by white Americans at the time.

Arguing for basic human rights for black people was only part of Lincoln's purpose in this speech. More importantly, he wished to demonstrate that African American men were part of "the people" who created the Constitution because they could vote in five states in 1787 (in fact, there were no race-based restrictions for voting in eleven states in 1787 and twelve states in 1789). Again, using an enslaved woman as an example, Lincoln argued that freedom was the best condition for human beings because all people should have the right to grant or withhold "consent," including over their own bodies. Alluding to the all too common rape of female slaves by their masters, Lincoln argued,

> We desired the court to have held that they [Dred Scott's daughters] *were citizens* so far at least as to entitle them to a hearing as to whether they were free or not; and then, also, that they were in fact and in law really free. Could we have had our way, the chances of these black girls, ever mixing their blood with that of white people, would have been diminished at least to the extent that it could not have been *without their consent.* But Judge Douglas is delighted to have them decided to be slaves, and not human enough to have a hearing, even if they were free, and thus left subject to the forced concubinage of their masters, and liable to become the mothers of mulattoes in spite of themselves. (Emphases added.)

Lincoln chose these words carefully and precisely. "Consent" today is frequently employed in discussions of sexual matters; in nineteenth-century America, it more often related to republican government—government by consent. Lincoln's argument, therefore, could not have been more clear: Even a lowly, despised slave girl deserved the certain inalienable rights that had been secured by the Founding Fathers, including the right to grant or withhold consent to her own body.[35] Lincoln furthered these ideas in his "House Divided" address the following year, criticizing Northern and Southern Democrats for "depriv[ing] the negro, in every possible event, of the benefit of this provision of the United States Constitution [article 4, section 2], which declares that—'The citizens of each State shall be entitled to all privileges and immunities of citizens in the several States.'"[36] African Americans—enslaved and free—it seemed, deserved at least some of the rights of citizenship. It is little wonder that Democrats in Illinois chafed that all Lincoln talked about was "'freedom,' 'liberty' and niggers."[37]

Lincoln reiterated his point about black citizenship even more explicitly two years later in his first inaugural address, on March 4, 1861. In that speech he stated that he would enforce the Fugitive Slave Act of 1850 because his oath of office required him to enforce all federal laws. However, he reminded his audience that the Fugitive Slave Clause of the US Constitution was ambiguous and did not state clearly whether the states or the federal government were responsible for the rendition of fugitive slaves. "If the slave is to be surrendered, it can be of but little consequence *to him* or to others by which authority it is done," Lincoln said (emphasis added). In this short sentence, Lincoln used the masculine pronoun to remind his audience of the humanity—the real, lived experience—of men, women, and children who were cruelly returned into bondage under the Fugitive Slave Act. While politicians and voters were having theoretical and political debates over who should enforce the Fugitive Slave Clause, *real people* were suffering. Moreover, Lincoln continued, any law pertaining to the recapture and reenslavement of human beings ought to contain "all the safeguards of liberty known in civilized and humane jurisprudence . . . so that *a free man* be not in any case surrendered as a slave" (emphasis added). To make his point unmistakably clear, Lincoln again pointed to article 4, section 2 of the Constitution, concluding, "And might it not be well at the same time to provide by law for the enforcement of that clause in the Constitution which guarantees that 'the citizens of each State shall be entitled to all privileges and immunities of citizens in the several States'?"[38]

Never before had an American president acknowledged or advocated for enslaved or free African Americans to be given citizenship rights. Lincoln's critics certainly understood exactly what he was getting at. "What this last sentence means, we all know," exploded the editors of the *Charleston Mercury.* "Does any one pause to ask what these questions signify, or is their signification palpable to the most obtuse intellect?" asked the editors of the *Baltimore Sun.*

The second interrogatory, almost in plain terms, suggests the passage of such laws as will declare *the status of the slave to be that of a citizen of the State from which he has fled!* Mr. Lincoln asks 'might it not be well to provide by law,' (either by Congress or the Legislatures of the free States) for the enforcement of that clause in the constitution which guaranties that [']the *citizens* (the runaway slave) of each State shall be entitled to all the privileges and immunities (the *habeas corpus* act, trial by jury, &c.) of citizens in the several States.' This we believe to be the literal meaning of Mr. Lincoln's interrogatory.

Still fulminating over this passage the next day, the editors continued, "Is it not plain that he means that the black man, being a citizen of Massachusetts, should be upheld and sheltered by the *law* in his visits to and residence in Virginia or Maryland, if it please him to go thither? Is it not plain that it means that all our laws of exclusion enjoined by penalties ought, in his judgment, to be declared unconstitutional, and the free negro be protected by law in the establishment of his domicil[e] where he will? What else does he mean?"[39] Of course, the *Sun*'s prediction had relevance not only for the South, but also for Northern states— like Illinois—which also had laws prohibiting black immigration. If these editors had known what Lincoln said privately—that he called the Fugitive Slave Act "very obnoxious" and "ungodly," and that he hoped to strip it of its "obnoxious features"—they would have erupted in even greater vitriol.[40]

It is little wonder that enslaved and free African Americans looked to Lincoln as the liberator of their race. Some slaves in Florida refused to work because they believed that Lincoln's presidency would bring about their freedom. In South Carolina, slaves were lashed for singing, "We'll fight for liberty / Till de Lord shall call us home; / We'll soon be free / Till de Lord shall call us home," when they heard of Lincoln's election. Meanwhile, in Missouri an enslaved woman was beaten and imprisoned in a slave trader's yard for hanging a picture of Lincoln in her room. In the North, black Philadelphians "were delighted and turned out in unusual numbers" to see Lincoln in February 1861, as he traveled to Washington, DC, for the inauguration.[41] In Rochester, New York, however, Frederick Douglass was not impressed, and he wrote several editorials critical of the incoming president for having proslavery policies. It would take three personal encounters with Lincoln for Douglass to come to see him the way these black Southerners already did.

When Lincoln rode between the White House and the Capitol for the inaugural ceremonies, a black man drove the open barouche. Lincoln's first interactions with African Americans in the capital would all be with servants—just as they had been when he lived at Mrs. Sprigg's boardinghouse more than a decade earlier. Some of these servants were people he had brought with him. And yet within six weeks he would meet another black man in a new setting—one that, by all surviving accounts, made an impression on him.

On April 18, an angry mob in Baltimore hurled insults and stones at Union soldiers as they passed through the city on their way to Washington, DC. One of the first casualties of this early engagement of the Civil War was a black man from central Pennsylvania named Nicholas Biddle. The sixty-five-year-old runaway slave had joined the Washington Artillery of Schuylkill County, Pennsylvania, as the servant of a white officer as soon as Lincoln had called for troops. On that fateful April afternoon, he marched proudly through the city in military attire—an action that infuriated the pro-Confederate mob. Someone in the crowd shouted, "Nigger in Uniform!" while another yelled, "Kill that —ed brother of Abe Lincoln!" Biddle received a horrifying blow to the face by a paving stone that had been thrown in his direction. As one of his comrades wrote the following day, "Nick Biddle had his head cut open to the bone with a stone thrown by one of the Sescess." The soldiers eventually made it to Washington, DC, and were quartered at the US Capitol. Biddle lay in pain, a pool of blood staining the floor where he slept that night.

Relieved that some troops had finally made it to the capital, President Lincoln, Secretary of State William H. Seward, and Secretary of War Simon Cameron went to the Capitol the following day to greet the weary soldiers. Lincoln remarked, "I did not come here to make a speech. The time for speech-making has gone by, and the time for action is at hand. I have come here to give the Washington Artillerists from the State of Pennsylvania a warm welcome to the city of Washington and to shake every officer and soldier by the hand, providing you will give me that privilege." Lincoln then shook hands with each man present—including Biddle. A black Union chaplain later wrote that Biddle's "pain was mixed with pleasure" at the Capitol on April 19, "for it was his privilege to be visited by Abraham Lincoln, to be taken by the hand, and to receive from the kindly President words of compliment and cheer." Until the day he died in 1876, the elderly black man "never tired of talking about those supreme hours of his life: the time of his wounding, and the time of Lincoln's call to see him, and sympathize with him; and the scar which he carried to his grave he proudly showed to people interested, as his military badge and brand of patriotism." Lincoln, too, must have been profoundly moved by this moment. As one historian has written, "Lincoln appears to have been particularly struck by the appearance of Biddle, whose head was wrapped with blood-soaked bandages. The president urged him to seek medical attention, but Biddle refused, preferring instead to remain with his company."[42]

By all accounts, Lincoln looked upon Nicholas Biddle as a soldier. While it was true that the Union government would not accept black men into the Union Army for nearly two more years, Lincoln showed no hesitance to treat Biddle—an officer's servant—as equal to every other soldier in the room. It was a handshake Nick Biddle never forgot.

INTERLUDE 1

The Office

Every American knows the White House. Millions of tourists visit Washington, DC, each year and snap pictures of it from the fence at E Street, or across Pennsylvania Avenue from Lafayette Square. Thousands get to enter the building for a public tour, after going through heightened security in the east wing. They walk from room to room of the grand and elegant ground floor, constrained in their movement by ropes, special carpets, docents, and Secret Service agents. Few visitors get to ascend the staircase to the second floor.

Things were very different in the nineteenth century. Indeed, it is difficult for twenty-first-century Americans to realize just how open the White House was in Lincoln's time. The president held office hours, much as college professors do today, and ordinary Americans could enter the building, ascend the staircase, and wait outside of his office for their opportunity to meet with the president. One Frenchman who visited the White House in 1865 was astounded that common citizens were invited into these sacred precincts. "I have been taught discretion by our customs to the point where I wouldn't dare go past its threshold without a guide or without a special invitation from the great personage who lives there," he wrote. Yet the doors of the White House "stand open to every American: like a church, it is everybody's house." He observed, "At all hours of the day, you will find curious or idle people milling about in the great reception room where the President holds his popular audiences. It is said that some visitors—country bumpkins, no doubt—cut pieces from the silk curtains to take home as souvenirs of their pilgrimage. You may think that a policeman or at least a guard has been posted. Not at all! There is only a notice asking visitors to respect the furnishings, which belong to the government."[1]

This sort of scene was common in Lincoln's White House. Early in his presidency, people jammed into the rooms, hallways, and stairwells to wait for their turn to see the president. They sought patronage appointments and other favors. For "hours and hours," wrote Lincoln's private secretary William O. Stoddard, "the anterooms and halls upstairs were so full that they would hold no more." The "broad staircase itself was also packed and jammed, stair by stair, from top to bottom, so that you could hardly squeeze your way up or down." And yet for Lincoln, it was important to meet with these supplicants. "Three or four hours do they pour in, in rapid succession, nine out of ten asking offices, and patiently does the President listen to their applications," wrote one observer. "They do not want much, and they get very little," Lincoln once remarked. "I know how I would feel in their place."[2]

Upon ascending the staircase on the east side of the building, visitors would enter a small vestibule before walking up a few more steps and passing through folding doors into the waiting room outside of Lincoln's office. Now they were standing above the grand East Room. One visitor in late 1860—when James Buchanan still occupied the space—said this waiting room had "a worn and not particularly clean carpet; old mahogany furniture, with old-fashioned horse-hair coverings; dusty walls and a few dusty busts of former Presidents; a few dusty prints of the 'Signers,' and a very dilapidated copy of the 'Declaration' in a soiled sandal wood frame." It was fitting that visitors to Lincoln's office would first pass by this large print of the signing of the Declaration of Independence. In 1857, Chief Justice Roger B. Taney and Sen. Stephen A. Douglas had argued that the Declaration did not include black men and women. Lincoln had countered that "the Declaration contemplated the progressive improvement in the condition of all men everywhere"—that the Founders could not attain perfect equality in 1776, but that the words of that document were written "for future use" to augment "the happiness and value of life to all people of all colors everywhere." Now as president, Lincoln would be able to help bring about this political and social change.[3] Over the next few years, black men as well as white men would pass by that copy of the Declaration on their way to meet with the president.

As visitors sat or stood in this waiting area near the picture of the Declaration, they would likely encounter Lincoln's private secretaries, John G. Nicolay and John Hay. Both young men had come to Washington in 1861 with Lincoln—the boss they affectionately called "the Tycoon." From their perch here it was their job to make sure that the president was not needlessly disturbed. Hay was young, quick-witted, handsome, poetic, and charming. Hay was educated at Brown University, and one Washington insider likened him to Lord Byron.

Nicolay could not have been more different. A German immigrant, he was quiet, reserved, and gruff. Stoddard later wrote, "People who do not like him—because they cannot use him, perhaps—say he is sour and crusty, and it is a grand good thing, then, that he is." Indeed, Lincoln needed assistants who could withstand the exasperating work of holding off the hundreds of people who would come to see the president. Nicolay was "the bulldog of the ante-room," according to Stoddard, and he "had developed an artificial manner the reverse of 'popular,' and could say 'no' about as disagreeably as any man I ever knew." This was just what Lincoln needed, and the president's decision to make Nicolay and Hay the guardians of his office reflected excellent judgment on his part.[4]

Lincoln's office was through the first door on the south side of the waiting room. It was long with high ceilings. Stoddard called this room "the nerve-centre of the Republic" and "a wonderful historic cavern to move about in." In the center of the room stood a large walnut table, surrounded by chairs. Lincoln held his Cabinet meetings on Tuesdays and Fridays at this table—the very same table that every Cabinet had used since Thomas Jefferson's administration. The table's surface was often covered in piles of paper, some bound into bundles with red string. On one particular day, a visitor noticed several books laying on it—a manual of parliamentary procedure, a thesaurus, and two books of humor: *The Orpheus C. Kerr Papers* and *Artemus Ward*. Lincoln needed humor to bring balance to his life, and he was known to read excerpts from humor books to his Cabinet officials (much to their chagrin). In fact, he read aloud a story from *Artemus Ward* in September 1862 before presenting a draft of the Emancipation Proclamation to the Cabinet. Lincoln found special delight in reading "Orpheus C. Kerr," which was meant to sound like "office seeker"—a perpetual thorn in his side.

Official government maps could be seen everywhere in the office. In the northwest corner of the room stood a rack with map-rollers. Folios were strewn on the floor and leaning against walls. By the end of the war, one visitor observed that the walls were "so thickly hung with maps" that the color of the wallpaper "cannot be discerned." They depicted every theater of combat, from the nearby Virginia countryside to the Shenandoah Valley, and from the Mississippi River to the Gulf of Mexico. Faint pencil lines traced the routes that the armies had taken, and disclosed plans for campaigns. Tiny pinholes revealed where Lincoln had pricked small red-, blue-, and black-headed pins into the maps, keeping track of movements in faraway places.

Lincoln's writing desk stood by a window at the room's exterior wall. Stoddard described it as a "second-hand mahogany upright desk, from some old furniture auction—or that is what it looks like." In fact, every president since

John Adams had worked at this old desk. Piled high on it on any given day were more bundles of papers, more pieces of correspondence, and more maps. From his high-backed chair at the desk Lincoln could pull a wire to summon a servant, or look out of his windows at the sites of the bustling city.

The carpet in the room was worn and faded by years and years of sunlight and foot traffic. The furniture, according to one observer, was formal, "stately and semi-comfortable." A sofa and two easy chairs sat against the wall on the eastern side of the room. James Buchanan had left an engraving of Andrew Jackson over the carved white marble fireplace. At the end of the war, the only picture on the mantel was a photograph of John Bright, the great English statesman who fought to prevent British recognition of the Confederacy.

Two windows let natural light into the room, supplementing the gaslight chandelier above the Cabinet table. On hot summer days, when Lincoln raised the window sash, a cool Potomac breeze would sweep through the room and rustle the papers and maps. From his south-facing windows he could see the grassy fields near the Capitol, the partially completed Washington Monument, the castle of the Smithsonian Institution, the glistening waters of the Potomac, and the heights of Arlington in the distance. Early in the war, Confederate flags fluttered in the breeze across the river, and thousands of tents were pitched on the grounds surrounding the White House and Capitol.[5] Lincoln looked southward out of his windows, not like many of his predecessors, who only sought to placate Southern slave owners. Now, as a wartime president, he would make war on his countrymen in order to bring them back into the republic. By 1865, it would be a very different nation.

Visitors who came to Lincoln's White House office encountered a man who exhibited what we would today call *authenticity*. He had genuine humility and showed real interest in his guests. His friend Joshua Speed remarked that Lincoln's "perfect naturalness" with visitors "threw such charm around him." He was, Speed continued, "true to every body and every thing about and around him—When he was ignorant on any subject no matter how simple it might make him appear he was always willing to acknowledge it—His whole aim in life was to be true to himself & being true to himself he could be false to no one." Another acquaintance recalled that Lincoln "was a very modest man in his demeanor. . . . In his freedom of intercourse with people he would seem to put himself of a par with everybody; and yet there was within him a sort of reserved power, a quiet dignity which prevented people from presuming on him, notwithstanding he had thrown down the social bars." According to this friend, Lincoln had a "psychic radiance"—a "magnetic influence . . . which brought him & the masses into a mysterious correspondence with each other." Another said, "He put on no airs. He did not hold himself distant from any man." Yet "there was something about him which we plain people couldn't explain that made us stand a little in awe of him. . . . You could get near him in a sort of neighborly way, as though you had always known him, but there was something tremendous between you and him all the time."[6]

Lincoln remained this personable, approachable fellow throughout his presidency, and yet the time he spent in his White House office also changed him. "I am very sure that if I do not go away from here a wiser man, I shall go away a better man, for having learned here what a very poor sort of a man I am," he told a friend one day. His view of national issues broadened as he realized the gravity of the problems that were resting on his shoulders. Those closest to him saw these changes taking place. After discussing emancipation with the president, John Hay wrote in his diary, "While the rest are grinding their little private organs for their own glorification the old man is working with the strength of a giant and the purity of an angel to do this great work."[7]

Today Lincoln's office is known as the Lincoln Bedroom, although he never slept in it (not in a bed, at any rate). In the 1860s it was a room where Lincoln spent untold hours meeting with politicians, dignitaries, and constituents, black as well as white.

2

"THE POLITICAL WONDERS OF THE YEAR"

Shortly after the presidential election of 1860, rumors circulated in the press that Abraham Lincoln had delivered a speech in Cincinnati in the presence of "some free negroes." Lincoln was bothered by this false account and wrote defensively to the editor of the *New York Times*, "I was never in a meeting of negroes in my life."[1] He was a man of his times, and he feared that being connected to African Americans in a personal way could hurt him politically, especially as the nation was cascading toward disunion. But soon the challenges of the wartime presidency would cause him to change his outlook, and he would welcome the opportunity to meet with black Americans.

The first African American to visit Lincoln's White House was Bishop Daniel Alexander Payne of the African Methodist Episcopal (AME) Church. Payne had been born to a free black family in Charleston, South Carolina, in 1811. His parents both died before he turned ten, at which point he was taken in by relatives. As a youth he was apprenticed as a shoemaker, a tailor, and a carpenter. In 1828, Payne opened a school for black children, but he was forced to close it in 1834 when South Carolina criminalized the education of African Americans (violators of this law would be fined and whipped). One day in Charleston a white man saw Payne standing on the street with a cane. The man became "indignant at the idea of a 'nigger' carrying a cane" and snatched it from Payne's hand. Payne fought back and was imprisoned for his actions. In 1835 he moved to Gettysburg, where he attended the Lutheran Seminary and supported himself as a bootblack and waiter. Although he did not graduate, he was licensed to preach in 1837. In the early 1840s, Payne left the Lutherans and joined the AME Church. He was elected bishop in 1852 and, during the Civil War, was based in Washington.[2]

Payne was optimistic for the plight of his people in April 1862, as were many African Americans in the nation's capital. Both houses of Congress had just passed a bill to abolish slavery in the District of Columbia. Now it only remained for President Lincoln to sign it. Anticipating that Washington's enslaved population would soon become free, Bishop Payne delivered a sermon entitled, "Welcome to the Ransomed, or, Duties of the Colored Inhabitants of the District of Columbia," on Sunday, April 13, at the Ebenezer Chapel in Georgetown, not far from the White House. His text was 1 Timothy 2:1–4, in which the Apostle Paul instructs the young minister Timothy to offer "supplications, prayers, intercessions, and giving of thanks . . . for all men," as well as "for kings, and for all that are in authority; that we may lead a quiet and peaceable life in all godliness and honesty." Payne implored his parishioners "to celebrate the emancipation, yea, rather, the *Redemption* of the enslaved people of the District of Columbia." And to the newly freed, he urged "not to *lounge in sinful indolence*, not to *degrade yourselves by vice*, nor to *corrupt society by licentiousness*, neither to *offend the laws by crime*," but to enjoy "*a well regulated liberty*." This meant being industrious and frugal, avoiding iniquity, believing in Jesus Christ, reading the Bible faithfully, cultivating their minds, saving what they earned, and educating their children. "Work, work, work!" he exhorted them. And "*run away* from whiskey, rum, and tobacco."

Payne also exhorted the congregation to pray for their governing authorities because God was using them to bring about their freedom and rights. "For the oppressed and enslaved of all peoples, God has raised up, and will continue to raise up, his Moses and Aaron," Payne declared. Only God could have "moved the heart of this Nation to have done so great a deed for this weak, despised and needy people!" He therefore urged his listeners to continue praying that God would grant wisdom to Congress, Lincoln, and the Supreme Court. They "need our prayers, they shall possess them," he said, so that justice may be "incorruptible" and "liberty governed by righteous law."

Ironically, Payne saw it as a blessing that black men were excluded from the Army because this gave them "the peculiar privilege" to have more opportunities to make "supplications, prayers, intercessions, and thanksgiving for these authorities." The prayers of the "colored" faithful, in other words, would be more effectual than bullets. He concluded that African Americans must also pray that the governing authorities find salvation in Jesus Christ so that when they "think, write, speak, act for the public weal, their own souls may be brought under the saving power of the Gospel, and with all the members of their respective families be made the heirs of the grace of life." In "the knowledge of the truth as it is in Christ Jesus" each would "become a holy, wise, and just man! Then will the laws be enacted in righteousness and executed in the fear of the Lord."[3]

Prayer was central to Payne's politics. He believed that praying for governing authorities—as the Bible commanded—would help bring about freedom and equality for African Americans. But Payne had it in mind to do more than simply offer supplications *for* the national authorities; he would also make supplications directly *to* them. On the very next day, Monday, April 14, Payne boldly went to the White House to meet with Lincoln. He first sent word that he would be coming, and when he arrived at the building, he presented his card. He wanted to ask Lincoln directly whether he planned to sign the DC Emancipation Bill. The bishop later recorded his impression of the meeting: "I found the President easy and urbane in manner, but not fluent in conversation, with a very careworn appearance and the countenance and expression of one who thinks deeply. The weight of the war was even then resting heavily upon him. He told me that he felt as though Providence had guided him, and enabled him to accomplish what he had accomplished."

When Payne arrived at the White House, Lincoln was in a room speaking with Sen. Elihu Washburn of Illinois. The president came to the door to greet the black minister. Taking Payne by the hand, Lincoln asked him, "Bishop Payne, of the African M. E. Church?" When Payne answered yes, Lincoln led him into the room "with my hand in his" and over to the fireplace, where he introduced him to Senator Washburn. Lincoln then seated Payne in an armchair between himself and Washburn. At that moment, Union General Carl Schurz came into the room and sat down. After a few more words, Payne turned to Lincoln and said, "I am here to learn whether or not you intend to sign the bill of emancipation?" Lincoln replied, "There was a company of gentlemen here to-day requesting me by no means to sign it." Schurz, a German immigrant, then interjected: "But, Mr. President, there will be a committee to beg that you fail not to sign it; for all Europe is looking to see that you fail not." Payne agreed. "Mr. President," he said, "you will remember that on the eve of your departure from Springfield, Ill., you begged the citizens of the republic to pray for you." Lincoln nodded. Payne continued: "From that moment we, the colored citizens of the republic, have been praying: 'O Lord just as thou didst cause the throne of David to wax stronger and stronger, while that of Saul should wax weaker and weaker, so we beseech thee cause the power at Washington to grow stronger and stronger, while that at Richmond shall grow weaker and weaker.'" Lincoln bent his head back and replied, "Well, I must believe that God has led me thus far, for I am conscious that I never would have accomplished what has been done if he had not been with me to counsel and to shield." Schurz and Payne continued to press him, but Lincoln would not answer their question directly.

After about forty-five minutes of conversation, Payne believed that he should prepare to leave. He handed Lincoln several copies of the *Christian Recorder*, the newspaper of the AME Church, and told him that if he "could find a leisure moment" and should peruse them he would "see what the A.M.E. Church was doing to improve the character and condition of our people in the republic." Payne likely hoped that Lincoln would see how African American religious leaders were instilling good moral values in their flocks. In a related way, Payne may have been subtly suggesting that colonization would not be necessary because black people would make good citizens.

Shortly after Payne's interview at the White House, the *Christian Recorder* remarked that the conversation he had with the president "will doubtless be profitable to our people in the future." The paper further surmised that Lincoln "without doubt sought to make himself more thoroughly acquainted with the wants and capacities of that portion of his much despised but loyal subjects. And all who are acquainted with the mental ability of Bishop Payne and his zeal for his race, are satisfied that by this interview the President was favorably impressed." A Washington correspondent for the paper added: "Bishop Payne assured his Excellency, 'That he had the prayers of the colored people; and since the booming of rebel cannon in Charleston harbor, first broke the stillness of morn, as the shot fell on Sumter's walls, he had prayed that God would stand behind the Government at Washington, as he stood behind the throne of David, and the Government at Richmond might wax weaker and weaker.'" According to this observer, Lincoln assured Payne "of his reliance on Divine Providence—expressing a hearty wish for the welfare of the colored race. The Bishop left the White House most favorably impressed."

Many years later, Payne reflected on what Lincoln was like during this conversation. "There was nothing stiff or formal in the air and manner of His Excellency—nothing egotistic," he wrote. "President Lincoln received and conversed with me as though I had been one of his intimate acquaintances or one of his friendly neighbors. I left him with a profound sense of his real greatness and of his fitness to rule a nation composed of almost all the races on the face of the globe." Payne had been to the White House in 1843, following the *Princeton* disaster, when he had preached a sermon at the funeral of one of President John Tyler's body servants, who had been killed by the explosion of a gun aboard that ship. Tyler had apparently not treated Payne with any dignity or respect, for he wrote that Lincoln "was a perfect contrast with President Tyler."[4]

Based on Payne's account, some historians believe that Lincoln was "hesitant" to sign the measure and that Payne's visit pushed him to do it.[5] However, Payne probably had little reason to worry. Lincoln had publicly supported emancipation in DC in his protest with Dan Stone in 1837 as well as in his own bill in 1849. He likely never wavered in his commitment to sign the bill, for he had no doubt that such a law was constitutional, and it contained two ingredients that Lincoln thought were essential: compensation for slave owners and voluntary colonization for freedpeople. The only provision it lacked, in Lincoln's mind, was a vote by the residents of the District. When the president signed the bill into law on April 16, he stated, "I have ever desired to see the national capital freed from the institution in some satisfactory way," and "I have never doubted the constitutional authority of congress to abolish slavery in this District."[6] It just might be that he was not ready to make that decision public when he met with Bishop Payne. A few days later, Sen. Charles Sumner of Massachusetts came to the White House and asked Lincoln for the pen he had used to sign the law. Lincoln took a handful of pens from his desk and replied, "It was one of these. Which will you take? You are welcome to all."[7]

African Americans throughout the nation celebrated the passage of this act. Payne later called it one of "the political wonders of the year," and said, "It was my fortune to be there when it occurred, and to participate in the joys of the occasion." On Sunday, April 20, black churches in Washington held special services for prayer and thanksgiving. In Baltimore, on May 1, the black community held a "jubilee and thanksgiving." In New York City, on May 5, African Americans began celebrating at 5 a.m., holding prayer meetings, a flag raising ceremony, and speeches. At the Cooper Union that night, Henry Highland Garnet paid "a lofty tribute to the worth and honesty of the President of the United States." At a meeting in Boston, wrote another black abolitionist, "there gushed forth from the grateful hearts of colored men and women their expressions of joy and thanksgiving for this inauguration of emancipation by President Lincoln, destined, as they humbly trust, to spread out, and inure the healing of the nation."[8]

Surprisingly, the newspapers took little notice of the bishop's historic visit to the White House on April 14. They did notice, however, when one or two other black men visited Lincoln later that week.

On April 17, the AME Church held its annual conference at the Israel Bethel Methodist Church, the second largest black congregation in Washington. Bishop Payne presided over the meeting, and other black leaders present included Rev. Richard H. Cain of New York, and two American-born émigrés who were serving as emigration commissioners from Liberia: John D. Johnson and Alexander Crummell.[9] Cain, Johnson, and Crummell were interested in one part of the DC Emancipation Act in particular—a provision that allocated $100,000 "to be expended under the direction of the President of the United States, to aid in the colonization and settlement of such free persons of African descent now residing in said District, including those to be liberated by this act, as may desire to emigrate to the Republics of Hayti or Liberia, or such other country beyond the limits of the United States as the President may determine." (In July 1862, Congress would appropriate an additional $500,000 for such purposes.)[10]

Little is known about John D. Johnson's background. In the 1840s and early 1850s he had been a barber and keeper of a "refreshment saloon" in Williamsburg, New York. In 1853, he settled with his wife and children in Monrovia, Liberia, where he became an affluent merchant. A strong advocate of colonization, Johnson became a Liberian citizen and, in 1859, helped charter a ship that brought thirty-three emigrants to Liberia. Among the migrants was Martin Delany, a black doctor who had previously been a harsh critic of Liberia, but whose views would soften as a result of this month-long visit. In the spring and summer of 1862, Johnson traveled to Washington, DC, where he met with members of Congress to discuss colonization.[11]

Crummell had been born to free black parents in New York City in 1819. His father, Boston Crummell, had been kidnapped in Africa and brought to America as a slave. As a young man, Crummell had tried to pursue a theological education so that he could enter the ministry as an Episcopal priest, but racial bigotry prevented his admission to his denomination's seminary in New York. Crummell received private instruction from clergymen in New England while also attending lectures, for no credit, at Yale. In 1844 he was ordained a priest. When the meeting place of his congregation burned down three years later, Crummell moved to England, where he attended Queens' College, Cambridge, taking a bachelor's degree in the spring of 1853. That summer, Crummell traveled to Liberia as a missionary—a place he could also raise his family "amid the political institutions of black men." He returned to the United States in April 1861 to lecture on behalf of the American Colonization Society and Liberia College. For the next year and a half he toured the United States, delivering lectures against racism and in favor of black migration to Liberia. "I believe that God is about to plant a new germ of civilization in Africa," he told an audience of the New Hampshire Colonization Society in June 1861, "and that we are fast rising to that lofty position designed by God for us."[12]

On April 9, 1862, Crummell and Johnson learned that they had been appointed by the Liberian government to serve as commissioners "to address colored people of this country [the United States] on Emigration." In this new capacity, one—or possibly both of them—decided to make an official visit to the White House. (As will be seen below, it is known for certain that Johnson met with Lincoln; it seems likely that Crummell joined him.) At the meeting, Lincoln said that he "was ready and would be glad" to use the money appropriated by Congress to assist free black people in emigrating to Liberia or other places, and that he would do all that the law of Congress permitted him to do to assist them. According to a news dispatch from Washington, dated April 17, "An agent of the Government of Liberia appeared before the President to-day, and urged the compulsory transportation of freed slaves to Liberia." While the dispatch spoke of just a single agent, it is possible that both Johnson and Crummell went to the White House to discuss the matter with Lincoln. No further account of the meeting appears to have survived, other than this one-sentence summary.

The thought of "compulsory" removal of freedpeople elicited "severe comments" in at least one newspaper, while a white leader in the colonization movement wrote to the head of the American Colonization Society to remind him that "our Society can have no part in any 'compulsory transportation'" of black people to Africa. He then asked, "Does President Lincoln perfectly understand this?" Concerned about the backlash, Johnson and Crummell "immediately" wrote to Lincoln asking him to "exonerate us from the imputation" contained in the news reports. Lincoln replied in a brief letter on May 5 "that neither you nor any one else have ever advocated, in my presence, the compulsory transportation of freed slaves to Liberia or elsewhere." Lincoln then informed the two Liberian commissioners, "You are at liberty to use this statement as you please." They very quickly published it in the press.[13]

In fact, Lincoln adamantly opposed anything but voluntary colonization, which he made clear at a Cabinet meeting in September 1862. When his postmaster general, Montgomery Blair, "made a long argumentative statement in favor of deportation," saying that it was "necessary to rid the country of its black population," and Attorney General Edward Bates followed up by saying that "compulsory deportation" was necessary because "the negro would not go voluntary [sic]," Lincoln "objected unequivocally to compulsion" and insisted that "emigration must be voluntary and without expense to themselves."[14]

John D. Johnson may not have been totally forthright with the president when he claimed not to support compulsory deportation of contrabands (slaves who fled to Union lines during the war). A few weeks after his White

House meeting, Johnson told Republican Congressman George W. Julian of Indiana that "the Contrabands turned adrift by the war . . . should be sent out of the country, whether they are willing to go or not" because "they were mere children in capacity, and needed the control of the superior race, and ought to have it, whether they desired or not." When Julian asked Johnson whether this would apply to all African Americans, whether free or enslaved, and from both North and South, Johnson replied that it did—"that the race was inferior, incapable of taking care of itself, and if they could not be persuaded to accept colonization, he would compel them to accept it."

Black leaders were outraged when they heard about Johnson's statements. In Washington, the Social, Civil, and Statistical Association (SCSA), a black organization that counted Lincoln's valet, William Slade, among its leaders, debated resolutions "to go at once and drive him (Johnson) from this city." After some debate, the resolutions were amended to create a committee of five to call on Johnson to "inquire of him if the remarks [attributed to him] were true, and to report to the next meeting."

On July 30, 1862, the SCSA drafted a letter to Johnson criticizing him for seeking "to influence [congressional] legislation against us" and for engaging "in acts inimical and treasonable to the interests of the colored people of this community and of the country generally." Moreover, they claimed that Johnson had heartlessly taken advantage of black refugees who had found status as contrabands in the nation's capital. The committee of five called upon Johnson, who, according to SCSA members, was "boiling over with rage and excitement." Initially, Johnson denied the allegations against him, but after some pressing, he "owned that he was guilty of the charges." At that point, two members of the SCSA who were not part of the committee of five—William Wormley and William Ringgold—violently assaulted Johnson. Another black organization, the Island Literary Association, then met and adopted resolutions "that Johnson be tarred and feathered" and that they would pool their resources to sustain members of the SCSA who might be prosecuted for "any action that they may see fit to exercise in relation to Johnson, and others of like stripe." This resolution was prescient, for violence against other black emigrationists soon occurred. A group of young black men gave Joseph E. Williams "a severe beating" for petitioning Congress in favor of colonization. According to one news report, "The colored people are now aroused, and unless these men leave the city it is feared that a general outbreak will follow."[15]

AME minister Henry McNeal Turner was disturbed by all of this lawlessness. He reported to the *Christian Recorder* that Johnson had been "most inhumanly mobbed . . . by the colored people of this city, or, I should have said, by a colored mob." Turner learned that Johnson had treated the men who called on him "contemptuously, which so angered them that they transformed themselves into a mob and let slip vengeance at him." According to Turner's sources, "nothing saved his life but the intervention of some young ladies." Turner was "sorry that our people acted so rudely in the matter, as I do not think it tends to their honor," but he was "equally sorry" that Johnson "wished to deprive us of that God-given right of choosing or refusing." Ultimately, Turner hoped that African Americans would not turn to violence to solve the problems in their communities. "I hope our people everywhere will soon begin to look upon mobs as the most contemptible, lowest, rottenest plan in all God's universe of carrying power. Let us come out and expose men's mean principles, but not injure their bodies, remembering that God made the latter, but never made the former; and it indicates an animal predominancy in its perpetrators."[16]

Johnson's two assailants, William Wormley and William Ringgold, were arrested and tried before the Criminal Court of the District of Columbia. At their trial, which took place on May 1, 1863, they offered no defense. The judge quickly found both men guilty and sentenced each to a fifty-dollar fine and ten days in jail. On the same day as the trial, two of Lincoln's Cabinet secretaries— Postmaster General Montgomery Blair and Navy Secretary Gideon Welles— wrote to Lincoln asking him to commute their time in prison. These "young men," they wrote, "have always sustained an excellent moral character as is well known to very many of our citizens." A Washington attorney who watched the trial and who was known for taking the cases of black defendants also wrote to Lincoln asking for commutation of the prison sentence. He told the president that "the case was so managed as to give the Court the worst possible opinion of the act of assault and battery for which they were indicted." Moreover, having known Wormley and Ringgold for at least two years, he informed Lincoln that they were "civil & polite young men" who should not be imprisoned. Lincoln acted quickly, issuing a remission of their prison sentence (but not the fines) on May 2, 1863.[17]

Despite the physical resistance that John D. Johnson was facing from the black community in Washington, he continued to press his case on behalf of Liberia. (He also contemplated suing his assailants for civil damages.) On March 3, 1863, Johnson sent Lincoln a letter reminding the president of their earlier meeting. Knowing the president's views of the matter, Johnson prudently spoke only of voluntary colonization. Shortly after writing this note, Johnson again called upon Lincoln at the White House. This time, however, the president seems to have blown him off.[18] By mid-1863, Lincoln was losing interest in colonization, and nothing came of this correspondence or meeting.

3

"A SPECTACLE, AS HUMILIATING AS IT WAS EXTRAORDINARY"

As much as Lincoln personally deplored the institution of slavery, he did not believe that he could abolish it simply because he was president. The Constitution did not authorize him to touch slavery in the states where it existed, and if he had done so in the first months of the war, the border slave states would have almost certainly joined the Confederacy. Nor was there much political support for emancipation among the Northern electorate early in the war. As much as abolitionists like Frederick Douglass and Charles Sumner wanted Lincoln to free the slaves, Lincoln knew that doing so would be futile. Northern support for the war effort would plummet and the armies might disintegrate. (The soldiers, after all, had volunteered to fight for the Union, not emancipation.) In other words, if Lincoln had taken a hard stance against slavery in 1861, he may have lost the Civil War right out of the gate—and slavery, then, would have been preserved in the South, anyway. So Lincoln adopted a moderate approach to the matter. He pledged to do what he could to stop slavery's expansion into the Western territories, he worked diligently to shut down the illegal trans-Atlantic slave trade, and he tried to induce Border State slaveholders to relinquish their "property" in exchange for compensation. (Slave owners in the Border States were never willing to accept this proposition.) Within this framework, Lincoln hoped that the prospect of colonization might alleviate the concerns of Northern whites that their labor market would be flooded with freedpeople.

Lincoln and the Republicans in Congress nevertheless took important steps to undermine slavery early in the war. In March 1862, Congress enacted a new article of war that forbade the Union soldiers from returning fugitive slaves to their masters. On July 17, Lincoln signed two laws that struck at the peculiar institution—the Second Confiscation Act, which declared free the slaves of masters who were convicted of treason, and the Militia Act, which allowed African American men to serve in "any military or naval service for which they may be found competent." Finally, on July 22, Lincoln informed his Cabinet that he planned to issue an emancipation proclamation. However, because the war was going badly for the Union at that time, Secretary of State William H. Seward urged Lincoln to postpone issuing such a proclamation until the North won a significant victory on the battlefield. Unfortunately, such a victory would not come until September 17, at Antietam.

Lincoln finally issued his preliminary emancipation proclamation on September 22. At a Cabinet meeting that day, he explained that he had "made a vow—a covenant—that if God gave us the victory in the approaching battle, he would consider it an indication of Divine will, and that it was his duty to move forward in the cause of emancipation." According to Secretary of the Navy Gideon Welles, "It might be thought strange, he said, but there were times when he felt uncertain how to act, that he had in this way submitted the disposal of matters—when the way was not clear to his mind what he should do. God had decided this question in favor of the slave. He was satisfied it was right. . . . His mind was fixed—his decision made."[1] Emancipation, in short, was the will of God.

The issue of emancipation had been on Lincoln's mind "by day and night, more than any other," he told a delegation of Christian ministers who came from Chicago to see him in September. On September 24, he told another audience at the White House, "What I did, I did after very full deliberation, and under a very heavy and solemn sense of responsibility. . . . I can only trust in God I have made no mistake." Some Northerners urged Lincoln not to carry through on his promise, for there were important elections looming throughout the North in October and November 1862, but Lincoln believed the decision was both "right and expedient." In truth, Lincoln was now firmly committed to emancipation as both a military necessity and as a moral good. To another group of Kentuckians in November, he said that he "would rather die than take back a word of the Proclamation of Freedom." But before Lincoln issued the preliminary emancipation proclamation in September, he took steps to help prepare the nation for the momentous transformation that was coming. One part of this strategy involved showing the Northern populace that he was fully committed to colonization.[2]

On August 4, Lincoln appointed Indiana minister James Mitchell as his colonization agent. On August 10, Mitchell sent word to black churches in Washington that the president wished to meet with a delegation of African

Americans. Representatives of several churches met at Union Bethel African Methodist Episcopal Church on August 14 and selected a group of men to visit the White House. The five men chosen were all well-educated members of Washington's black elite. Edward M. Thomas, the chairman, was president of the Anglo-African Institute for the Encouragement of Industry and Art and was well known for his personal library and fine art collection. John F. Cook Jr., a graduate of Oberlin College, was the son of the founder of the Fifteenth Street Presbyterian Church, Washington's preeminent black congregation. Benjamin McCoy had established a private school before founding the Asbury Methodist Church. John T. Costin was a grand master in the Freemasons. The least prominent among the group was Cornelius Clark, a hackman (driver) in the nation's capital.[3]

Lincoln met with the five delegates on the afternoon of August 14. Shortly before they arrived, he had a meeting with Joseph Jenkins Roberts, the former president of Liberia, and William McLain, a white officer of the American Colonization Society. Roberts had been born into a well-to-do free black family in Norfolk, Virginia, on March 15, 1809—just four weeks after Lincoln's birth. In 1829 he had emigrated to Liberia with his mother and younger brothers, where he became a wealthy trans-Atlantic shipping merchant and coffee farmer. Very quickly, Roberts gained the favor of Liberia's white governor for his efforts in suppressing hostile Africans. In 1833 he was elected the high sheriff, in 1838 he was appointed lieutenant governor, and in 1842 he became the first person of color to be appointed governor of Liberia. Upon the establishment of the Republic of Liberia in 1847, Roberts was elected the nation's first president, and he was reelected in 1849, 1851, and 1853. During this period, he met with other leaders of the Western world, including Queen Victoria of England, Napoleon III of France, and King Leopold I of Belgium.[4] By the time he met with Lincoln in 1862, he was used to negotiating with the great leaders of the world.

Roberts told Lincoln that between three and four hundred thousand people were now living in Liberia, many of whom were the descendants of American émigrés. Another twelve thousand had recently arrived from the United States. According to McLain, Lincoln "had said that for all the colored race who wanted to be any thing & do any thing for themselves & their race, Lib[eri]a was the place for them."[5]

Lincoln took a much different approach in his meeting with the delegation of black Washingtonians, which began about a half hour after Roberts and McLain left the president's office. Unlike the meeting with Roberts, which received virtually no press attention, Lincoln had a stenographer in the room for this second meeting so that his remarks would quickly appear in newspapers throughout the nation. Mitchell introduced the five men to the president and, after they had shaken hands and sat down, Lincoln made "a few preliminary observations," informing them that Congress had appropriated funds for colonization, "thereby making it his duty, as it had for a long time been his inclination, to favor that cause."

Lincoln asked the men, rhetorically, why "the people of your race" should be colonized and where they should go. He then answered his own questions. "You and we are different races," he began. "We have between us a broader difference than exists between almost any other two races. Whether it is right or wrong I need not discuss, but this physical difference is a great disadvantage to us both, as I think your race suffer very greatly, many of them by living among us, while ours suffer from your presence. In a word we suffer on each side." If Lincoln's black visitors could admit that this was true, then, he thought, "it affords a reason at least why we should be separated."

At this point, Lincoln asked the men if they were free men. "Yes, sir," one of them replied. "Perhaps you have long been free, or all your lives," the president surmised. This was the only time he asked a question that he was interested to hear their answer in the moment.

Lincoln then proceeded to make the case that since African Americans were not well treated in the United States, they would be better off elsewhere in the world. "Your race are suffering, in my judgment, the greatest wrong inflicted on any people," he said. And even if emancipation were to come to this country, black people were far from ever "being placed on an equality with the white race." White people had many "advantages" in life that people of color did not enjoy, and though African Americans may aspire to achieve equality, there was "not a single man of your race" on the entire continent who had ever been "made the equal of a single man of ours."

Such discrimination was "a fact with which we have to deal," Lincoln told them. "I cannot alter it if I would. It is a fact, about which we all think and feel alike, I and you." He then continued with some of the most infamous lines from this address—words that seemed to convey his greater concern for white people than for the suffering enslaved. "I need not recount to you the effects upon white men, growing out of the institution of Slavery," he said. Its "general evil effects on the white race" had brought the United States to its "present condition—the country engaged in war!—our white men cutting one another's throats." The "truth" of the matter, Lincoln continued, was that "but for your race among us there could not be war, although many men engaged on either side do not care for you one way or the other. Nevertheless, I repeat, without the institution of Slavery and the colored race as a basis, the war could not have an existence." Here,

Lincoln blamed the war on the *presence* of African Americans—*not* on the sin of slavery itself, or on the many white Americans who profited or benefited from it. Thus, he concluded, "It is better for us both, therefore, to be separated."

Lincoln understood that many free black people would not likely want to leave the country, in part because they might not be convinced that things would be better for them elsewhere. Naturally, they would rather stay in their homes and communities in the United States. To those who held these views, Lincoln said, "This is (I speak in no unkind sense) an extremely selfish view of the case." He continued: "There is an unwillingness on the part of our people, harsh as it may be, for you free colored people to remain with us." If these "intelligent," free black leaders would only lead the way, then those "whose intellects are clouded by Slavery" might follow and "much might be accomplished." Moreover, if white people saw colonization as a success, it might encourage them to "open a wide door for many to be made free." Thus, he told them, "It is exceedingly important that we have men at the beginning capable of thinking as white men, and not those who have been systematically oppressed."

Lincoln called on the delegation to make sacrifices for "the sake of your race," just as George Washington and the revolutionary generation had done. He recognized that some might rather remain in the land where they were born, but he could not understand why they would want to do this. "I do not know how much attachment you may have toward our race," he remarked. "It does not strike me that you have the greatest reason to love them. But still you are attached to them at all events."

Lincoln mentioned Liberia as a possible place to settle, but then spent most of his efforts describing the Chiriqui region of what is now Panama. It was closer than Africa and, unlike Liberia, "it is on a great line of travel—it is a highway." African Americans could prosper there if they utilized its "great natural resources and advantages"—such as coal mines, which Lincoln described in some detail. Making a pseudoscientific argument so common among white Americans at the time, he also said that African Americans could prosper there "because of the similarity of climate with your native land—thus being suited to your physical condition."

Lincoln told the delegation that he was willing to spend the colonization funds that Congress had allocated on this enterprise. "The Government may lose the money," he said, "but we cannot succeed unless we try; but we think, with care, we can succeed." Lincoln admitted that Central American politics were unstable, but he stated that the political leaders there "are more generous than we are here" and that "I would endeavor to have you made equals, and have the best assurance that you should be the equals of the best."

Lincoln wanted to know if the black delegation could find one hundred able-bodied and "tolerably intelligent" men with wives and children to lead the way. "I want you to let me know whether this can be done or not. This is the practical part of my wish to see you." Finally, he asked them "to consider seriously" this proposition, not merely for themselves, but "for the good of mankind" in future generations. The chairman of the delegation, Edward M. Thomas, briefly replied that they "would hold a consultation and in a short time give an answer." Lincoln then concluded, "Take your full time—no hurry at all."[6]

Newspaper reaction to the meeting was mixed. The *New York Sun* believed the "spectacle" of the president meeting with African Americans would "forever remain one of the chief marvels of history." The editors praised Lincoln for using language that "assumed a tone of apology suitable for the occasion" and words that "seemed to spring from a heart filled with mingled emotion of tenderness and sorrow." Another paper said it would "cheer on the experiment" if it meant hastening the end of the war, while a third claimed, "This effectually puts the quietus to the oft-repeated assertions of the Democrats, that the Republicans were endeavoring to bring about in this country 'an equality of the races.'"[7] The Philadelphia *Press* offered a particularly optimistic take: "The negro may well say that under President Lincoln he has had his first hearing in the White House. Other Presidents have bought and sold him, and driven him from the territories, and closed their eyes to the nefarious system under which he was captured in Africa and dragged over the ocean in chains. But President Lincoln has listened to his story and given him counsel and advice."

Others, however, were less sanguine. Upon reading the analysis in the Philadelphia *Press*, the editors of the *Syracuse Journal* exploded: "It is true the negro has had his first admission to the White House,—audience it was not. He went, not to receive a hearing but a lecture on the difference between his race and ours." Instead of lecturing his guests, Lincoln should have listened to their "story of wrong and outrage, extended through many a century of barbarian history, down to the present enlightened age, that would make the very stones cry out." Another white editor argued that rather than support colonization, black people should simply be treated fairly in the United States: "It therefore appears that the white man has only to be just, to make the position of the black man in this country a very pleasant one. We do not believe that colonization is the way out of slavery." William Lloyd Garrison's *Liberator* called Lincoln's address "a tissue of absurdities and false assumptions." Meanwhile, one Copperhead woman joined in the criticism, although for a very different reason. In a letter to the editor of the Columbus *Crisis* she argued that colonization schemes were ill-advised because they would remove black people from their natural state of bondage.[8]

Two days after the meeting, Edward Thomas sent Lincoln two short letters. In the first, he asked for "a *personal* interview" of only "a *few* minutes" on Monday morning, August 18, at 8:30 or 9 a.m. In the second note, he informed Lincoln that the members of the delegation would confer with black leaders in Philadelphia, New York, and Boston regarding the president's recommendations. "We were entirely hostile to the movement until all the advantages were so ably brought to our views by you," Thomas wrote, and he believed that other Northern black leaders would "heartily" join in the movement "when the Subject is explained by us to them."[9]

If Thomas was persuaded by Lincoln's arguments, however, other black leaders were not. After reading about the meeting in the newspapers, Frederick Douglass was angered by the condescending tone of Lincoln's lecture. He thought the speech made Lincoln "appear silly and ridiculous, . . . showing all his inconsistencies, his pride of race and blood, his contempt for Negroes and his canting hypocrisy." Douglass doubted that Lincoln had any "sincere wish to improve the condition of the oppressed" and instead "merely [had] the desire to get rid of them." Lincoln's "tone of frankness and benevolence" toward the black delegation reminded Douglass of "the politeness with which a man might try to bow out of his house some troublesome creditor or the witness of some old guilt." In a concluding sentence that reflected Douglass's anger more than a reasoned assessment of Lincoln's ability as a speaker, the black abolitionist explained that Lincoln's "plain" and "coarse" speech to the black delegation was emblematic of the president's "decided awkwardness in the management of the English language."[10]

Other African Americans had similar reactions, for the truth was that few wanted to leave the United States. In Brooklyn, Rev. James N. Gloucester told an audience that the "contrabands" should be armed as soldiers, not expelled from "the land of their birth." Lincoln's colonization "schemes," he said, were "unnecessary, impolitic and unjust." Instead, the president should "put arms in their hands, and God would see to it that this system of oppression against which she is struggling would find its quietus." According to Gloucester, "they were loyal citizens of the government, and should be allowed to assist her in her struggle against her enemies." (The following year, Gloucester would meet with Lincoln to discuss the recruitment of black troops.) On Long Island, a mass meeting of African Americans adopted resolutions denying that "we are a 'different race of people,' as God has made of one blood all nations that dwell on the face of the earth." The United States was "our country by birth," they continued, and "we are acclimated, and . . . better adapted to it than to any other country." Having sacrificed so much to build this country, they simply wanted the rights embodied in the Declaration of Independence to apply to them. They reminded Lincoln that there were "no colored rebels" and that "we colored people are all loyal." Rather than ask black people to leave the nation, Lincoln should arm them to put down the rebellion. White abolitionists were equally infuriated. In her diary, Julia Wilber said that Lincoln's "heartless cold-blooded speech" was a "disgrace" for the "President of a Republic which declares that all men are born free & equal."[11]

Few moments in Lincoln's presidency appear as regrettable as this one. On the one hand, it is noteworthy as the first time that a sitting president invited a group of African Americans to the White House for an interview. On the other hand, Lincoln's words were terribly condescending. William Lloyd Garrison's Boston newspaper, the *Liberator*, noted the complicated nature of this moment, calling it "a spectacle, as humiliating as it was extraordinary."[12]

Lincoln's harshest modern critics have used this meeting to bludgeon Lincoln as a racist. Other historians, however, have argued that Lincoln was acting strategically. Lincoln almost certainly hoped that newspaper reports of this meeting would appeal to the racist white constituency in the North and in the Border States—voters who needed to be prepared for the emancipation edict he was preparing to make public. He also wanted to appeal to voters who might be souring on the Republican Party in the lead-up to the 1862 elections. Lecturing black leaders about the benefits of colonization, writes historian James Oakes, "might make emancipation more palatable." The meeting thus represented both Lincoln's shrewd political calculations and his belief "that the voluntary emigration of blacks was the best thing for everybody."[13]

If Lincoln's desire was to appeal to Northern Democrats, he at best achieved mixed results. The New York *Caucasian* opined that the "great Virginians of other days"—George Washington, Thomas Jefferson, and James Madison—would have reacted with "horror" and "overwhelming disgust" should they have seen Lincoln talking to "darkies in the Mansion house of the people!"[14] Another antiwar Democrat, writing under the pseudonym "Major Jack Downing," argued that Lincoln showed too much empathy for the black men at the meeting. In a fictional conversation with Lincoln, Downing said, "You talk to these niggers jest as if they were white people, all except their color. You seem to think that they will do something for their posterity, sacrifice something, but they won't. The nigger only cares for the present. The mulattoes have some of the talents of the white men, but the nigger not a bit." Downing continued in this racist vein, saying that African Americans will always be "the same uncivilized, heathin people when white folks did not have control of 'em. You send 'em to Centril America, an in a gineration or so they will be again eatin lizards an worshipping snakes, as they do in Africa now."[15] The disturbing language of this satire can help modern readers recapture the social, cultural, and political contexts of Lincoln's meeting. From this Democrat's perspective—a Democrat who reflected the views of a significant voting bloc in the North—it was not that Lincoln offered his black visitors too little respect, but that he treated them as equals.

Of course, Lincoln had not treated the men as equals in his office that day, but he had created an unprecedented situation. Not only had he invited the five black men to meet with him in his office, but, ultimately, he had set things up so that he would have to wait for their response and listen to what they had to say. Henry McNeal Turner recognized this unusual opportunity, and he urged the readers of the *Christian Recorder* to take hold of the favorable circumstance they had been given. When he learned that the five delegates were preparing a reply to the president, he wrote, "I hope they will make it speak in power, for if we do not speak now, at a time when the chief magistrate is bound to hear us, I very much doubt another opportunity being offered. May God teach them what to say."[16]

Turner's observations were exactly right. In this moment, Lincoln would have to listen to the black delegation and accept their response. For despite the political posturing and lecturing tone of Lincoln's words, he had invited them into his office and asked them to do something. They did not have to answer the way Lincoln wanted them to. He could not force them to do so. And they did not. The black delegation ultimately adopted resolutions in which they deemed discussion of colonization to be "inexpedient, inauspicious and impolitic" and that "we judge it unauthorized and unjust for us to compromise the interests of over four and a half millions of our race by precipitous action on our part."[17] This was a radical new development in American politics.

It is worth repeating that the tone of Lincoln's lecture to the black delegation should not skew how we understand his other interactions with African Americans. This meeting was unlike any other. Never again did he lecture a black guest. The infamous meeting of August 1862, in short, is the exception that proves the rule.

4

"THE LORD HAS WORK FOR ME HERE"

Although most African Americans rejected the idea of moving to faraway and unfamiliar lands, Lincoln's highly publicized meeting with the black delegation caused a small number to begin making plans. Some sold their homes and other property in anticipation of an imminent departure, but they grew anxious when the Lincoln administration did not direct them on how to proceed. Frustrated with this situation, a delegation of nine black emigrationists went to the White House on October 27, 1862, "to express their disappointment in the delay at going to Central America." The most prominent among them, J. Willis Menard of Illinois, would in six years become the first African American elected to Congress. Three of the men were from Washington, DC, two came from Pennsylvania, and three from New York.

The delegation wrote a memorial that asked Lincoln "when we can take our departure to the land promised us by yourself in the address made to us in this, your Executive mansion." They explained that many black families had already sold their homes, "acting upon your promise to send us as soon as one hundred families were ready." Now they had nowhere to live, and winter was fast approaching. "We are not willing to believe that your Excellency would invite us to make arrangements to go—would tell us that we could not live prosperously here—would create hopes and stimulate us to struggle for national independence and respectable equality," they said, and then not fulfill his "promise" to send them to a better land. They therefore asked Lincoln to give "the explicit orders to sail, before the cold weather sets in to pinch us here" or a voyage by sea would be too dangerous.

One of Lincoln's private secretaries informed the delegation that the president "was as anxious as he ever was for their departure" and that he had placed the matter of colonization in the hands of Sen. Samuel C. Pomeroy of Kansas. The secretary also told them that Lincoln could not meet with them that day, but that he would do so soon.[1] It does not appear that Lincoln ever met with them.

A few days later Lincoln met with two other supporters of colonization. The more prominent of the two, George W. Samson, was president of Columbian College (now George Washington University). The other, Rev. Chauncey Leonard, was "an esteemed colored" Baptist minister.[2] Born in 1822 in Connecticut, Leonard was ordained in 1853 and ran the Saratoga Street Colored Institute, a school for black children in Baltimore, for three years in the mid-1850s. Then, in 1858, he moved to Washington, DC, to shepherd First Baptist Church. In 1861, Leonard opened a school for black children and the Washington *Evening Star* reported that his pupils were well trained and could quickly and accurately answer questions from visitors—an experience that "would do credit to any school in the land." Sadly, arsonists destroyed the school in 1862.[3]

On November 1, 1862, Samson and Leonard went to the White House to meet with Lincoln. The president told them that he would draw up to $500 from his colonization fund to send Leonard to Liberia on a scouting mission, if the secretary of the American Colonization Society (ACS) thought it was in "the interest of the colored people" of Washington, DC. Lincoln further stated that he believed fifty other black residents of Washington could be ready to depart in a vessel called the *M. C. Stevens* "if she delays sailing one week." Samson was confident that Lincoln would pay the passage and steerage of these fifty migrants if R. R. Gurley, the corresponding secretary of the ACS, presented a list to him.[4]

In January 1863, R. R. Gurley and Philadelphia minister Thomas S. Malcolm met with Lincoln to make arrangements for Leonard to sail for Monrovia. Gurley suggested that Lincoln provide $200 from the congressional colonization fund, which the president readily agreed to.[5] In February, Leonard sailed from Boston as "a pioneer of about fifty Baptists, who are to follow on the 1st of May."[6] From Sierra Leone in April, he wrote, "The Lord has work for me here."[7] Unfortunately, Leonard suffered from sickness while in Liberia and was not able to do as much teaching and other work as he had hoped to accomplish. Moreover, as a result of his illness, Leonard's expenses increased dramatically while he was in Africa, and he had to appeal to Lincoln for more money to cover his debts.[8] He returned to the United States in late 1863.

On July 9, 1864, Leonard sent a brief note to Lincoln. Writing from Alexandria, Virginia, he implored the president: "Being anxious to accomplish the greatest amount of good to the Colored Soldiers, of the United States Army; I most respectfully ask to be appointed Hospital Chaplain, at the Hospital for Colored Troops in this place." Lincoln must have remembered his former visitor, for upon reading Leonard's note he instructed his private secretary, John Hay, to send a letter to Secretary of War Edwin M. Stanton appointing Leonard to the position.[9] Leonard accepted the appointment in early August, and for the next year and a half he served as chaplain at the L'Ouverture Hospital in Alexandria—a facility named after the Haitian revolutionary, Toussaint L'Ouverture. There he would care for the physical and spiritual needs of sick and wounded black soldiers as well as black civilian refugees. One surgeon at the hospital described Leonard as having "a modest manly bearing" with a deep concern for the wellbeing of "the people of his race."[10] At L'Ouverture, Leonard established a school for the convalescents. He also regularly shared the Gospel with the wounded, preached sermons, led Bible studies, baptized converts, distributed religious tracts, lectured on his travels to Africa, helped bury the dead, and had the sad and solemn duty of writing letters informing families that their loved ones had died.[11] Many years later he recalled his work at L'Ouverture as being "to them as a father among strangers when the last moments of life was dying out."[12]

Leonard became severely ill with dysentery in the summer of 1865. Following the war, he traveled around as a missionary and pastor, spending time in Washington, DC, as well as several cities and counties in Virginia where he organized churches for freedmen. About the time of the Centennial celebration he returned to Philadelphia for a few years. From 1878 to 1883 he resided in Springfield, Massachusetts, before returning to Providence, Rhode Island, in 1883, where he served as minister at the Fourth Baptist Church (Colored). He suffered chronic dysentery in the postwar period and received an inadequate salary from his ministerial duties, forcing him to accept financial assistance from anyone willing to help, including white clergymen of other denominations. In 1884, Elisha Hunt Rhodes—the Union soldier made famous by the Ken Burns *The Civil War* documentary—wrote on Leonard's behalf for a pension. Rhodes described Leonard as "a colored man very much respected here, and is in feeble health and very destitute." Without support from the Pension Office, Rhodes continued, Leonard "cannot last long." By the 1890s he had become the chaplain for the Grand Army of Rhode Island. When he died in 1892, his meeting with Lincoln was still considered one of the central events of his life. His brief obituary noted, "At the time of the proposition to colonize the slaves in Africa, President Lincoln appointed three men to learn the condition of the locality named, and the probable results. Mr. Leonard was one of the members of that committee."[13]

~

Abraham Lincoln's earliest meetings with African Americans reveal his willingness to welcome black leaders into his orbit when discussing great matters of state. This was something that no other president had ever done. These early meetings focused almost entirely on the subject of colonization. Alexander Crummell, John D. Johnson, Joseph Jenkins Roberts, the several black delegations, Edward M. Thomas, and Chauncey Leonard were all deeply interested in the subject. The meetings may help explain part of Lincoln's sustained interest in colonization during the first two years of the war. Several of these men supported the enterprise, while others came to endorse it after meeting with him. Such meetings may have given Lincoln a false sense of enthusiasm among African Americans for colonization.

In late 1862, it appears that Lincoln also met with Henry McNeal Turner, who at the time was only twenty-eight years old. Shortly after Lincoln issued his preliminary Emancipation Proclamation in September 1862, Turner reported to the *Christian Recorder* that Lincoln "wrote his proclamation in good faith. I believe Mr. Lincoln embodied his conscientious promptings when he wrote that proclamation." Knowing that many African Americans had been angered by Lincoln's condescending lecture to the black delegation the previous month, Turner informed his readers that "Mr. Lincoln is not half such a stickler for colored expatriation as he has been pronounced (I am responsible for the assertion), but it was a strategic move upon his part in contemplation of this emancipatory proclamation just delivered. He knows as well as any one, that it is a thing morally impracticable, ever to rid this country of colored people unless God does it miraculously, but it was a preparatory nucleus around which he intended to cluster the raid of objections while the proclamation went forth in the strength of God and executed its mission." Turner then added cryptically and suggestively, "I do not wish to trespass upon the key that unlocks a private door for fear that I might lose it, but all I will say is that the President stood in need of a place to *point to*."[14]

Turner's remarkable letter to the *Christian Recorder* may be the only surviving piece of evidence that offers direct insight into Lincoln's political strategy for inviting the black delegation to the White House. As suggested in the previous chapter, Lincoln used that meeting to help prepare the Northern electorate for emancipation (although not all historians accept this interpretation). Lincoln appears to have explained that strategy to Turner. Turner may therefore be the only person in whom Lincoln so candidly confided his plan. At the same time, Lincoln knew that Turner's dispatch would reach the eyes of thousands of black readers. He wanted *them* to know that his heart was in emancipation, *not* colonization. Turner concluded his report, "Mr. Lincoln loves freedom as well as any one on earth, and if he carries out the spirit of his proclamation, he need never fear hell. GOD GRANT HIM A HIGH SEAT IN GLORY."[15]

Lincoln nevertheless continued to push for colonization even after he issued the Emancipation Proclamation. But after several failed attempts—including one that led to the deaths of eighty-five black migrants on an island off of the coast of Haiti in 1863—he finally abandoned the scheme. By the summer of 1863, Lincoln told Gen. Nathaniel P. Banks that he hoped that voters in Louisiana would accept the Emancipation Proclamation and "adopt some practical system by which the two races could gradually live themselves out of their old relation to each other, and both come out better prepared for the new." Lincoln quickly added, "Education for young blacks should be included in the plan." In the summer of 1864, Lincoln's private secretary John Hay wrote in his diary, "I am glad the President has sloughed off that idea of colonization. I have always thought it a hideous & barbarous humbug."[16]

Lincoln would continue to meet with black advocates for emigration but not to discuss colonization. On April 11, 1864, a black New Yorker named Lewis H. Putnam came to the White House to see the president. Putnam had been born in North Carolina and spent some time in Canada before moving to New York City. He was an advocate for black rights who had assisted fugitive slaves on the Underground Railroad, and prior to the war he had been a proponent of black emigration to Liberia. (In the mid-1850s, Putnam was accused of swindling fellow African Americans through colonization schemes. He later sued for libel. An 1853 letter to the editor of *Frederick Douglass' Paper* called Putnam "decidedly one of the most remarkable black men of our time," but proceeded to describe him in derogatory terms.)[17] Virtually nothing is known about his visit to the White House other than that, at the conclusion of the meeting, Lincoln penned a short note to Edwin Stanton asking him to "please see L. H. Putnam, whom you will find a very intelligent colored man; and who wishes to talk about our colored forces, their organization."[18] Lincoln was likely willing to speak with Putnam in April 1864 since the topic of conversation was arming black men, not colonizing them.

INTERLUDE 2

Foreign Diplomats

In his annual message to Congress in December 1861, Lincoln stated, "If any good reason exists why we should persevere longer in withholding our recognition of the independence and sovereignty of Hayti and Liberia, I am unable to discern it." Lincoln therefore asked Congress to consider passing a law that would offer diplomatic recognition to the world's two black republics. Heeding this call, Charles Sumner, chairman of the Senate Committee on Foreign Affairs, reported such a bill on February 4, 1862. Lincoln signed it into law on June 5.[1]

When this issue came up for debate in the Senate, Kentucky slaveholder Garrett Davis sounded the alarm over the social and political implications of the proposal. If such a measure were adopted, he argued, Haitian and Liberian diplomats "would have to be received by the President and by all the functionaries of the Government upon the same terms of equality with similar representatives from other Powers." To make matters worse, they and their families would have to be given some measure of social equality at the White House. "If a full-blooded negro were sent in that capacity from either of those countries, by the laws of nations he could demand that he be received precisely on the same terms of equality with the white representatives from the Powers of the earth composed of white people," complained Davis.

When the President opened his saloons to the reception of the diplomatic corps, when he gave his entertainment to such diplomats, the representatives, of whatever color, from those countries would have the right to demand admission upon terms of equality with all other diplomats; and if they had families consisting of negro wives and negro daughters, they would have the right to ask that their families also be invited to such occasions, and that they go there and mingle with the whites of our own country and of other countries that happened to be present. . . . Now, sir, I want no such exhibition as that in our capital and in our Government.[2]

In the House of Representatives, Ohio Democrat Samuel S. Cox echoed these concerns, saying, "If they send negro ministers to Washington city, . . . they shall be welcomed as ministers, and have all the rights of Lord Lyons and Count Mercier. They cannot send any one else than negroes, as representatives of their nations." Cox then added with derision, "How fine it will look, after emancipating the slaves in this District, to welcome here at the White House an African, full-blooded, all gilded and belaced, dressed in court style, with wig and sword and tights and shoe-buckles, and ribbons and spangles, and many other adornments which African vanity will suggest! How suggestive of fun to our good-humored, joke-cracking Executive!"[3]

The bigoted fears expressed by Davis and Cox reflected how many Northerners viewed the two black republics, underscoring that Lincoln had little to gain in electoral politics by urging their diplomatic recognition. Several Democratic newspapers decried the imminent arrival of "a darkey Minister" to Washington. "This Administration and Congress are going it loud on the nigger question," opined one editor. Not only had Republicans "put Sambo on an equality with our brave white private soldiers," but now black diplomats would be welcomed to the national capital. "This is quite an innovation on old established customs. Fancy a big darkey among the favored diplomatic corps, paying his respects to Abraham the First, while 'the white trash' must stand back until 'dis colored gemman' retires."[4]

The fears of Senator Davis, Representative Cox, and these Democratic editors soon came to fruition. Lincoln let it be known that he would not object if the president of Haiti sent a black man as an emissary to Washington, telling one journalist, "Well—you can tell Mr. Geffrard that I shan't tear my shirt if he does send a negro here!" Over time, this story evolved to have Lincoln say, "send a nigger here!" but the original source from 1862 does not use that slur.[5]

Radical Republicans and African Americans rejoiced at Lincoln's new foreign policy. Martin R. Delany wrote to Frederick Douglass that he was pleased that Lincoln would recognize someone "from among ourselves." Similarly, a correspondent to the African Methodist Episcopal (AME) Church's *Christian Recorder* proclaimed, "I am of the opinion that it is the duty of every colored man to uphold the present administration, because it is doing more for his race than has ever been done since the organization of the government. Never has a President, or cabinet officer stood forth to vindicate the rights of black men before." As evidence, this writer affirmed that diplomatic recognition of Haiti and

Liberia "demonstrate[s] that this administration is the friend of the black race, and desires its prosperity no less than the good will of all the races of men."[6]

In February 1863, Haitian diplomat Ernest Roumain arrived in Washington, DC. Within a short time he was meeting with Lincoln and Secretary of State William H. Seward. In March, Seward hosted an elaborate formal dinner for the new honored guest. Attendees included ambassadors from England, France, and Russia, as well as Secretary of the Treasury Salmon P. Chase, Postmaster General Montgomery Blair, Senator Charles Sumner, and other high-ranking officials. Some evidence also suggests that Roumain frequently attended White House levees. One Iowa woman who met Roumain at a dinner party said she "felt queerly, as though I were having a very funny dream" when she met the "elegant colored" Haitian diplomat and his secretary wearing white kid gloves and "conversing in Spanish, French and English, yet most unmistakably darkey!" Roumain, she wrote, "is tall, very fine looking and bright copper colored. His hair is like that of an Indian, his features Spanish, and his manner very French." The two black gentlemen "were modest and reserved, acting with perfect dignity," and yet, she wrote, "I confess I stared more at them than was quite polite, and found it a little hard to keep my face straight, for any one who has been raised in a slave State finds it a little ludicrous to be entertaining people from Hayti." She soon found, however, "that it was not at all difficult to pay proper attention and respect to these Haytien dignitaries . . . whose manners were so gentlemanly."[7] Roumain's presence at events in Washington's social circles forced white Americans to reconsider the ways they viewed people of color. As Frederick Douglass concluded, "We have recorded few more important facts in the history of the relation of this Government to the colored part of mankind."[8]

Sadly, Roumain was not treated well by most of the Washingtonians he encountered. According to a correspondent to the *Anglo-African*, Lincoln and his Cabinet "received him as they did other foreign representatives," but other residents of the District "did not give him the same reception that they did to others." This witness observed that the Haitian minister had "become disgusted with the general treatment received at the hands of the majority of the white citizens of this city." And so, in late 1863, Roumain left for Manhattan, a more ethnically diverse urban metropolis. Nevertheless, in Lincoln's welcoming of the first black diplomat into the city, African Americans saw hope for the future. The *Anglo-African*'s correspondent took heart that he was living in "an age of progress" and that African Americans "are making rapid strides onwards against all the prejudices with which we have to contend." Accordingly, he believed that "the time is not far distant when we shall occupy *social and political positions*, where we shall not be known by *our color*."[9]

5

"THE PROMISE BEING MADE, MUST BE KEPT"

When Abraham Lincoln issued the Emancipation Proclamation on January 1, 1863, he transformed the nature of the war. The proclamation freed the slaves in areas of rebellion, thus turning the Union armies into armies of liberation. As Union soldiers moved forward, they would bring freedom to the enslaved in the Confederacy. Moreover, the proclamation made no mention of colonization or of compensation for slave owners, important steps forward in Lincoln's thinking. Finally, Lincoln's edict permitted the raising of black regiments—a radical action that would ultimately lead to the enlistment of nearly two hundred thousand black Union soldiers. For two years, black men had been offering their services to the Union, but they were almost universally rejected by state and federal authorities (except to serve as laborers). Now, Lincoln said, black men "will be received into the armed service of the United States to garrison forts, positions, stations, and other places, and to man vessels of all sorts in said service." How striking that Lincoln signed this revolutionary document in his White House office—the very room in which he had met with black emigrationists and with the black delegation just a few months earlier. Lincoln was now more interested in using black men to help restore the country, not in sending them out of it. And he had come to this decision, he wrote, invoking "the considerate judgment of mankind, and the gracious favor of Almighty God."[1]

It is unclear when exactly Lincoln came to support the recruitment of black soldiers. He opposed arming black men both publicly and in private conversations during the summer and fall of 1862.[2] A meeting with one of the war's most famous fugitive slaves may have helped push him toward accepting black soldiers.

On May 13, 1862, Robert Smalls and several other South Carolina slaves captured the CSS *Planter* in Charleston and sailed her to the Union fleet, achieving their own freedom in the process. Smalls received a hero's welcome in the North, and two weeks later Lincoln signed a law authorizing the Navy to give Smalls half of the value of the *Planter* as salvage.[3] In late August, Smalls traveled to Washington, DC, where he told his story to an audience of 1,200 at Israel Church. After hearing the thrilling narrative, Henry McNeal Turner called Smalls "a living specimen of unquestionable African heroism." While in Washington, Smalls also met with Lincoln. He almost certainly told Lincoln the story of his escape as he urged the president to arm black men. As a congressman in 1886, Smalls recalled, "Proceeding to Washington I was honored with several interviews with President Lincoln and Stanton, and from them bore an official letter to General [David] Hunter authorizing the formation and mustering in of several regiments of colored soldiers."[4] The story has evolved over time. Recently, the *Washington Post* erroneously claimed that Smalls "sat at the conference table next to Frederick Douglass as they tried to convince President Abraham Lincoln that African Americans should be allowed to fight for their own freedom."[5] Douglass, however, did not meet with Lincoln until August 1863—*after* black men had been serving in the Union armies for almost a year. Nevertheless, Smalls's meetings with Lincoln helped encourage the president to arm black men against the Rebels. Black men would now fight for the freedom of their race, just like Robert Smalls had done to achieve his own freedom in May 1862.

Recruitment of black soldiers began in earnest in the spring of 1863. "The bare sight of fifty thousand armed and drilled black soldiers on the banks of the Mississippi would end the rebellion at once," Lincoln wrote optimistically to Andrew Johnson of Tennessee in March 1863. "And who doubts that we can present that sight, if we but take hold in earnest?" Lincoln soon took hold in earnest in Washington. On Monday, April 27, journalist Jane Swisshelm reported, "The colored men of the District have been notified to appear before the President on Wednesday, day after to-morrow. It is expected that all regiments will be raised here, but the regulations are that all the officers are to be white men. I do not see that the colored men can do much about raising troops; but the world moves; and if they prove as good soldiers as their friends think they will, their merits will be acknowledged in the right to fill the offices as well as the ranks."[6] No record of this meeting appears to exist, but Lincoln did tell a Washington delegation around this time: "Now, what I want of you is to bring on your *men*, and I will find service for them. I am anxious for them. I want them now."[7]

The black community of Washington was initially reluctant to show enthusiasm for enlisting because they had faced a violent backlash following the issuance of the Emancipation Proclamation a few months earlier; however, a recruiting station was soon established. Rumors circulated that William Slade wanted to be appointed quartermaster of the regiment. In early May, black leaders held a war meeting at Israel Church on South Capitol Street. The congregation sang, "Am I a Soldier of the Cross?" and heard speeches by several black and white leaders, including Henry McNeal Turner. Those present elected a committee to assist with the efforts, among whom was John F. Cook Jr., one of the five men who had met with Lincoln in August 1862. Another member of the committee, William Wormley, was one of the men who had assaulted the Liberian emigration commissioner, John D. Johnson, and subsequently received a pardon from Lincoln. Another meeting was held at the Fifteenth Street Presbyterian Church on May 11 to make final arrangements for the organization of the First US Colored Infantry. "We hope there will be a full attendance of our colored friends, as this is the best course for them to prove that they deserve freedom," reported a local paper. By late June, the First USCT was mustered into the federal service. Lincoln appointed Reverend Turner the regimental chaplain.[8] A year later, on August 25, 1864, Turner's wife delivered a baby girl, whom the happy parents named Lincolnia.[9]

Further north, black leaders in Poughkeepsie, New York, began organizing "the Fremont Legion." They hoped to find at least ten thousand black volunteers to serve under Union General John C. Fremont—a man that African Americans had greatly admired since he ran for president in 1856. In mid-March 1863, a delegation from Poughkeepsie arrived in Washington for the purpose of tendering their services to the Union. The chairman of the delegation, H. Parker Gloucester, was a light-skinned son of a Kentucky slave who had spent six years in Europe and was known by an acquaintance as "a polished gentleman." Parker and his fellow delegates had "several interviews with the President," and Parker said Lincoln "most cordially received" them. According to Henry McNeal Turner, Gloucester met with "President Lincoln nearly every day for over a week. He has also been the frequent guest of Mrs. Lincoln on one or two occasions." During one of the meetings, the delegates presented Lincoln with a petition that thanked him "for proclaiming liberty to the suffering millions of our oppressed fellow countrymen, whose groans have ascended to that God who is our refuge and help in time of trouble." Alluding to the Old Testament book of Proverbs, they praised God for raising up Lincoln "as a deliverer, and a lamp by which our feet are guided into the paths of liberty." They reminded

Lincoln that black men had fought for the nation during the American Revolution and War of 1812, and quoted "our brother," Patrick Henry, who had said in 1775, "I know not what course others may take, but as for me, give me liberty or give me death." Now, like "our fathers," these black New Yorkers told Lincoln that they, too, were ready to fight for their country. "We have been called cowards," they said. "We deny the charge. It is false." To prove their manhood, they called upon Lincoln to accept the services "of ten thousand of the sable sons, called the Fremont Legion, to be led to the field of battle."[10]

During another of these meetings, Gloucester went to the White House in the evening and found the president and first lady sitting in the parlor with their old friend Dr. Anson G. Henry. Mrs. Lincoln offered Gloucester her hand and a cup of tea, and the black man joined them in pleasant conversation for two hours. A few days later, Gloucester told journalist Jane Swisshelm about this encounter. She reported to her readers, "He told me incidents of his reception at the White House, and expressions of President Lincoln which I do not feel at liberty to repeat, but which go to show, not only that the President has agreed to accept the services of colored men, but that he enters into the spirit of the project with a zest and heartiness which must inspire confidence in the measure—which must give the black men who enlist in the service the unspeakable advantage of feeling that they are respected by the Commander-in-Chief, as men, and cared for as soldiers, which will give them opportunity to prove themselves worthy of confidence, and command, for them, the respect of other branches of the service." Swisshelm stated that Lincoln was "slow-and-steady" and would win "the race." Presciently, she concluded, "As President Lincoln keeps along, with his face in the right direction, never stops for a nap, never slips backward, he will be likely to reach the goal in good season."[11]

Parker Gloucester was impressed by his interactions with the president and Mrs. Lincoln. In April he told a New Bedford, Massachusetts, audience "many facts in connexion with conversations he had had with the President and his wife, which showed old Abe's firmness and determination to put down the rebellion, and his wife's loyalty and patriotism." Moreover, he continued, "Mr. *Lincoln* was opposed to colonization. He was in favor of colored soldiers, colored chaplains, and colored physicians."[12] The editors of the *Anglo-African* rejoiced that this was "evidence of great change in high quarters."[13]

At 10 a.m. on May 30, Parker Gloucester returned to the White House with his brother, Rev. James N. Gloucester of Brooklyn, and two white men who were interested in promoting the enlistment of black soldiers. According to one Washington acquaintance, James was "a man of not only large property, but deep interest in the improvement of his race." Massachusetts senator Charles Sumner presented them to the president.

When the group arrived, Lincoln was meeting with Secretary of the Treasury Salmon P. Chase, but, according to one witness, he "received the committee in his own business-like, bland, and genial manner." Lincoln listened to their appeal "with attention and respect" and assured them "of his profound interest in their mission, his willingness to serve his country to the entire extent of his ability, his unshaken adherence to the claims of humanity and his implicit confidence in God." He also affirmed for them that it was "the settled purpose of the Government" to bring black soldiers "into its active service."

According to the *New-York Tribune*, Lincoln declared that he "would gladly receive into the service not ten thousand but ten times ten thousand colored troops" and he "expressed his determination to protect all who enlisted, and said that he looked to them for essential service in finishing the war." The *New York Times* reported that Lincoln "listened . . . with earnestness, and indeed solemnity, and replied that the policy of the Government, so far as he represented it, and his will controlled it, was fixed, and that the Government would avail itself of any plausible instrumentalities to obtain the cooperation of the emancipated slaves of the South as a military organization." Lincoln said "that we had been drifting to this result, and had partly been compelled to it by the exigencies of the war" but that he was "thoroughly in earnest in this purpose." Indeed, Lincoln added that the arming of black men was "essential . . . to an early and complete success of the Union arms." Pointing to a map of the vicinity of Vicksburg, Mississippi, Lincoln continued, "My view of it is, that the colored people will have to take those places, and will have to hold them. . . . I desire to accomplish this result." One newspaper correspondent opined, "O that the ear of the nation might have heard the cheering, eloquent words of counsel, as well as merited reproof, that fell from his lips as he discoursed upon the affairs of the nation."

During the conversation, James N. Gloucester presented Lincoln with two leaflets he had produced as president of the American Freedmen's Friend Society in Brooklyn. As the delegation prepared to leave, they scheduled another interview with Lincoln for the following morning, although no record of that meeting has been located. The *Tribune* concluded, "The Committee was profoundly impressed by the earnestness of the President, and his determination to employ all within this reach to the suppression of the Rebellion."[14]

Upon learning how kindly Parker Gloucester had been received at the White House, the black community of Poughkeepsie adopted resolutions thanking

"President Lincoln and his excellent lady, Mrs. Lincoln." Meanwhile, another black Poughkeepsian remarked that Lincoln's kind reception of Gloucester was "a good rebuke" of the sort of "American snobbishness" that black travelers encountered on segregated streetcars. Even more important, news of Lincoln's kindness "has awakened a spirit of enthusiasm among the colored men here, to enter the service. Let the Americans stop snubbing colored men, and they will find them true to the Government." Democratic newspapers, by contrast, read these reports and chafed that Lincoln was going to commission black generals— "the nigger idea of a nigger liberator."[15]

In July 1863, the black community in Poughkeepsie appointed a committee to raise between ten and twenty thousand black volunteers in the state of New York. Paschal B. Randolph, the famous black spiritualist, served as its secretary and spoke at their convention. The solution to defeating the rebellion, Randolph exhorted, could be found "in the shape of warm lead and cold steel, duly administered by 200,000 black doctors."[16] The New Yorkers invited William Whiting, solicitor of the War Department, to address their convention, but Whiting was unable to attend. Instead, he sent a public letter that soon received wide circulation in the press. On the matter of emancipation, Whiting wrote, "The policy of the Government is fixed and immovable. . . . Abraham Lincoln takes no backward step. A man once made free by law cannot be again made a slave. The Government has no power, if it had the will, to do it. Omnipotence alone can re-enslave a freeman. Fear not that the Administration will ever take the back track." Whiting also assured the attendees at the convention that the War Department would gladly welcome their services. "The President wishes the aid of all Americans of whatever descent or color, to defend the country," he wrote. "He wishes every citizen to share the perils of the contest, and to reap the fruits of victory." Unfortunately, New York's Democratic governor, Horatio Seymour, would not support the enlistment of black soldiers, so black New Yorkers had to go to other states to join the Union Army.[17]

Lincoln may have been slow to turn to black soldiers, but once he made the decision, he enthusiastically supported their recruitment into the ranks. He recognized that bringing black men into the Army—especially refugee slaves— would simultaneously strengthen the Union and weaken the Confederacy by taking away the labor source of the Rebels. As he explained to William T. Sherman, "our colored forces . . . unlike white recruits, help us where they come from, as well as where they go to."[18]

Some Northerners publicly called upon Lincoln to retract the Emancipation Proclamation, but he utterly refused to do so because, as he explained, "the promise being made, must be kept." Indeed, Lincoln knew that "the promise of freedom" was the "strongest motive" for black men to enlist and fight—and he could not renege on that. From Lincoln's perspective, these soldiers were making noble efforts on behalf of the Union and freedom. With "silent tongue, and clenched teeth, and steady eye, and well-poised bayonet," he wrote, they were helping "mankind on to this great consummation."[19]

Despite the initial enthusiasm among enlistees, black soldiers faced intense discrimination. They were recruited into segregated regiments with white officers, and initially were only permitted to do fatigue duty—manual labor—rather than fight. Moreover, the weapons they received were of subpar quality. Finally, although military recruiters promised black men the same pay as white soldiers—thirteen dollars per month—the War Department determined to pay them only ten dollars per month with a further deduction of three dollars for clothes. This decision was not arbitrary—it was based on the pay structure laid out for black laborers in the Militia Act of 1862. But it rightly struck black soldiers and their families as immoral and unjust. On top of all of this, the Confederate government threatened to execute or enslave black men found in arms against the Confederacy. It is little wonder that African American soldiers and civilians protested these policies. Writing under the pseudonym "Bought and Sold," one black soldier told the *Christian Recorder* that he "felt very patriotic" when he enlisted but that letters from his suffering wife "have brought my patriotism down to the freezing point, and I don't think it will ever rise again; and it is the case all through the regiment." A noncommissioned officer in the Fifty-Fourth Massachusetts likewise complained about how this "wrong and insult" from the "Lincoln despotism" had reduced his wife "to beggary" and dependence "upon another man."[20] As enthusiastic as black men were to fight for their liberty, they also soon found that they had to fight for equality as well.

6

"I FELT BIG THERE"

Frederick Douglass was doubtful that Lincoln would be a strong antislavery president, and when he read Lincoln's first inaugural address in the newspapers—with its pledges to enforce the Fugitive Slave Act of 1850 and to not touch slavery in the Southern states—he was livid. In the pages of his newspaper, *Douglass' Monthly*, he called Lincoln the abolitionist movement's "most powerful enemy" and "an excellent slave hound" who had "complete loyalty to slavery." A likeminded black abolitionist similarly remarked that African Americans must "pray that Pharaoh Lincoln may be made to take another step, and another, until Liberty is proclaimed to every slave in this land."[1]

By the midpoint of the war, however, Douglass found reason to hope. "That this war is to abolish slavery I have no manner of doubt," he told an audience a few days before Lincoln issued the final Emancipation Proclamation. As the Lincoln administration moved forward in the process of enlisting black men, Douglass became an enthusiastic recruiter. While urging "Men of Color, to Arms!" he remarked that "the slave was the best defense against the arm of the slaveholder." Douglass called on black men to fight with honor, like those who had gone before to secure liberty in "our Country." He knew that black men could prove their worth on the battlefield and thus make claims to "political and civil liberty."[2]

Working with Massachusetts abolitionist George L. Stearns, Douglass helped raise the famous Fifty-Fourth Massachusetts Infantry—a regiment that included two of his own sons, Charles and Lewis. The black abolitionist was proud of his sons' service, and that so many black men heeded his call to enlist, but he was enraged that the federal government paid black soldiers six dollars per month less than white soldiers. Douglass had promised black recruits that they would receive equal pay because federal authorities had told him they would. He was also incensed that Lincoln had not responded to the Confederate policy of executing or enslaving black Union soldiers, rather than treating them as prisoners of war. "The slaughter of blacks taken as captives," wrote Douglass, "seems to affect him [Lincoln] as little as the slaughter of beeves for the use of his army." Douglass wanted vengeance and retaliation against the Rebels.[3]

Unbeknownst to Douglass, Lincoln had already issued an order of retaliation that pledged to execute one Confederate soldier for every black soldier "killed in violation of the laws of war," and to place a Confederate "at hard labor on the public works" for "every one enslaved by the enemy or sold into slavery." Such a policy would remain in force until the Confederate government began treating US Colored Troops as lawful prisoners of war. Since he did not yet know about this order, Douglass wrote to Major Stearns that his faith in Lincoln was "now nearly gone" and that he could no longer in good conscience recruit black men into the Army. In an article in *Douglass' Monthly*, the black orator asked, "What has Mr. Lincoln to say about this slavery and murder? What has he said?—Not one word. In the hearing of the nation he is as silent as an oyster on the whole subject. . . . And until Mr. Lincoln shall interpose his power to prevent these atrocious assassinations of Negro soldiers, the civilized world will hold him equally with Jefferson Davis responsible for them."[4]

Stearns did not want to lose Douglass as a recruiter, so he sent him a copy of Lincoln's retaliation order and urged him to go meet with the president. Without any invitation from Lincoln, Douglass boarded a train for Washington, DC, passing through his native state of Maryland. He arrived in Washington on August 9, 1863, and met with Lincoln the following day. Years later, in his autobiography, Douglass described the "nerve" it took for him to visit the chief magistrate of the nation. "The distance then between the black man and the white American citizen was immeasurable," he wrote. "I was an ex-slave, identified with a despised race, and yet I was to meet the most exalted person in this great republic." Douglass was reluctant to perform this "unwelcome duty," for he did not know how Lincoln would receive him. "I might be told to go home and mind my business," or "I might be refused an interview altogether," he later observed. Nevertheless, Douglass "felt bound to go." And he was glad he did. As he later wrote, "I shall never forget my first interview with this great man."

Douglass approached the White House with Sen. Samuel C. Pomeroy of Kansas. Once inside, he found himself "the only dark spot" among a crowd of white people who had come to have an audience with the president. Douglass expected to have to wait for hours before he would be summoned into Lincoln's office, but within two minutes of presenting his card he was called in. While elbowing his way through the masses, he heard one man remark, "Yes, damn it, I knew they would let the nigger through."

Upon entering Lincoln's office, Douglass wrote, "I was never more quickly or more completely put at ease in the presence of a great man than in that of Abraham Lincoln." The president was seated in a low armchair with his feet stretched out to the floor. Piles of documents were everywhere, and his private secretaries were scurrying around the room. Everyone appeared to be "much over-worked and tired," but Lincoln's face "lighted up" when Douglass's name was announced. As Douglass approached the president, Lincoln stood up and "extended his hand, and bade me welcome." Douglass later recalled, "I at once felt myself in the presence of an honest man—one whom I could love, honor, and trust without reserve or doubt." Douglass began to tell him who he was and why he was there, but Lincoln "promptly, but kindly" stopped him and said, "I know who you are, Mr. Douglass; Mr. Seward has told me all about you. Sit down. I am glad to see you." The two then sat down together, and Douglass told him how black recruitment had slowed down in recent months "because there was a feeling among them that the government did not, in several respects, deal fairly with them."

Lincoln asked for specifics. Douglass replied that black men wanted equal pay, protection from the Confederacy's barbaric policies, and the ability to become commissioned officers. Lincoln "listened with patience and silence to all I had to say," Douglass later wrote. "He was serious and even troubled by what I had said and by what he himself had evidently before thought upon the same points. He, by his silent listening not less than by his earnest reply to my words, impressed me with the solid gravity of his character."

Lincoln explained that the recruitment of black soldiers "was a great gain to the colored people." Popular prejudice would not have allowed black men to enlist earlier in the war, and there still were many white Northerners who opposed employing black soldiers. Black men, he said, "had larger motives for being soldiers than white men," and they "ought to be willing to enter the service upon any condition." In other words, having a lower pay rate was a temporary but "necessary concession" to white racism—a way to ease white Northerners into supporting the use of black soldiers. Nevertheless, Lincoln assured Douglass, they would "ultimately . . . receive the same" pay.

On Douglass's second point—that black soldiers receive equal protection as prisoners of war—Lincoln called retaliation "a terrible remedy, and one which it was very difficult to apply." Lincoln worried that if one side started retaliating against the other that "once begun, there was no telling where it would end." If he could capture the Confederate soldiers who were known to have committed atrocities, Lincoln "could easily retaliate." But the thought of executing men "for a crime perpetrated by others" was "revolting" to Lincoln's feelings. He was confident that the Confederates would "stop such barbarous warfare" and he had heard some reports that they had already begun treating black men as prisoners of war. (In fact, Lincoln never carried out his order of retaliation.) In this moment, Douglass later wrote, "I saw the tender heart of the man rather than the stern warrior and commander-in-chief of the American army and navy, and, while I could not agree with him, I could but respect his humane spirit."

On the third and final point, Lincoln said that he "would sign any commission" for black officers that Secretary of War Stanton should send him. Douglass concluded, "Though I was not entirely satisfied with his views, I was so well satisfied with the man and with the educating tendency of the conflict that I determined to go on with the recruiting."[5] Before Douglass departed, Lincoln endorsed a pass for him "to travel, unmolested . . . everywhere as a free man, and a gentleman." The plan was for Douglass to recruit black soldiers in the Mississippi River Valley, although he never wound up serving the Union cause in this way.

At some point during the conversation, Lincoln remarked that he had read a speech in the newspapers in which Douglass criticized him for being "tardy, hesitating and vacillating." In his own down-to-earth way, Lincoln objected to the accusation. "Mr. Douglass, I have been charged with being tardy, and the like," he said. And he admitted that he "might seem slow." But as to the charge of vacillating, Lincoln insisted, "Mr. Douglass, I do not think that charge can be sustained; I think it cannot be shown that when I have once taken a position, I have ever retreated from it."[6] Emancipation and the arming of black men, in other words, would be irrevocable as long as Lincoln was the chief executive.

Douglass's meeting with Lincoln transformed his view of the president, and he relished the opportunity to tell audiences about his experience. In a speech to the American Anti-Slavery Society a few months later, on December 4, 1863, Douglass told the crowd, "I have been to Washington to see the President; and as you were not there, perhaps you may like to know how the President of the United States received a black man at the White House." Douglass then said that "he received me . . . just as you have seen one gentleman receive another!" At this, Douglass paused while the audience erupted in applause. He then continued, "with a hand and a voice well-balanced between a kind cordiality and a respectful reserve. I tell you I felt big there." At that line the audience laughed.

Walking into Lincoln's office, Douglass found Lincoln "sitting in his usual position, I was told, with his feet in different parts of the room, taking it easy." (This joke about Lincoln's height and demeanor elicited more laughter from the crowd.) Lincoln then arose and reached out to shake Douglass's hand, saying, "Mr. Douglass, I know you: I have read about you, and Mr. Seward has told me about you," which put Douglass at ease. Douglass told the audience that he wished Lincoln had been quicker in declaring "equal protection" to black soldiers and prisoners of war. Here Douglass paraphrased Lincoln's response: "he said the country needed talking up to that point. He hesitated in regard to it when he felt that the country was not ready for it. He knew that the colored man throughout this country was a despised man, a hated man, and he knew that if he at first came out with such a proclamation, all the hatred which is poured on the head of the negro race would be visited on his Administration. He said that there was preparatory work needed, and that that preparatory work had been done." Lincoln then added, "Remember this, Mr. Douglass; remember that Milliken's Bend, Port Hudson, and Fort Wagner are recent events; and that these were necessary to prepare the way for this very proclamation of mine [Lincoln's order of retaliation]."

Douglass told the audience that Lincoln "impressed me as being just what every one of you have been in the habit of calling him—an honest man. I never met with a man, who, on the first blush, impressed me more entirely with sincerity, with his devotion to country, and with his determination to save it at all hazards."[7]

Douglass also described his meeting to an audience at the Cooper Union in New York City: "I have been to see the President—a man in a low condition, meeting a high one," he joked. "Not a Greek meeting Greek, exactly, but railsplitter meeting nigger. Perhaps you would like to know how I, a negro, was received at the White House by the President of the United States. Why, precisely as one gentleman would be received by another." At this the audience applauded. Douglass told of how Lincoln "extended me a cordial hand, not too warm or too cold," and he laughed when he added, "he addressed me as *Mr. Douglass.*"[8]

Douglass had a reason to be proud of his efforts. He was one of the first people to confront the president in person with the issue of equal pay. Pressure on Lincoln would continue to mount—so much so that in 1864 he signed a bill into law equalizing pay for many black soldiers (although those who had been enslaved in April 1861 would not receive equal pay until 1865).[9] Lincoln would also soon begin appointing black field officers in the Army. On another level,

Douglass's meeting with Lincoln offered encouragement to African Americans nationwide. Lincoln had not lectured his guest as he had done with the black delegation in August 1862. Instead, he "listened with patience and silence to all [Douglass] had to say." When African Americans read about Douglass's experience at the White House—and heard about how kindly Lincoln treated him—it no doubt inspired some of them to go see the president for themselves.

7

"WITHOUT MOLESTATION OR INSULT"

Wicked winds blew through the streets of Washington, DC, on January 1, 1864, toppling shop signs and sending ladies' hats flying into the air. "If the weather may be taken as an index we shall have lively times in 1864," predicted the editors of the Washington *National Republican*.[1] Little did they know that something strange and wonderful was about to happen at the Executive Mansion that very day.

For years, presidents and first ladies had hosted New Year's receptions. The festivities in 1864 began at 10 a.m. Foreign ministers were the first group admitted to see the president. Secretary of State William H. Seward led the way, followed by diplomats from France, England, Russia, Brazil, and other nations. At 11 a.m. officers of the Navy and Marine Corps were welcomed in. After them came the officers of the Army, including Union generals Henry Wager Halleck, Abner Doubleday, and George H. Thomas. At noon, the doors were opened to the general public. Eager crowds had been assembling at every gate of the White House since the early morning hours, each person wanting "to take by the hand and wish a Happy New Year to the Nation's Chief Magistrate." A large police force was brought in to keep order, along with Lincoln's self-appointed bodyguard, Ward Hill Lamon. After the Army officers had finished shaking the president's hand, reported the Washington *Evening Star*, the gates were opened, and "then commenced the rush for the door." The space was thick with visitors. Among the people "getting a good squeeze," reported the *Star*, were the mayor of Washington and a federal judge. The crowd surged into the White House, trampling upon one another's feet, and "doing some considerable damage to hats, bonnets and fine dresses." Each visitor passed through the

Green, Blue, and Reception Rooms. Along the way, they shook hands with the president and met Mrs. Lincoln. They then passed out of a window in the East Room that had been converted into an exit. Pickpockets worked the various spaces, making small fortunes off of unsuspecting guests. Many revelers then returned to their homes and raised glasses to the health of the president.[2]

This sort of frivolity was to be expected at the White House on New Year's Day, but something new and different also happened on this first anniversary of the Emancipation Proclamation. As the Washington *Daily Chronicle* reported on January 2, "Yesterday four colored men, of genteel exterior and with the manners of gentlemen, joined in the throng that crowded the Executive mansion and were presented to the President of the United States." The paper added, "Years ago had any colored man presented himself at the White House at the President's levee . . . he would in all probability have been roughly handled for his impudence." But times were quickly changing. The paper concluded, "We are neither amalgamationists nor the advocates for the leveling of all social distinctions; but we rejoice that we have a President who is a democrat in fact as well as by nature."[3]

One of the four black attendees, Rev. Henry Johnson of Ithaca, New York, described the "privilege" he had of calling upon the president. In former years Johnson had been enslaved in Washington, DC, and had been locked up in the slave pens of Alexandria, Virginia, from which point he was sent to the Deep South. Fortunately, Johnson escaped, but not before being "dogged by bloodhounds" and shot by his master. For the rest of his life he would carry "four buckshot in his leg, mementos of the tender mercies of the 'patriarchal institution.'"

Johnson found Lincoln to be "a gentleman, straight and tall, modest, with pleasing features; firm and determined doth he look, and as I think he is." He also met Secretary of State Seward, who "took me by the hand and introduced me to his daughter and the ladies present," Johnson recalled with evident pride. "As great as the crowd was of gentle and noble men, these privileges were granted me without molestation or insult." That night Johnson attended a gathering at the Israel African Methodist Episcopal Church to celebrate the one-year anniversary of the Emancipation Proclamation, where, echoing Frederick Douglass, he told the audience that "the President received him as one gentleman ought to receive another." It was a momentous day in Washington.[4]

Joining Johnson were abolitionists Charles Lenox Remond and John J. Smith of Massachusetts. (The fourth may have been abolitionist and emigrationist George T. Downing, who spent considerable time with Remond and Smith around this time.) Remond, the namesake of one of Frederick Douglass's sons, was a lawyer who was known as a "champion of human rights." Smith had been born free in Virginia, but said that he moved to Boston when Virginia "became too hot for him." Shortly after attending the White House reception, Smith told an integrated Washington audience that "the colored people should accept nothing less than recognition as men" and should "never occupy a position where they would not be recognized as equals if they behaved themselves."[5] (Smith later served in the Massachusetts legislature and on the Boston Common Council.)

Accounts of this unusual scene at the White House circulated widely in the press. A sympathetic journalist remarked that if these four black men had tried to enter the White House "three years ago, they would have got their heads broke for their presumption." Now, however, they were welcomed by the president—an event that was likely to "throw some negrophobes into convulsions." This observer was right. Democratic editors expressed outrage over what happened. An Ohio paper, which carried the motto "White Men Shall Rule America" on its masthead, said that Lincoln was "fishing for nigger votes" and might soon appoint "some intelligent contraband" for a position in the Cabinet. In like manner, a Maine paper complained, "What a hideous travestie this is— what an abject and shameful truckling to the shocking and unnatural doctrine of negro equality—what a terrible humiliation at any time—and what a shameless boast at a period when the nation is undergoing the horrors of civil war, engendered by this same insane craving for negro equality, forbidden by the decrees of the Almighty." An Indianan conceded that Lincoln could mingle with African Americans "as a private individual," but when he welcomed them into the White House "as the representative of a great nation, he chooses to inaugurate a reign of social equality between the white and black races." For this, the editor stated, "democrats . . . have the right to enter their emphatic protest." In Chicago, the anti-Lincoln *Times* similarly crowed that "filthy buck niggers, greasy, sweaty, and disgusting, now jostle white people and even ladies everywhere, even at the President's levees." Another Midwestern paper snarled that when Lincoln greeted the "Four niggers" he "was, no doubt, highly pleased to make their acquaintance."[6] When Confederates learned of the New Year's reception they reacted with outrage, but not disbelief. Edmund Ruffin, the notorious Virginia secessionist who had fired the first shot on Fort Sumter in April 1861, wrote in his diary: "At a late public reception by President Lincoln, among the honored guests were four negro men, who had no other claims to distinction than their color, & their appearing in genteel clothing." Ruffin groused at how Republican newspapers greeted "the occurrence with applause, as indicating the true democratical principles of the President."[7] White Southerners like

Ruffin could feel satisfied that their decision to secede from the Union had been justified. Lincoln, as seemed all too apparent to them, was welcoming African Americans into polite society and the body politic, acknowledging their social equality.

The four men who boldly entered the White House on that bright, cold, windy January day set the stage for an even more remarkable encounter that would take place the following month. In February 1864, two black Army surgeons—Alexander Thomas Augusta and Anderson R. Abbott—also decided to enter the White House, uninvited, for a public reception. They likely had read in the papers about the four black men at the New Year's reception and felt inspired to try it for themselves. They, too, would make national headlines. And in approaching the chief magistrate of the nation Drs. Augusta and Abbott made a claim to the rights of US citizens at a time when African Americans were legally excluded from that status.

Born in 1825 to free black parents in Norfolk, Virginia, Alexander T. Augusta wanted to be a doctor from a young age. His family likely left the Old Dominion in the 1830s after Nat Turner's failed slave insurrection, which led to new, oppressive measures against slaves and free blacks. In his twenties Augusta worked as a barber in Baltimore—an occupation that afforded black men the opportunity to attain a modicum of economic empowerment and respectability. He later spent three years in California during the Gold Rush in the early 1850s. When he applied to the University of Pennsylvania Medical College in Philadelphia, he was denied admission on account of his race. Instead, he matriculated at Trinity Medical College in Toronto, where he earned his MD in 1856. The president of the college later remembered Augusta as one of his "most brilliant students." The newly minted black physician practiced medicine in Canada for about six years, where he advertised "Patent Medicines, Perfumery, Dye Stuffs, etc.," as well as "Leeches applied. Cupping, Bleeding, and Teeth Extracted." In Toronto he mentored a young black medical student named Anderson R. Abbott, whose parents had fled from Alabama to Canada in 1835.[8]

After a decade in Toronto, Augusta recognized an opportunity to return to the United States. Lincoln's Emancipation Proclamation of January 1, 1863, declared that black men would be given the opportunity to serve in the Army, and Augusta was inspired to lend his skills as a doctor to the Union war effort. On January 7, he penned a short letter to Lincoln seeking appointment as a physician in the Union army. "Having seen that it is intended to garrison the US forts &c with coloured troops, I beg leave to apply to you for an appointment as surgeon to some of the coloured regiments, or as physician to some of the depots of 'freedmen,'" he wrote. Augusta explained how he had been "compelled to leave my native country, and come to this on account of prejudice against colour, for the purpose of obtaining a knowledge of my profession." Now that he was a licensed physician, he concluded, "I am now prepared to practice it [medicine], and would like to be in a position where I can be of use to my race." Augusta sent a similar letter to Secretary of War Edwin M. Stanton the same day.[9]

Despite his obvious qualifications, Augusta faced intense discrimination throughout the application process. When he arrived before the Army Medical Board in March 1863 to be examined, the president of the board, Meredith Clymer, was surprised to see that he "appeared" to be "a person of African descent." Augusta explained to the members of the board, "I have come near a thousand miles at great expense and sacrifice, hoping to be of some use to the country and my race at this eventful period; and hope the Board will take a favorable view of my case." But the board was unmoved. Clymer and Surgeon General William A. Hammond both wanted Augusta's invitation "recalled." Fortunately, Secretary of War Stanton refused their racially motivated request and ordered the examination to proceed. On April 1, Augusta passed the board's examination and was commissioned a major in the Army—the first African American to receive an Army commission in US history. According to one account, "Dr. Augusta was then put through a squeezing process which few surgeons, in or out of the service, could have sustained unscathed. The fun of the thing is, that it is highly probable that Augusta knew more than all his questioners." Afterward, Surgeon General Hammond asked the examining physician, "I say Cronyn how did you come to let that nigger pass?" Dr. Cronyn replied, "The fact is, general, that the nigger knew more than I did and I could not help myself."[10]

Augusta wore his officer's uniform with great pride. One African American in Washington wrote, "The Doctor wears his well-earned honors with all becoming dignity and sports his shoulder-straps, leaf, and double-breasted coat with the ease of a Major whose rank he takes." He "furnish[es] a fine example to our young men of talents which should lead others to speedily follow."[11] Initially Augusta examined black recruits and soldiers at a contraband camp near Alexandria, Virginia. On April 16, he went into Washington to attend a celebration of the first anniversary of DC Emancipation, held at the Fifteenth Street Presbyterian Church. The organizers of the event included Mary Lincoln's seamstress Elizabeth Keckly and President Lincoln's valet, William Slade. The service opened with a prayer invoking blessings upon the members of Congress who had voted in favor of emancipation in the District, as well as for "the President who had done so much for liberating the slaves of the country." According to one reporter, the person "whose presence gave apparently the most delight to the colored folks, male and female, was Dr. A. T. Augusta, colored, wearing the gold leaf epaulets of a major." When the black poet J. Willis Menard looked down from the pulpit and noticed Augusta, he congratulated the audience, saying, "For the first time in the history of this country, epaulettes were seen upon the shoulders of a black man!" He then joked that when he finally saw "a major general's epaulettes on a black man, he would cease to be an emigrationist."[12]

Despite his newfound celebrity among African Americans, Augusta continued to face discrimination from white officers and civilians, many of whom could not stomach the thought of a black man wearing shoulder straps. On a few occasions he was also the victim of unprovoked violent assaults.

At 9:15 a.m., on May 1, 1863, Augusta left an overnight lodging in Baltimore in order to catch a 10 a.m. train for Philadelphia. No one interfered with him as he made his way in full Army uniform to President Street Station. At the depot he purchased a ticket from the agent "without the usual bond required of colored persons wishing to proceed North" and took his seat in the car. After a few minutes, however, he heard people talking behind him. Then, out of nowhere, a fifteen-year-old white boy came up from behind, cursed at him, and ripped off his right shoulder strap. Augusta jumped up from his seat and turned to face the boy. Standing next to him was the conductor who had directed Augusta into the car. As Augusta chastised the boy for what he had done, the conductor pulled off Augusta's other epaulette, "while at the same time the boy threatened to strike me with a club he held in his hand." Seeking an exit, Augusta turned toward the door but "found I was surrounded by about eight or ten roughs." He knew he could not confront them or they "would pounce upon me." He concluded that the best course of action was to sit quietly back down.

Eventually the assailants left the train. A policeman entered and approached the black surgeon. "If you are a policeman, I claim your protection as a United States officer, who has been assaulted without a cause," Augusta demanded. When he learned that there were provost guards on the train, he sought them out, explained what had happened, and asked for their protection. At that point Augusta could have continued on the train for Philadelphia, but he decided that it would be better to find the men who had attacked him. He exited the car and went to the provost marshal's office to report what had transpired. Fortunately, the provost marshal promised to protect Augusta "to the fullest extent," deputizing Lieutenant William E. Morris to return to the station to arrest his attackers. Morris instructed Augusta to place his hand upon the assailant's shoulder and "claim him as my prisoner," at which point Morris would "take charge." Augusta "knew this was an extraordinary step for me to take in Baltimore, but I told him I would do it."

The two men returned to President Street Station, where Augusta saw the older assailant crossing the street. He went up to him, accused him of taking his shoulder straps, placed his hand on his shoulder, and arrested him. "I then ordered the guard to take him into custody, which he did." Augusta next "hunted around the depot for the boy, but could not find him." As the black surgeon and Lieutenant Morris walked the streets of Baltimore, a white man named Charles W. Hancock approached Augusta and assaulted him. Augusta called for the guard and had Hancock arrested.

The morning had not gone at all as Augusta had planned. By the early afternoon he had thought he would be in Philadelphia, not searching for these "roughs" on the streets of Baltimore—a city notorious for its proslavery and anti-Union sentiments. Now, finally, at 12:30 p.m., Augusta again departed the provost marshal's office to catch the 1 p.m. train. As the black surgeon and Lieutenant Morris walked toward the station a crowd gathered around them. With each step they took the mob grew larger and larger. When they got to the corner of Pratt and President streets, a young man named James Dunn stood in their way and then dealt Augusta "a severe blow on the face, which stunned me for a moment and caused blood to flow from my nose very freely." Lieutenant Morris grabbed Dunn by the collar, while Augusta, "not knowing that there was anyone else in the crowd to protect me, made for the first door I saw open." A woman standing in the doorway pushed Augusta back to prevent him from entering her home, while the large crowd began to chant, "kill him" and "hang him." The black surgeon wheeled around and saw a man holding "my cap and a revolver." The man told Augusta "to stand still, that I was protected." Augusta came down the steps of the woman's house and walked with the stranger and another armed guard to the station. The guard arrested a few other men connected with the incident and sent them to Fort McHenry for trial. Several armed soldiers stayed with Augusta until the train departed. Another Union officer told Augusta that he would "protect me at the risk of his own life," and two armed cavalrymen were detailed to protect him in Philadelphia.

A Washington correspondent for the *Anti-Slavery Standard* was outraged by the treatment Augusta received. "If we are to have a negro army, the government must give to it all the rights and privileges of a white army," he began.

There must be no hesitation on that point. Better burn Baltimore even with the ground than permit any agent of the government to be deliberately mobbed in the streets. This brutal attack upon Dr. Augusta is the first outbreak in the border country against the policy of employing colored men to fight in this war. As it is the *first*, the government must show that it is determined to defend its deliberately-chosen position with all the military power at its command. If Mr. Lincoln hesitates in this matter, he is lost. I have noticed in Washington that but one thing availed against colorphobia, and that is *military power.*

The Baltimore press reported that Augusta had provoked the first assault by the use of profane language against the train conductor, but Augusta vehemently denied the accusation. Moreover, he wrote, "I hold that my position as an officer of the United States entitles me to wear the insignia of my office, and if I am either afraid or ashamed to wear them anywhere, I am not fit to hold my commission, and should resign it at once." Alluding to the infamous *Dred Scott* decision—which held that African Americans had "no rights which the white man was bound to respect"—Augusta wrote that his ordeal "has proved that even in *rowdy Baltimore* colored men have rights that white men are bound to respect."[13]

From May 27 to October 2, 1863, Augusta served as the surgeon in charge of the Contraband Hospital in Washington, making him the first African American to head a hospital in the United States. Observers praised him for how he brought order and cleanliness to the place. According to one visitor, Augusta and his fellow black doctors found the hospital "in a very deplorable condition; so much so, that they have had to revolutionize everything out there" to protect the lives of the African American convalescents. This black observer thought it was "a great victory gained" for black people to have "Dr. A. placed over the medical department." Another visitor reported, "The hospitals are in elegant order. The sick have every attention that they can desire, and the Doctor spares neither time nor trouble to make them comfortable. I hear of no complaint whatever."[14]

During this time, Augusta got embroiled in another controversy that would eventually reach the floor of the US Senate. It all began at 3 p.m., on August 17, 1863, when Pvt. George Taylor, a twenty-one-year-old coal miner in the Twenty-Fifth Ohio Volunteers, violently assaulted an unidentified black man at the rear of the Carver Hospital in Washington. Taylor had fought "with more than ordinary gallantry" in six battles, and been wounded three times. He was presently receiving medical care at Carver for a "severe" injury to his nose that he had received at Chancellorsville in May 1863. Taylor apparently saw the black man and called for him to come over, but the stranger replied that he had to go to supper. Enraged—and possibly drunk—Taylor picked up a stone and threw it at the man, knocking him down. He then kicked and "pounded" him, even stomping on his face, until two other soldiers pulled him off. One witness later testified, "The colored man was very badly cut up,—his head was very bloody,—and was full of gashes. He was laying on his belly without moving."

The victim was taken to Carver Hospital and treated with "milk punch"—a stimulant consisting of milk and whiskey. Two days later, on August 19, the poor sufferer was placed on an open cart and transferred about a mile to the Contraband Hospital, still "in a state of unconsciousness and insensibility." There, three black doctors—William P. Powell, Alexander T. Augusta, and Anderson R. Abbott—examined him. At first the three physicians agreed that a certain procedure would be necessary to help alleviate the swelling in the skull, but on second thought they decided not to perform the operation since the man was so near to death. The patient died at 5:30 p.m. on August 20. The doctors estimated that he was between thirty and forty years old. The next day, Powell and Augusta performed an autopsy. After removing the top of his skull and examining the area around his brain, they concluded, "Death was caused by congestion and inflammation of the brain." They never learned the victim's name.

Private Taylor was arrested and arraigned before a military court, but before the trial could commence, he was sent to St. Elizabeth's Hospital an insane asylum in Washington—for two months. There, a surgeon with training in "psychological science" examined him, concluding that there was "no reason to suppose that he was insane" when he committed the crime "or at any other period of his life." The only mitigating circumstances that the surgeon could see were that Taylor had grown up without "any education or moral training" and that from a young age "his competitive association with rough boys and men seems to have nourished a vindictive temper and habits of dissipation which he probably both inherited and imitated."

A new trial commenced on January 26, 1864. Taylor pleaded not guilty to a charge of murder, and his lawyer implausibly tried to argue that the blunt trauma to the victim's head had not been the cause of death. Two of the black surgeons, Powell and Augusta, were called to testify before the court. Prior to their testimony, the court questioned their qualifications, but ultimately both were permitted to speak. The judge advocate later called Augusta "a gentleman whose rank, acquired by his undoubted proficiency should entitle him to the position of a reliable authority on the case at issue." After a trial that took more than a month, the court found Private Taylor guilty of manslaughter and sentenced him to be dishonorably discharged from the service and imprisoned at Fort Delaware at hard labor for five years.[15]

It is noteworthy that Augusta was able to testify in court against Private Taylor, as most state and federal courts at the time prohibited black people from testifying against white defendants. (During the war, military courts began ignoring state laws that prohibited black testimony and it became quite common for free and enslaved African Americans to testify against white and black defendants in military trials.) Aside from the legal hurdles, however, Augusta also faced physical resistance when he attempted to go to court. Augusta was initially called to testify on February 1 (by now he had been surgeon of the Seventh US Colored Infantry for four months), but an unfortunate incident prevented him from appearing at the trial until February 8. When Augusta attempted to board a streetcar along Pennsylvania Avenue on February 1, the conductor "pulled me back, and informed me that I must ride on the front with the driver, as it was against the rules for colored persons to ride inside." When Augusta objected to this discriminatory policy, the conductor replied that he "should not ride at all." The conductor "then ejected me from the platform, and at the same time gave orders to the driver to go on," Augusta wrote. "I have therefore been compelled to walk the distance in the mud and rain, and have also been delayed in my attendance upon the court." The black surgeon then sent a letter to the Army judge advocate in Washington "respectfully request[ing] that the offender may be arrested and brought to punishment."

Upon reading about this "outrage" in the newspapers, Massachusetts senator Charles Sumner introduced a resolution in the Senate calling for an investigation. This incident, he declared, "is worse for our country at this moment than a defeat in battle." Moreover, he continued, "it is a disgrace to this Government which sanctions it under its eyes. It is a mere offshoot of the slavery which happily we have banished from Washington." Within days of Sumner's resolution being adopted, Augusta traveled to the Capitol building where he attempted to attend a Supreme Court hearing. Unfortunately, he was turned away from the courtroom by one of the officers of the Court, the justices unaware that he had come to watch the proceedings. But even this incident, like the Baltimore fight and the streetcar scuffle, made its way into the newspapers.

Democrats in the Senate reacted to Sumner's resolutions with incredulity. In the first place, they could not believe that a black man had been commissioned a major in the Union Army. Several wondered whether the news reports were mistaken. Moreover, they maintained that black men and women had their own cars to ride, so they ought not to complain about their circumstances. Sumner's motion, one Indiana Democrat proclaimed, was part of a push for "the political equality of the negro . . . to be forced upon the white race." Sen. Willard Saulsbury, a slave owner from Delaware who was renowned for coming into the Senate drunk, even went so far as to express gratitude to the conductor. "I must take occasion to say that I most heartily approve the action of the officer on board that railroad car," he declared. "I think he deserved the thanks of the community. When these negroes go about sticking their heads into railroad cars, and among white people, and into the Supreme Court room, I think an officer is perfectly right in telling them they have no business there; because it is evident that the reason they do so is simply to gain notoriety, and to see if they cannot bring themselves into conflict with the officers of the railroad cars or the officers of the Supreme Court."

A Senate committee report concluded that "colored persons are entitled to all the privileges" of riding on the streetcars "which any other persons have" as well as the right to sue the railroad company if their rights were infringed. As a consequence, the Senate decided that no further legislation was needed at this time to protect the rights of black passengers. Nevertheless, Democratic newspapers responded to Sumner's motion with outrage. Wanting to "mix up blacks and whites promiscuously in the cars," according to an upstate New York editor, "is certainly the recognition of the social equality of the blacks and whites." Privately, Lincoln's Attorney General Edward Bates adopted a similar position. The "dark doctor," he wrote in his diary, ought to consider this an "*outrage* [that] was personal to himself" since it was done by a civilian employee of the streetcar company. If he had been wronged, he should sue the individual and not "call upon a *Judge Advocate* to *arrest and punish the offender*." Bates worried that using the military to arrest men for offenses like these would lead to the utter subversion of civil law by "military power."[16] It is unknown whether the conductor was ever arrested. Ironically, Augusta may have watched this debate from the Senate galleries. One journalist reported, "The negro 'Dr.' Augusta, with the uniform of a Major on, daily ingratiates himself into a seat in the Senate gallery among the large number of battle stained and war-worn private soldiers. Many of them change their seats or go out of the gallery altogether, for when you come down to the real essence of the thing the hatred of a soldier to this negro equality business has no equal."[17]

Augusta now had a national reputation, although many white Northerners had nothing but contempt for him. A Democratic paper in Ohio sneeringly reported that a "NEGRO MAJOR, in full uniform, was put off the street cars, in Washington . . . and made to walk." The editors concluded, "Let him go to the White House for consolation. There he will be received as 'one gentleman receives another'"—a mocking allusion to how Frederick Douglass had described his 1863 meeting with Lincoln.[18] While Augusta would not have been aware of this derisive, condescending story, that is precisely what he decided to do—he would go meet his ally and commander in chief at the White House, just as any ordinary white citizen or soldier could do. On the evening of February 23, 1864, he and fellow surgeon Anderson Abbott walked up to the Executive Mansion unannounced and entered during one of Lincoln's weekly public receptions. The two men had maintained their close friendship during the war.

When Abbott suffered from symptoms of malaria or bronchitis in September 1863, Augusta cared for him at the home of Elizabeth Keckly.[19] Now they would have to rely on each other for support as they embarked on one of the most significant and exhilarating adventures of their lives.

The weekly levee at the White House on Tuesday, February 23, overflowed with dignitaries. Among the crowd were Assistant Secretary of State Frederick W. Seward, historian George Bancroft, Speaker of the House Schuyler Colfax, generals and admirals, diplomats from Sweden and Spain, Supreme Court justices, congressmen, and senators. Several escaped prisoners from Richmond's Libby Prison were also among the guests, and Union General Daniel Sickles, who had recently lost a leg at Gettysburg, sat in the Oval Room surrounded by his staff and friends. One journalist noted that "Mr. Lincoln was in good spirits" while Mary Lincoln "was dressed very charmingly" and "tastefully" in a white silk dress that was heavily festooned with black lace. She also wore a pearl necklace and a headdress made of pearls. The "penitential season" of Lent did not bring down the atmosphere at the White House at all.[20]

As Augusta and Abbott approached the White House dressed in their military uniforms, they could hear music coming from the building. Carriage after carriage drove up past them, filled with "handsomely dressed ladies, citizens, and soldiers" who represented "the elite of Washington." At the north portico, white Union soldiers stood guard. The two black doctors passed through the porch, just as the other guests did, and gave their winter wraps to servants inside. "The White House was a blaze of light," Abbott later recalled. "Music was wafted to our ears from the Marine Band, which was stationed in the Conservatory." As they stepped further in they saw ushers, lackeys, waiters, servants, and messengers "scurrying here and there attending to guests."

Inside the building the two men met Benjamin Brown French, the commissioner of public buildings. After presenting French with their cards, he "conducted us with all the urbanity imaginable to the President who was standing just inside the door." French first introduced Augusta. According to Abbott, "Mr. Lincoln, on seeing Augusta, advanced eagerly a few paces forward" and "grasped his hand." About six paces away stood Mary Lincoln with the president's eldest son, Robert, who was home from Harvard. Robert approached his father as he "held the Doctor's hand" and asked him, "Are you going to allow this innovation?" Without any hesitation, Lincoln replied, "Why not?" Nothing more was said between the president and his son, and Robert slinked back to his mother's side. At that, Lincoln turned back to Augusta and "gave his hand a hearty shake." The president next shook Abbott's hand, and the two surgeons then passed on to the First Lady.

Augusta and Abbott next walked into the East Room, which was "crowded and brilliantly lit up." All attention immediately turned to them. "I never experienced such a sensation before as I did when I entered the room," Abbott later recalled. "We could not have been more surprised ourselves or created more surprise if we had been dropped down upon them through a skylight." Abbott supposed that their military uniforms made them even more conspicuous. "Colored men in the uniforms of US Military, officers of high rank, had never been seen before," he wrote. "I felt as though I should have liked to crawl into a hole. But as we had decided to break the record we held our ground. I bit my lips, took Augusta's arm, and sauntered around the room endeavoring or pretending to view the very fine pictures, which adorned the walls. I tried also to become interested in the beautiful music discoursed by the Marine Band but it was the first time that music had failed to absorb my attention."

As they walked about the large, elegant, brightly lit room, the white guests cleared the way before them so that no matter where they stood they were "the center of a new circle of interest." No one in the room seemed able to conceal their innermost feelings. Some stared at them through monocles and opera glasses "merely from curiosity," while others bore an "expression of friendly interest." Still others "scowled at us in such a significant way that left no [doubt] as to what views they held on the negro question." After about thirty minutes, the two men returned to the anteroom to retrieve their winter wraps. A reporter asked them for an interview and they handed him their cards. With that, they passed out into the cold winter night. "So ended our first visit to the White House," Abbott wrote.[21]

People who witnessed the scene were amazed by what they saw. "I shall never forget the sensation produced at a levee by the appearance of two tall and very well dressed Africans among the crowd of those who came to pay their respects," wrote Lincoln's private secretary William O. Stoddard. "It was a practical assertion of negro citizenship, for which few were prepared." Lincoln nevertheless "received them with marked kindness" and after a short while they "went on their way with great self-possession. . . . It was as good as a play." Another witness to the scene wrote that "no visitor could discover that Mr. Lincoln considered them black. They were greeted with the same cordiality and freedom that he bestowed upon white men," and that Lincoln "treated the affair as of ordinary occurrence, much to his credit and renown." Meanwhile, Copperhead papers expressed outrage. The *New York Freeman's Journal* snarled that "filthy black niggers" now mingled with white people at the White House. The *Detroit Free Press* sought to undermine the accomplishments of these two surgeons, writing contemptuously, "Prominent among the distinguished people there were 'Dr.' Augusta, and 'Dr' Abbott, two negro Surgeons in the uniform of a Major." The *Free Press* added, "The ladies were very much disgusted with the social equality thus attempted." Some Democrats publicly cursed Lincoln in the streets for having admitted black guests.[22]

While Lincoln may have received Augusta and Abbott cordially, others did not. About this same time, seven white surgeons in black regiments petitioned Lincoln to remove Augusta from his position as surgeon of the Seventh US Colored Troops (USCT) so that they would not have to suffer the "degradation" of serving with a black commissioned officer. "We claim to be behind no one, in a desire for the elevation and improvement of the Colored race, in this Country, and we are willing to sacrifice much, in so Grand a cause, as our present positions may testify," they wrote without any sense of irony. "But we cannot in any cause, willingly compromise what we consider a proper self respect." Two months later, a white surgeon assigned to the Seventh USCT fired off an angry letter to Ohio Senator John Sherman, expressing "my surprise and indignation, when upon joining my Regiment I found my *Superior* Medical Officer, a *colored* man." The surgeon called on Sherman to help "right this *wrong*, which to my mind is *grave, unjust,* and *humiliating*."[23] Unfortunately, the War Department caved to the pressure and in October 1864 reassigned Augusta to examine black recruits, although the department refused to strip him of his rank. Abolitionist Julia Wilbur was appalled by the opposition Augusta faced, writing in her diary, "His white enemies & despisers have succeeded it seems in having him removed. I am disgusted with mankind. Especially those who are living on the government."[24]

Following the war, Augusta spent about a year working in Freedmen's Bureau hospitals near Savannah, Georgia, before returning to Washington, DC, to practice medicine. In July 1867, he was brevetted lieutenant colonel "for faithful and meritorious services," making him the highest-ranking black officer of the Civil War era. In the postwar period he became known by the leading citizens of the District of Columbia as a man of "ability and integrity."

Augusta would go on to have a number of other impressive "firsts" for African Americans. He had been the first black doctor to graduate from a medical school in British North America, the first black commissioned officer in the Union Army, and the first African American to run a hospital. In 1868 he joined the faculty at Howard University, becoming the first black person to teach medicine in the United States. The following year he received an honorary degree at Howard, becoming the first black man to receive such an honor from an American university. Even in death he had one final "first"—the first black officer to be buried at Arlington National Cemetery, when he died at the age of sixty-five on December 21, 1890.[25]

INTERLUDE 3

The Ballot

Today the right to vote is central to what it means to be a US citizen, but it has taken Americans a long time to come to this understanding. For much of our history, voting has been considered a "privilege," not a "right." Moreover, the US Constitution, as ratified in 1788, largely left the states with the power to determine who could vote. In the Founding era, black men with property were eligible to vote in as many as a dozen states, just as white men with property could. (Women with property could also vote in New Jersey in the 1790s and early 1800s.) Unfortunately, that right was stripped away in most states during the Age of Andrew Jackson.[1] By the time of the Civil War, very few African Americans could vote, and support for black male suffrage among the white electorate was virtually nonexistent.

Most politicians in the Founding Era clung to the idea that people needed a stake in society—ownership of property—to be eligible to vote. Eventually, political leaders came to believe that military service also qualified men for the ballot. If a man was willing to fight and die for his country then he ought to have a say in how it was governed. As early as 1836, Abraham Lincoln publicly declared that even white women should be allowed to vote if they paid taxes or served in the military (although they did not serve in the military at this time). "I go for all sharing the privileges of the government, who assist in bearing its burthens," he wrote as a candidate for the Illinois state legislature. "Consequently I go for admitting all whites to the right of suffrage, who pay taxes or bear arms, (by no means excluding females.)"[2] This was a remarkable statement for an unknown, provincial political candidate to make at this time, but it was consistent with the belief that those who had a stake in society should also have a voice in it. Twenty-five years later, those sentiments could be applied to black men as well. Nearly two hundred thousand free blacks and ex-slaves served in the Union armies between 1862 and 1865. Clearly, they too were assisting in "bearing its burthens."

Yet Lincoln did not immediately support black suffrage when black men began enlisting. In fact, as a young politician in Illinois in the late 1830s and early 1840s, he had publicly mocked the idea of black men voting.[3] His views began to change in the mid-1850s, however, as he realized the strength of "the Slave Power" in the United States. He had thought slavery was on a path toward ultimate extinction, but the Kansas-Nebraska Act of 1854 shook his faith in the wisdom of America's leaders. This infamous law allowed white settlers in the territories of Kansas and Nebraska to decide whether or not they would permit slavery to exist within their borders (previously the Missouri Compromise of 1820 had forbidden slavery from entering these territories). Sen. Stephen A. Douglas of Illinois touted this measure as "popular sovereignty"—the right of the people of the territories to govern themselves.

In response to the Kansas-Nebraska Act, Lincoln argued that there was something immoral about denying black people the right of government by consent. He responded to Douglas's "popular sovereignty" arguments with one of his most powerful statements on democracy. In his Peoria Address of 1854 Lincoln articulated his "faith" in the "right of self-government." He then asked whether popular sovereignty actually qualified as self-government. The answer to this question, Lincoln declared, "depends upon whether a negro is not or is a man. If he is not a man, why in that case, he who is a man may, as a matter of self-government, do just as he pleases with him. But if the negro is a man, is it not to that extent, a total destruction of self-government, to say that he too shall not govern himself?" Lincoln then hit the point home. "When the white man governs himself that is self-government; but when he governs himself, and also governs another man, that is more than self-government—that is despotism. If the negro is a man, why then my ancient faith teaches me that 'all men are created equal;' and that there can be no moral right in connection with one man's making a slave of another." Popular sovereignty, in short, was *not* self-government because it denied African Americans the sacred right of consent that was promised to all people in the Declaration of Independence.[4]

Lincoln did not explicitly endorse black suffrage in this speech; in fact, he stated that his own "feelings" did not support making former slaves "politically and socially, our equals." Four years later, in 1858, he would utter his infamous statement at Charleston, Illinois, that "I am not, nor ever have been in favor of bringing about in any way the social and political equality of the white and black races,—that I am not nor ever have been in favor of making voters or jurors of negroes, nor of qualifying them to hold office, nor to intermarry with white people."[5]

How could Lincoln articulate these seemingly incompatible views? One answer is that he recognized a difference between the natural rights that were articulated in the Declaration of Independence, and political rights, which are granted by a community. In the Peoria Address he stated that even if he supported granting political rights to African Americans, he knew that "the great mass of white people" would not support such a project. "Whether this feeling accords with justice and sound judgment, is not the sole question, if indeed, it is any part of it," Lincoln continued. "A universal feeling, whether well or ill-founded, can not be safely disregarded."[6] This leads to the second reason that Lincoln could take seemingly incompatible positions: historical context. Lincoln knew that arguing explicitly for black political and social equality was a nonstarter. Consider what Stephen Douglas had to say on the subject at the first Lincoln-Douglas Debate in 1858:

> I ask you, are you in favor of conferring upon the negro the rights and privileges of citizenship? ("No, no.") Do you desire to strike out of our State Constitution that clause which keeps slaves and free negroes out of the State, and allow the free negroes to flow in, ("never,") and cover your prairies with black settlements? . . . If you desire negro citizenship, if you desire to allow them to come into the State and settle with the white man, if you desire them to vote on an equality with yourselves, and to make them eligible to office, to serve on juries, and to adjudge your rights, then support Mr. Lincoln and the Black Republican party, who are in favor of the citizenship of the negro. ("Never, never.") For one, I am opposed to negro citizenship in any and every form. (Cheers.)

Douglas argued that the US government "was made on the white basis . . . for the benefit of white men and their posterity for ever." At this, the crowd shouted, "Good for you," and "Douglas forever." With sneering sarcasm, Douglas added, "I do not question Mr. Lincoln's conscientious belief that the negro was made his equal, and hence is his brother, (laughter,) but for my own part, I do not regard the negro as my equal, and positively deny that he is my brother or any kin to me whatever." When Douglas finished this line, the crowd cheered and shouted, "Never" and "Hit him again." Local Democratic newspapers, meanwhile, reported that Lincoln's "niggerism has as dark a hue as that of Garrison or Fred Douglass."[7]

Within this context, Lincoln's remarks opposing black political rights make more sense. He was trying to make a moderate argument that could appeal to a broad swath of white voters in a state that believed that government was only for white men. He was trying to shape public sentiment. He knew he could not persuade most white voters in Illinois to grant political rights to African Americans, but he hoped that he might help them live up to the ideals set out in the Declaration of Independence—a document most Americans at least professed to revere.[8]

The issue of black political rights faded from Lincoln's mind during the first two years of his presidency. It took seeing black soldiers in the field, and at least three meetings with black delegations from the South, to win over his support.

"TO KEEP THE JEWEL OF LIBERTY WITHIN THE FAMILY OF FREEDOM"

Following the Union's capture of New Orleans in April 1862, wealthy free black men of the city began pushing federal authorities for the full rights of citizenship. Unlike any other place in the Confederacy, a vibrant, affluent free black community existed in the Crescent City. These men possessed a number of important civil rights, including the ability to inherit and bequeath inheritances, to sue in civil courts, to testify against white people in criminal prosecutions, and to not be testified against by slaves. However, the ability to wield the ballot had always been denied them. This, they hoped to change.

Initially these well-heeled men of color showed little interest in advocating for universal manhood suffrage. They believed that their "industry and education" gave them "all the qualifications necessary to exercise the right of suffrage in an intelligent manner." In other words, they claimed to have a stake in society, unlike poor black men who had until recently been held in bondage. As one black newspaper in New Orleans explained, the debate over extending the franchise to black people should not "confuse the newly freed people with our intelligent population."[1] These issues would come to the fore as political leaders sought to bring Louisiana back into the Union. Indeed, reconstruction gave the state's elite black population an opportunity to press for the full rights of citizenship.

Lincoln badly wanted Louisiana to have a loyal civil government that would bring the state fully back into the Union, and for the last six months of 1863 he urged his military commanders to call for an election of civil office holders and to set up a constitutional convention. After substantial pushing by the president, Union General George F. Shepley, the military governor of Louisiana, called for an election to take place on December 3. Shepley also issued an order enfranchising white Union soldiers. Wealthy men of color in New Orleans hoped that they, too, might be included in this process. The free black community of the city sent petitions to Shepley and Union General Nathaniel P. Banks asking for access to the ballot box, just as white Union soldiers had been given. (They also sent a separate petition to Shepley, which carried ten and a half pages of signatures, asking for protection from harassment and illegal arrest on the streets.) Much to their chagrin, however, Shepley and Banks never responded to their requests. So the free black population of New Orleans decided to take their case directly to Washington. "If we cannot succeed with the authorities here," they declared, "we will go directly to President Lincoln."[2]

In January 1864, two Creole citizens of New Orleans—E. Arnold Bertonneau and Jean Baptiste Roudanez—drafted a lengthy petition addressed to Lincoln and Congress, urging them to enfranchise "all the citizens of Louisiana of African descent, born free before the rebellion" so that they could "participate" in the creation of the new, loyal civil government in the state. Although one newspaper correspondent wrote that they had "quite dark complexions, yet European cast of features," photographic evidence seems to indicate that they were light skinned. Both men had French fathers and "African" mothers, and Bertonneau's death certificate many years later described him as "white." Their petition captured their belief that *they* were equipped to vote, unlike the masses of darker-skinned ex-slaves, who were not.

In language that echoed the Declaration of Independence, the petitioners stated that they "are ready to sacrifice their fortunes and their lives" for "the Country and the Constitution." They touted the fact that they were wealthy and paid taxes, that they had respectable occupations, and that they had sacrificed much for the nation during the War of 1812. These attributes, they maintained, made them "fitted to enjoy the privileges and immunities belonging to the condition of citizens of the United States." The petitioners also pointed to the ways that the free black population of New Orleans was fighting for the Union cause. Just as their forebears had done, they had "hastened to rally under the banner of Union and Liberty" and had "spilled their blood, and are still pouring it out" in defense of the nation. As Union soldiers, they pledged to defend the Constitution "so long as their hands have strength to hold a musket." In light of their military service, the personal sacrifices they had made, and their stake in society, the signers sought "those inalienable rights which belong to the condition of citizens of the great American Republic." "We are men; treat us as such," they implored. The petition was signed at New Orleans on January 5, 1864. The first two signatures belonged to Roudanez and Bertonneau. Roughly one thousand other names followed, including those of twenty-eight elderly black men who had fought with Andrew Jackson during the War of 1812.[3]

On Thursday, March 3, Roudanez, an engineer, and Bertonneau, a wine merchant, approached the White House to present their petition to Lincoln. It was cold that morning in the nation's capital—twenty-eight degrees at 7 a.m. By the afternoon the temperature had risen to the mid-forties. The men must have been anxious as they walked through the city streets toward the Executive Mansion. The press reported that Lincoln received them "cordially." He told them that he "must finish the big job on his hands of crushing the rebellion, and in doing that, if it became necessary to prevent rebels from voting, he should do so." For Lincoln, restoring the Union was "paramount to all other questions," and he "would do nothing that would hinder that consummation or omit anything that would accomplish it." If giving black men the right to vote became "necessary to close the war, he would not hesitate," he said, for he saw "no reason why intelligent black men should not vote." But black suffrage was "not a military question," and he believed it had to be handled by the constitutional convention in Louisiana. As president, Lincoln said that he "did nothing in matters of this kind upon moral grounds, but solely upon political necessities." Since the petition based its claim for suffrage "solely on moral grounds" it "did not furnish him with any inducement to accede to their wishes." In other words, the black Louisianans had not demonstrated that giving black men the right to vote would help to win the war. Still, he assured them that he would support their request "whenever they could show that such accession would be necessary to the readmission of Louisiana as a state in the Union."[4]

Secretary of the Treasury Salmon P. Chase correctly predicted that the "petition of the colored Creoles to the President and to Congress will bring the subject before the Country."[5] During their time in Washington the two men also met with Sen. Charles Sumner of Massachusetts, a powerful advocate for black voting rights, who persuaded them to broaden their appeal to include *all* black men of Louisiana. (Sumner would later introduce their petitions on the floor of the US Senate.) On March 10, Roudanez and Bertonneau wrote out a new petition asking for the right to vote for all black men in Louisiana, including those who were poor, uneducated, and had been born in bondage. This new memorial argued that the federal government had the authority to alter the qualifications of suffrage in Louisiana, and that "justice" required that those who had been "born slaves" should also be given the franchise. Expanding the suffrage in this way, they now contended, would give "full effect . . . to all the Union feeling in the rebel States, in order to secure the permanence of the free institutions and loyal governments now organized therein." Such rights "especially" ought to be given to black men "whether born slave or free . . . who have vindicated their right to vote by bearing arms."[6] In other words, the only way to effectively subdue disloyal sentiment in the Confederacy would be to create a new class of loyal black voters.

Roudanez and Bertonneau had listened to Lincoln. He'd told them that he could not publicly support the expansion of suffrage solely for "moral" reasons. In response, they crafted a rationale for black voting rights that connected black suffrage to winning the war and then sustaining the peace by maintaining pro-Union majorities in the South.

The two men may have returned to the White House on March 12 to present their new petition to the president. (Over the past few decades many historians have placed the date of Lincoln's meeting with Roudanez and Bertonneau as March 12; it may be that he met with them twice—March 3 and 12.) A witness to one of their conversations with Lincoln—likely on March 3 but possibly on March 12—observed that Lincoln showed real sympathy for his guests. "I regret, gentlemen, that you are not able to secure all your rights, and that circumstances will not permit the government to confer them upon you," he told them. "I wish you would amend your petition, so as to include several suggestions which I think will give more effect to your prayer, and after having done so please hand it to me."

One of the men replied, "If you will permit me, I will do so here." Lincoln then asked him, "Are you, then, the author of this eloquent production?" "Whether eloquent or not," came the answer, "it is my work." Lincoln and the Louisianan then sat down side by side and amended the document. According to one witness, "The [white] Southern gentlemen who were present at this scene did not hesitate to admit that their prejudices had just received another shock." A few weeks later, Roudanez told an audience in Boston, "He listened attentively to our address, and sympathized with our object,—but said he could not aid us on moral grounds, only as a military necessity."[7]

It is not known exactly what changes Lincoln recommended. Nevertheless, Lincoln's engagement with Roudanez and Bertonneau clearly had an important effect on the president. On March 13, he sent a letter to Michael Hahn congratulating him for his recent election as governor of Louisiana. The majority of Lincoln's letter consisted of a "private" suggestion—that Hahn consider extending the franchise to "some of the colored people . . . for instance, the very intelligent, and especially those who have fought gallantly in our ranks." Such voters, Lincoln continued, "would probably help, in some trying time to come, to keep the jewel of liberty within the family of freedom."[8] In other words, just as the Louisiana Creoles had argued, Lincoln accepted the view that black voters would be an essential component to preserving liberty in the United States after the Civil War was over. The protection of their rights would ultimately come from their own ability to have a voice in government, not from the courts, or even from the federal government. The language of the "jewel of liberty" eventually became public (Hahn reportedly showed it to many delegates at the state constitutional convention), and black leaders would quote Lincoln's letter to Hahn as they continued to fight for the right to vote in the immediate postwar period. Congressman James G. Blaine would later write that Lincoln's "meaning was one of deep and almost prophetic significance. It was perhaps the earliest proposition from any authentic source to endow the Negro with the right of suffrage."[9]

Lincoln's suggestion to Governor Hahn is remarkable in several ways. Most importantly, it was the first time that a sitting president had suggested extending the right to vote to any persons of color. Clearly, he had begun to accept the arguments put forward by the Louisiana delegation that black men who paid taxes or served their country deserved the right to vote. The ideas that he had articulated about white women in 1836 now, in Lincoln's mind, could be extended to black men. Lincoln also recognized that giving them the ballot would help secure loyal Union majorities in electoral politics in Louisiana. Finally, it is worth noting that Lincoln advocated for a broader expansion of suffrage than even Roudanez and Bertonneau had desired when they first arrived at Washington.

The month after the meeting(s) with the two Louisiana Creoles, a delegation of ex-slaves and free blacks from North Carolina came to Washington to petition Lincoln for the right to vote. This delegation was much different. Its leader, Abraham H. Galloway, had been born to an unmarried slave woman and a white father in coastal North Carolina in 1837. Under the laws at the time, Galloway was born into bondage because his mother was enslaved. At about the age of ten, he was apprenticed to a brick maker. Ten years later, he and another slave stowed away aboard a ship loaded with turpentine and escaped to Philadelphia. There the two runaways encountered the famous abolitionist and Underground Railroad conductor William Still. "The blood was literally drawn from them at every pore in frightful quantities," Still later wrote, describing the effects of the turpentine upon Galloway's and his friend's bodies. "But as heroes of the bravest type they resolved to continue steadfast as long as a pulse continued to beat, and thus they finally conquered."[10] Fearful of being captured and sent back into bondage, Galloway and his companion kept moving northward on the Underground Railroad, eventually settling in Kingston, Ontario. From there Galloway occasionally made trips back into the Northern states to deliver fiery abolitionist lectures. In January 1861, on the eve of the Civil War, he traveled to Haiti, where he appears to have had a hand in planning some sort of slave rebellion in the South.

As the nation faced imminent civil war in April 1861, Galloway made his way back into the South. He worked as a spy for Union General Benjamin F. Butler in Virginia, and then traveled with Butler to New Orleans in 1862. There, Galloway was captured by the Confederates, but he somehow managed to escape, making his way back to the Union-controlled towns of New Bern and Beaufort, North Carolina. Here he became a leader in the local black community, and Union authorities quickly realized that they would have to deal with him if they were going to get freedmen into the Army.

In late May 1863, Galloway consented to meet with Edward Kinsley, a thirty-four-year-old abolitionist from New England who had come to North Carolina to recruit black soldiers for the Union Army. At midnight one night, local African Americans brought Kinsley to the home of a black leader in New Bern and took him up to the attic where "by the dim light of the candle" he could see that the room was filled with black faces. Standing right in front of him were Galloway and "another huge negro, both armed with revolvers." Galloway made it clear to Kinsley that black men from the area would only join the Union Army if they were guaranteed equal pay, care for their families, and education for their children. After hours of negotiations, they came to an understanding. As Galloway's biographer writes, "Kinsley later described the next few moments as the most harrowing of his life. While [Isaac K.] Felton and another of the black leaders held revolvers to Kinsley's head, Galloway compelled [him] to swear a personal oath that the federal Army would meet their conditions. After Kinsley did so, at five o'clock in the morning, the former slaves released him into the predawn air."

Although Kinsley was not able to keep up his end of the bargain, some five thousand black men from New Bern and the surrounding countryside soon mustered into the federal service. Galloway was willing to support this black recruitment effort because he understood that Union victory was the best way for him to accomplish his goals. For Lincoln, the paramount object of the Civil War was to reunify the nation. Galloway, by contrast, wanted liberty and equality for his people. But Galloway recognized the necessity of working within Lincoln's war effort. He could not accomplish what he wanted for his community unless the Union won the Civil War and the Confederacy was destroyed.[11]

In April 1864—about a year after his meeting with Kinsley—Galloway, now twenty-seven years old, made his way to Washington, DC, where he personally presented a written petition to Lincoln. Joining him were a merchant and farmer named E. H. Hill; two barbers, Clinton D. Pierson and John R. Good; an older minister named Isaac K. Felton (mentioned above); and a baker named Jarvis M. Williams. Four of the six men had been born into slavery. It is unknown whether Galloway and Felton brought the revolvers they had carried at their meeting with Kinsley.

April 29 was a pleasant spring day in Washington, with temperatures reaching sixty-five degrees by mid-afternoon. As the delegation approached the White House they were directed to enter the building through the front door. This was an unexpected experience for black men from the South since they never would have been welcomed through the front door into a white person's home or office in North Carolina. Reverend Felton later remarked that it would have been considered an "insult" for a person of color to seek to enter the front door "of the lowest magistrate of Craven County, and ask for the smallest right." Should such a thing occur, Felton said, the black "offender" would have been told to go "around to the back door, that was the place for niggers." In words that alluded to the Sermon on the Mount, Felton likened Lincoln to Christ: "We knock! and the door is opened unto to us. We seek the President! and find him to the joy and comfort of our hearts. We ask, and receive his sympathies and promises to do for us all he could. He didn't tell us to go round to the back door, but, like a true gentleman and noble-hearted chief, with as much courtesy and respect as though we had been the Japanese Embassy he invited us into the White House."

When they entered the president's office, Lincoln shook each man's hand. The black delegation then presented their petition to him. Although Galloway was illiterate, the ideas embodied in the document were almost certainly his. The six men approached Lincoln as "colored citizens of North Carolina, composed alike of those born in freedom, and those whose chains of bondage were severed by your gracious proclamation." They then made an appeal that must have resonated with Lincoln, for it echoed words and ideas he had been articulating most of his adult life—that they "cherish[ed] in our hearts and memories, that ever to be remembered sentence, embodied in the Declaration of Independence, that 'all men are created free and equal.'"

The delegation reminded Lincoln that free men of color had voted in North Carolina from 1776 to 1835, and that some Northern states had extended the franchise to black men "with eminent success and good results." In light of this evidence, they asked Lincoln "to finish the noble work you have begun" by granting them "that greatest of privileges, when the State is reconstructed, to exercise the right of suffrage, which will greatly extend our sphere of usefulness, redound to your honor, and cause posterity, to the latest generation, to acknowledge their deep sense of gratitude." The petitioners then pledged to continue in their efforts to suppress the rebellion "until every cloud of war shall disappear, and your administration stand justified by the sure results that will follow."

Lincoln told his visitors that he "had labored hard and through many difficulties for the good of the colored race, and that he should continue to do so." He gave them the "full assurance of his sympathy in the struggle the colored people of North Carolina are now making for their rights," and he told them that he "would do what he could for us." But as voting "was a matter belonging to the State it would have to be attended to in the reconstruction of the state." Still, Lincoln said that he "was glad to see colored men seeking for their rights," especially since "this was an important right *which we, as a people, ought to have*" (emphasis added). After a "lengthy talk with him on matters and things," recalled John Good, "we again joined hands, took a hearty shake and bid farewell!" "Their interview was a pleasant one," reported the *Anglo-African*, "and they received from Mr. Lincoln assurances of his sympathy and earnest cooperation."

The men were elated by what had happened. Upon returning home to New Bern, they reported back to their neighbors about their experiences, extolling Lincoln for the kindness he had shown them. "The President received us cordially and spoke with us freely and kindly," Good told the audience. Felton joked that he "expected to vote for Mr. Lincoln if he had to go to Massachusetts to do it." Galloway was more circumspect. Recognizing that Lincoln was not going to do anything right away, he urged black Americans to realize that "the best way to secure the help of others is to show a disposition to help yourselves."[12] Their gratitude for Lincoln would endure. A year later, four of these men participated in a large meeting in North Carolina that adopted resolutions honoring "Our noble President, Abraham, the Great as well as Faithful," who, under God's will, "has worked out the freedom of millions of bondmen."[13]

Lincoln met with other delegations of African Americans who also came to talk about the right to vote, although it is unknown how many came to see him. In the spring of 1864, a "mass meeting" of black Virginians met in Norfolk and elected two men, George W. Cook and James Moseley, to go to Washington "to inform the President and Congress of our desire of having access to the ballot box as citizens of the United States."[14] While no report of their meeting with Lincoln appears to survive, a former slave from Norfolk, Rev. Richard H. Parker, left an account of his time at the White House. Parker's master had forbidden him from visiting Washington, but after his enslaver died, Parker thought, "I reckon my time has come to go to Washington." Upon reaching the city, he toured the Capitol, the Treasury, and the Patent Office. Outside of the

White House, he sat down on a bench in Lafayette Square and stretched out his arms and legs. "Ah, this, this is the air of freedom," he said to himself as he looked over at the Executive Mansion.

Upon entering the building, Parker felt like the Queen of Sheba must have felt when she met with King Solomon in ancient Israel. Inside of Lincoln's office, however, he was in for something of a shock. Parker thought that Lincoln must be out, "as I didn't see any one there that looked *peart* enough for the Chief Magistrate." All he saw was "a plain, farmer-like looking man, tall and thin, and about as handsome in the face as I am." The man stood "right up as soon as we entered, and when he knew who we were, made us a hearty welcome, and offered us seats." Parker thought, "*What* an honor, to have our *President* offer *me* a *cheer!*" The men introduced themselves and spoke with Lincoln. According to Parker, Lincoln said, "Don't be in a hurry, friends, you'll get all your rights by and by,—you'll get them just as soon as you are prepared for them, and know how to use them." According to Parker, "I knew [as] soon as I heard that man speak, and saw his kind face, that he would be a good friend to my people; and I've never had cause to change my mind." After this meeting, Parker said, "I had no more to see in Washington, and came home contented, with a *full heart*."[15]

Lincoln's responses to the black delegations were consistent with how he spoke about presidential power throughout the war. He consistently maintained that he could only take actions that were consistent with his oath to preserve, protect, and defend the Constitution. Controversial actions could be justified if they were a "military necessity"—meaning, essential to winning the war and preserving the Union. But he did not believe that he could do anything he wanted simply because he was president. In fact, on March 26, 1864—about the same time as his meetings with the delegations from Louisiana and North Carolina—Lincoln told a delegation of white Kentuckians that he "never understood that the Presidency conferred upon me an unrestricted right to act officially" upon his deeply held personal beliefs. Rather, he explained that his oath of office "imposed upon me the duty of preserving" the Constitution and the nation "by every indispensable means."[16] If giving black men the right to vote would help win the war, then he would support it.

Initially, Lincoln believed that the only thing he could do was persuade state leaders to enfranchise African Americans. In the spring of 1864, he told a delegation of white visitors that voting rights for black men "must come soon. It must come pretty soon, and will." One witness to this scene observed, "It pleased me to know that the President had firmly stipulated for a free state and that he saw the coming of Negro suffrage in Louisiana."[17] Nevertheless, some abolitionists were dissatisfied with Lincoln's constitutional interpretation. One correspondent to the *Liberator* suggested that the president could use his power to enfranchise black men during the process of Reconstruction through the Guarantee Clause of the Constitution (article 4, section 4), which requires the federal government to ensure that every state has a republican form of government. The Declaration of Independence holds out rights for "all men," and the Preamble of the Constitution declares, "We the People," this correspondent argued, "not we the white people, nor we the black people." He continued, "Now, negroes are governed, and they are taxed, and republicanism requires that they should have the right of suffrage."[18]

Other Radical Republicans were also frustrated by Lincoln's moderate approach to black voting rights. "Mr Lincoln is slow in accepting truths," wrote Charles Sumner. "I have reminded him that if he would say the word we might settle this question promptly & rightly. He hesitates." From Sumner's perspective, "Too much blood & treasure have been spent to allow these states to come back again until they are really changed. The whole social & political system must be remodeled. *Union govts. cannot be organized with out the <u>blacks</u>.* Of this I am sure." By March 1865, however, Sumner was becoming more hopeful. "I think that his mind is undergoing a change," he wrote.[19]

Sumner was right.

Indeed, these three (or more) groups of Southern African Americans appear to have had quite an impact on Lincoln's thinking about black political rights. In a letter written to Union General James S. Wadsworth in early 1864, the president argued that it was almost a "religious duty" to protect the rights of all Americans—including those "of the colored race" who had "so heroically vindicated their manhood on the battle-field." Black soldiers who had fought "to save the life of the Republic," he continued, had "demonstrated in blood their right to the ballot, which is but the humane protection of the flag they have so fearlessly defended." In the fall of 1864, Lincoln also told his private secretary William O. Stoddard, "Do all you can, in any and every way you can, to get the ballot into the hands of the freedmen." Just as the second Louisiana petition had argued, Lincoln reasoned, "We must make voters of them before we take away the troops. The ballot will be their only protection after the bayonet is gone, and they will be sure to need all they can get." He then added, however, "The time is not ripe for saying all this publicly, but that time will come."[20]

When the time appeared right, Lincoln did eventually go public with his advocacy for black voting rights. On April 11, 1865, he publicly called for limited black suffrage in a speech he delivered from the balcony of the White House. (This speech is discussed in greater detail in chapter 17.) The meetings with these Southern delegations had helped push him to accept the idea of black men wielding the ballot along with the bullet. None other than Frederick Douglass realized what a great step forward it was for Lincoln to take such a public stance on such a controversial issue. It "meant a great deal," Douglass later said. "It was just like Abraham Lincoln. He never shocked prejudices unnecessarily. Having learned statesmanship while splitting rails, he always used the thin edge of the wedge first—and the fact that he used it at all meant that he would if need be, use the thick as well as the thin."[21]

Tragically, John Wilkes Booth was in the audience the night of April 11 and he was furious. Like Douglass, Booth realized that Lincoln was putting in the thin edge of the wedge first. Like Douglass, Booth expected full black citizenship rights to follow. In his mind, Lincoln's words in favor of black suffrage fully justified what he was about to do.

Figure 1. Elizabeth Keckly. Courtesy of Moorland-Spingarn Research Center, Howard University.

Figure 2. Thomas "Blind Tom" Bethune. Courtesy of the Thomas Harris Collection.

Figure 3. Nicholas Biddle. Courtesy of the Thomas Harris Collection.

Figure 4. Bishop Daniel A. Payne.
Courtesy of the Library of Congress.

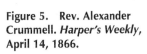
Figure 5. Rev. Alexander
Crummell. *Harper's Weekly*,
April 14, 1866.

Figure 6. Liberian President Joseph Jenkins Roberts. Courtesy of the Library of Congress.

Figure 7.   Rev. Chauncey Leonard (far right) with US Colored Troops at L'Ouverture Hospital, Alexandria, Virginia. Courtesy of Charles Joyce.

Figure 8.   Rev. Henry McNeal Turner. Courtesy of the Library of Congress.

Figure 9. Robert Smalls. Courtesy of the Library of Congress.

Figure 10. Charles Lenox Remond. Courtesy of the Boston Public Library.

Figure 11.   John J. Smith.
Courtesy of the Massachusetts
State Library.

Figure 12.   Dr. Alexander T. Augusta.
Courtesy of the Oblate Sisters of
Providence Archives, Baltimore,
Maryland.

Figure 13.   Dr. Anderson R. Abbott. Courtesy of the Toronto Public Library.

Figure 14.   E. Arnold Bertonneau. Courtesy of Thomas Bertonneau.

Figure 15. Abraham H. Galloway. From William Still, *The Underground Rail Road: A Record* (Philadelphia: Porter and Coates, 1872).

Figure 16. Rev. Leonard A. Grimes. From William J. Simmons, *Men of Mark: Eminent, Progressive and Rising* (Cleveland: Geo. M. Rewell and Co., 1887).

Figure 17. Rev. Richard H. Cain. From William J. Simmons, *Men of Mark: Eminent, Progressive and Rising* (Cleveland: Geo. M. Rewell and Co., 1887).

Figure 18.   Paschal B. Randolph. From *Beyond the Veil: Posthumous Work of Paschal Beverly Randolph* (New York: D. M. Bennett, 1878).

Figure 19.   Flag of the Sixth US Colored Troops. Courtesy of the Library of Congress.

Figure 20.   Rev. Alexander Walker Wayman. From Benjamin W. Arnett, ed., *Proceedings of the Quarto-Centennial Conference of the African M. E. Church, of South Carolina, at Charleston, S.C., May 15, 16, and 17, 1889* (Xenia, Ohio: Aldine Printing House, 1890).

Figure 21.   Photograph of a painting of Abraham Lincoln and Sojourner Truth examining the Bible given by the Baltimore ministers. Courtesy of the Library of Congress.

Figure 22. Maj. Martin R. Delany. Courtesy of the Gettysburg National Military Park.

Figure 23. Solomon James Johnson. Courtesy of Moorland-Spingarn Research Center, Howard University.

Figure 24. William Slade. Courtesy of the Abraham Lincoln Presidential Library and Museum, Springfield, Illinois.

Figure 25. Contrabands in Washington, D.C., preparing to sing for Lincoln. Courtesy of the Library of Congress.

Figure 26. Charlotte Scott. Courtesy of the Library of Congress.

9

"THE OBJECT IS A WORTHY ONE"

The Civil War opened up new mission fields for Christian ministries in the North. As early as 1861, major organizations began sending large numbers of missionaries into the South to evangelize and teach black refugees. Most of these groups—like the American Missionary Association and the American Bible Society—were run by Northern white elites. Black-run organizations similarly longed to enter the South to spread the Gospel and education, but they often lacked funds. Nor did they have donor bases with deep pockets, like many white ministries did. They soon realized, however, that they might be able to find a patron in Abraham Lincoln. He had access to $600,000 in colonization funds, and the White House itself might even become useful for fundraising purposes.

On August 21, 1863—less than two weeks after Frederick Douglass's first meeting with Lincoln—eleven black ministers of the American Baptist Missionary Convention traveled to the White House to ask for financial assistance for their ministry. The leader of the delegation, Leonard A. Grimes, had been born free in Virginia in 1815. As a young man in the 1830s, he was imprisoned in Richmond for helping slaves escape from bondage. Upon his release, Grimes moved to Boston where he was reputed to have helped "hundreds of escaping slaves" on their way to Canada. During the Civil War he recruited black soldiers, including some for the Fifty-Fourth Massachusetts.[1]

Joining Grimes were Sampson White of Philadelphia; Edmund Kelly of New Bedford, Massachusetts; Noah Davis and William Williams of Baltimore, Maryland; Samuel Madden, Alfred Boulden, Collen Williams, and Daniel G. Muse of Washington, DC; William E. Walker of Trenton, New Jersey; and William J. Walker of Fredericksburg, Virginia. Kelly had been born a slave in Tennessee in 1818 to an enslaved woman and an Irish immigrant. When he was six years old his mother was sold away. In the 1830s, he was hired to a primary school teacher, where he bribed young children to teach him how to read by giving them "*bon bons* from his master's table." He joined a Baptist church in 1837 and was licensed to preach in 1842. Eventually he spent $2,800 to purchase the freedom of his wife and four children. As a free man, Kelly authored several articles on behalf of his "deeply wronged race."[2]

The ministers presented a note to one of Lincoln's secretaries, "respectfully" requesting "an inter view of a few moments, for a deligation of Ministers of the Gospel, now in session in the City of Washington." Reverend Kelly also brought the president a short letter that contained images of his children, along with a newspaper clipping of an article he had written titled "The Colored Man's Interest in the Present War."

After the men were ushered into Lincoln's office, Grimes opened the conversation: "Mr. President:—We, the committee appointed by the American Baptist Missionary Convention, now in session with the First Colored Baptist Church, Washington, DC, desire to know what protection we might have from you toward sending missionaries on Southern soil to promulgate the Gospel of Christ within the lines of the military forces of the United States."[3]

According to a newspaper report, Lincoln "made some interesting remarks" during the meeting and then granted the delegation's request. He handed them a brief note stating, "To-day I am called upon by a committee of colored ministers of the Gospel, who express a wish to go within our military lines and minister to their brethren there. The object is a worthy one, and I shall be glad for all facilities to be afforded them which may not be inconsistent with or a hindrance to our military operations."

Lincoln's endorsement of the black ministers' work may have made a difference. From Washington, Grimes traveled to Arlington, Alexandria, Hampton, Norfolk, New Bern, and Roanoke to look into the affairs of the freedpeople. The American Baptist Missionary Convention would go on to send Christian missionaries to the South to evangelize and educate former slaves. Initially they sent missionaries into Virginia, the Carolinas, and Georgia, but within a few years they would aim to take their ministries to the Gulf States. "No other single contribution meant so much to us as these men," wrote a black Baptist preacher who had been reached by these missionaries. "Being bone of our bone, their dress and mannerism created a model in many ways and proved real character makers, and an inspiration to those preachers, who like ourselves, had been slaves and came with us from bondage."[4] Lincoln's support of these ministries enabled them to spread both the Gospel and education to former slaves across the war-torn South.

The following month, on September 23, three leaders from the Grand United Order of Odd Fellows in America—John A. Simms, John F. N. Wilkinson, and Thomas Cross—met with Lincoln to ask for "protection in case of molestation" at their upcoming eighteenth-anniversary celebration in Washington, DC. This black fraternal organization had done valuable philanthropic work thus far during the war, paying out $5,000 to aid the sick, and $4,000 to assist in burials. Upon receiving their request, Lincoln endorsed it: "While I think it probable that the protection sought within will not be needed, it is altogether proper that it should be given if needed, and I doubt not would be given without any direct interference of mine." A few weeks later, Simms, Wilkinson and Cross sent Lincoln an invitation to the celebration.[5] Unfortunately, the invitation arrived just one day before the event and Lincoln already had a Cabinet meeting scheduled for that day. Nevertheless, he did provide the celebrants police and military protection for the parade.

Some three hundred "colored Odd Fellows" from Boston, Alexandria, Baltimore, New York, Philadelphia, and Canada joined in the festivities on October 9, marching in a parade down Pennsylvania Avenue while being serenaded by two bands of black musicians, one of which was the regimental band of Alexander T. Augusta's Seventh US Colored Troops. Leading the parade was Past Noble Father John F. N. Wilkinson, one of the men who had met with Lincoln, and the choir leader at Henry McNeal Turner's church. Artist David Bustill Bowser served as grand master. The marchers carried flags, wreaths, and banners, one of which featured two men—one black and one white—handing a purse of money to a widow and her child. According to one news report, the streets of the city "were completely thronged with the masses of humanity of every hue. Such a sight was never before witnessed in the Federal City." By one estimate, twenty thousand people came out to watch the procession.

When the parade reached the White House grounds, the band played a song entitled "Red, White and Blue." Upon reaching the Executive Mansion itself, they commenced "The Star-Spangled Banner." The revelers gave three hearty cheers for Lincoln as well as more huzzahs for Lincoln's Cabinet, but as those men were in a meeting, they were unable to come out and pay their respects. At City Hall, the mayor stepped out and bowed. One black observer rejoiced to think of what went through Chief Justice Roger B. Taney's mind as he sat "at his window" on Indiana Avenue while the "procession of BLACK ODD FELLOWS march[ed] past his house, GUARDED BY A COMPANY OF WHITE SOLDIERS."

The procession finally ended at Henry McNeal Turner's Israel Church on Capitol Hill. There, the assembly prayed, sang songs, and heard messages. (Henry Highland Garnet was supposed to speak but was unable to attend.) From the pulpit, Rev. James A. Handy rejoiced that Lincoln had "demolished" the "corner-stone" of the Confederacy "by the blow struck, January 1st, 1863." Lincoln was a warrior, patriot, philanthropist, and statesman, Handy continued, who "with one twirl of his pen has raised four million of slaves to freedom, and increased his army with thousands of men." For all future time, January 1 would be a day of celebration, and Lincoln would be a hero to the black community. "In coming time unborn generations will, with music, song and sentiment, celebrate January 1st, 1863," Handy intoned, "and when the dust and rubbish shall be cleared away from this eventful year, the faithful chronicler will write January 1st, 1863, brighter, larger, higher." Then, he thundered, "what a perpetual flow of heart-felt eulogy will to a thousand generations commemorate the virtues, the labor, and the triumph of Abraham Lincoln, the Negro's friend, the Blackman's hope, the oppressed American's Liberator."

Republican papers nationwide praised the progress that this event symbolized. "Our National Capital witnessed a novel sight yesterday, and one which would hardly have been permitted there had it not followed along the progress of events," observed one Massachusetts paper. "War is a strange leveler of castes and prejudices, and men are obliged to march forward to keep pace with the tide of events." Democrats, by contrast, made fun of "the needless and ridiculous fears of the negroes" in thinking they needed armed "white" protection. This, of course, was a highly disingenuous position to take since more than one hundred people, most of whom were black, had recently been killed in the New York City draft riots. In fact, an attendee later remarked, "That this great demonstration could take place in the city of Washington without disturbance of any kind is one of the marvels of these wondrous times."[6]

A month after the Odd Fellows parade, James Mitchell, Lincoln's commissioner of colonization, arranged for a "short interview" between the president and the officers of the African Civilization Society (ACS). Founded by Henry Highland Garnet in the 1850s and incorporated in the state of New York on May 5, 1863, the ACS sought to promote "the civilization and Christianization of Africa, and of the descendants of African ancestors in any portion of the world, wherever dispersed." The organization also hoped to help end the Atlantic slave trade by bringing "lawful commerce" to Africa, and to ensure "the elevation of the condition of the colored population of our own country and other lands." They prided themselves on being the "only Institution of the kind on our Globe managed wholly by coloured Gentlemen." The only problem was that they lacked funds—but they knew that Congress had recently allocated $600,000 for colonization, and the person in charge of those funds was Lincoln.[7]

At 4 p.m. on November 5, Lincoln met with five representatives of the ACS. George Washington Le Vere was the pastor of St. Paul's Congregational Church in Brooklyn. Henry M. Wilson, a graduate of Princeton Theological Seminary, had been a Presbyterian minister in New York since the 1840s and became a proponent of emigration in the late 1850s. Richard H. Cain, a native of Virginia whose mother was Cherokee and whose father was African, had attended Wilberforce University in Ohio and in April 1862 was ordained an elder in the African Methodist Episcopal Church by Bishop Daniel A. Payne. As a student at Wilberforce, Cain was one of 115 young black men to volunteer their services for the Union Army in 1861; however, the governor rejected them on account of their race. As treasurer of the Legal Rights Association, Peter S. Porter had successfully fought against segregation on New York streetcars in 1856, but not before being "most ferociously" beaten in his attempt to ride in a segregated car. Little is known of the fifth visitor, William Anderson, who served as a trustee of the ACS. (Bishop Payne also served as a vice president, and Martin R. Delany was among its trustees, although they did not attend this meeting.)[8]

After greeting the president, the five delegates presented him with a petition. The document let Lincoln know that they were praying for him and stated their belief that he had been "raised up in the wisdom of Jehovah to reform this great nation and deliver millions of captives, just as trully and certainly as Moses (once an exiled Hebrew) was to deliver God's ancient covenant people the Jews from Egyptian bondage." As representatives of the ACS, they thanked Lincoln for "your many timely services recently rendered a suffering portion of our race in this land." The society needed Lincoln's help, however, to accomplish its mission "to give civilization, the Gospel, Science and commerce to our people where-ever they may need them." In order to continue this work, they asked Lincoln to allocate at least $5,000 to the society, that they could use to accomplish their holy work.[9]

According to news reports, Lincoln gave the delegates "a patient hearing, and said he would bestow upon their written communication due consideration." Le Vere later called it a "highly satisfactory interview with President Lincoln." Around the time of the meeting—probably in advance of it—James Mitchell prepared an executive order for Lincoln to sign that would have released $5,000 of federal colonization funds to the ACS. However, Lincoln does not appear to have signed the document—possibly because the funds were legally allocated for "the relief of contrabands."[10] A few months later, Cain sent a letter to Lincoln asking for permission to create schools for freedmen within the lines of the Union armies in the South. Such educational institutions, Cain argued, would help prepare ex-slaves "for citizenship, and the high duties of Moral, and social, as well as spiritual life by leading them to comprehend their high destiny in the future." Lincoln's private secretary John G. Nicolay forwarded Cain's letter to Secretary of War Edwin M. Stanton.[11]

The meeting between Lincoln and the delegates of the ACS received some attention in the press. One Massachusetts paper caustically opined, "If their object is to civilize New York up to the African standard, he ought to give them the money."[12] Richard H. Cain responded to another critic by pointing out the Society's successes—that it had sent its first black teacher to work with the freedpeople, as well as Bibles, books, and copies of the *Anglo-African* and *Christian Recorder*. "Also," he continued, "we will send colored gentlemen and ladies among our brethren in the South, who will see that they are not wronged and cheated out of their rights."[13] Several of the members of the ACS who met with Lincoln went on to achieve significant things on behalf of the Union. In 1864, Lincoln appointed George W. Le Vere chaplain of the Twentieth USCT. After the war he worked as a missionary to freedpeople in East Tennessee. Cain would eventually be elected to Congress from South Carolina, serving two terms in the 1870s during which he fought for equal rights for both African Americans and women. (Unfortunately, by the time he died in 1887, he had witnessed the collapse of Reconstruction in the South.)[14]

Soon black ministers devised a new way to use the White House for religious support without having to ask the president directly for money. In the summer of 1864, Charles I. White, the white pastor of St. Matthew's Church in Washington, DC, expressed concern for the black Catholics who were meeting in the basement of his church. White believed that a new facility should be built for the black parishioners, and he organized a committee of three to call upon President Lincoln to ask for permission to hold a fundraising event on the White House lawn. The head of the committee, Gabriel Coakley, was a leader of the black Catholic community in Washington. Coakley also has an unusual distinction in Washington, DC, history. When Congress passed the DC Emancipation Act in April 1862, giving compensation to "loyal" owners, Coakley successfully petitioned for compensation for his wife and children, since he had purchased their freedom in earlier years. He was one of only a handful of black Washingtonians to make a claim like this. The federal government paid him $1489.20 for eight slaves that he "owned" (he had claimed their value at $3,300).[15]

On June 27, 1864, Coakley and his two fellow committeemen went to the White House where they found the president sympathetic to their request.

"Certainly you have my permission," Lincoln told them. "Go over to General French's office and tell him so." The men then hurried off to see Benjamin Brown French, the commissioner of public buildings. Before going, though, Coakley penned a brief note to French, informing him that they had the president's permission and asking for "a written permit to use the grounds for the purpose above stated . . . in order to avoid difficulty with those who might question our right to be there." Coakley was unable to meet with French, so the delegation left the letter with a clerk. On June 30, a messenger brought Coakley a letter from French, which stated, "The leave asked by the annexed letter is hereby granted, provided the assent of the President is given as stated by Mr. Coakley."

Coakley immediately rushed back to the White House to get the president's signature. He waited in the corridor outside of Lincoln's upstairs office for several hours until Lincoln finally came out. "General French has not refused you that permit, has he?" Lincoln asked. "No, Mr. President," replied Coakley, "but it must have your signature." Lincoln took the permit back into his office and endorsed it, "I assent. / A Lincoln / June 30, 1864." He then handed it back to Coakley and told him he hoped the festival would successfully raise money for the church.[16]

The event took place on July 4. "The entire colored population of Washington was out to-day with flags, music, &c., celebrating the Fourth by pic-nics, parades, &c.," reported the Washington correspondent for the Philadelphia *Inquirer*. "A very large pic-nic was held by them in the public square between the White House and War Department. They had colored bands and colored speakers, and conducted themselves in a very orderly manner."[17] Lincoln's private secretary John Hay observed the scene and recorded his observations in his diary. "They were very neatly & carefully dressed very quietly & decently behaved," he wrote, "the young fellows buckishly & the young girls like ill bred boarding school maids. There were many of both sexes, perfectly white and blue-eyed."[18] The painter Francis Carpenter, too, was fascinated by the scene, writing that "altogether no celebration of the day presented a greater appearance of enjoyment and success." Coakley later recalled in 1885 that Abraham and Mary Lincoln made a brief appearance at the festival.[19]

Journalist Lois Bryan Adams heard about the "splendid picnic in the beautiful shaded park" and went to see it. "It was really a sight worth going miles to see," she wrote. "There were several thousands of both sexes and of all shades and ages decked out in a brilliancy of coloring, dazzling to behold. A fine brass band of colored musicians, discoursed sweet music in one part of the grounds; there were groups of sable singers in another; tables loaded with refreshments were spread promiscuously under the trees, and general joy and gladness seemed to prevail." After standing and watching for a moment, Adams saw an old black woman who probably did not have any money to pay the admission fee. Instead, she "contented herself with looking through the iron railing at the jubilee within." Adams approached her. "Well, Aunty," she said, "they seem to be having a happy time in there." "O, my God, I reckon dey is!" exclaimed the old woman. "I reckon dey is *so*! A mighty good time, bress de Lor! Gov'ment done made de colored pop'lation happy dis time—'deed dey is! . . . O, my God, I reckon dey is happy onst!"[20]

The success of the Catholic picnic on the Fourth of July—it raised $1,200—inspired other black religious leaders to follow suit.[21] On July 21, 1864, J. R. Pierre, the superintendent of the Third Baptist Sabbath School (Colored) sent a brief note to Lincoln praising God for endowing him with concern for "the oppresed and down trodden of those who have to share the fate of the African decent." Pierre informed Lincoln that he wished to create a large "*Banner of Freedom*" that would feature a life size image of "your noble personage" and an image of a slave departing the plantation for a church. He asked Lincoln for permission to hold a gathering of his Sabbath School union on Thursday, August 4, "on the same grounds which were occupide by the Catholic friends on the fourth of July 1864, for the demonstration of there greate fullness to your honor and to the gentlemen that voted for the freeing of the slaves in the District of Columbia." This event would help raise funds for the banner, Pierre explained. Pierre's letter was referred to Benjamin Brown French, who replied on July 23 granting permission, provided the president approved, "otherwise not." Without hesitation, Lincoln approved.[22]

On August 3, Pierre excitedly placed a notice in the Washington *Evening Star*: "PERMISSION HAVING BEEN GRANTED for the use of the grounds adjacent to the President's Mansion, for a demonstration of the appreciation of the colored people of the much-desired and highly appreciated privileges they are permitted to enjoy since the freeing of the slaves and abolishing of the black laws of the District of Columbia, the Sabbath Schools of the District will assemble on the grounds, on THURSDAY, August 4, 1864." There would be preaching at 11 a.m. and 3 p.m., and addresses at 4 p.m. A choir and full band would be present. Admission was twenty-five cents for adults and ten cents for children. "The proceeds are to be applied to the purchase of a banner, to be known as the 'Banner of Freedom.'"[23]

August 4 was an important day. In response to a joint resolution from Congress, Lincoln had set it apart "as a day of national humiliation and prayer." Such a day seemed necessary to many leaders in Washington. Secretary of the

Navy Gideon Welles wrote in his diary: "There is much wretchedness and great humiliation in the land, and need of earnest prayers." Attorney General Edward Bates concurred, writing, "surely no people ever stood more in need of self-abasement, for our persistent wickedness and perverse obstinacy in wrong."[24]

The Third Baptist Sunday School assembled at the White House grounds at 10 a.m. and the religious exercises began at noon with a sermon by Alfred Boulden (one of the eleven black ministers who met with Lincoln in August 1863). Boulden preached from Habakkuk 2:11. "After these exercises were concluded the assembly gave themselves up to social enjoyment," reported the Washington *Evening Star*. They ate watermelons, cantaloupes, smaller fruits, cakes, lemonade, and other refreshments. They hung swings from the branches of trees while "promenading parties continually moved about." Everyone present seemed to be enjoying themselves "hugely." Outside of the picnic area, many tables were set up for the sale of refreshments "and trade was brisk. A large number of colored people remained outside of the enclosure, some not feeling able, and others not willing to pay the price of admission."

By 3 p.m., about four to five hundred people were present, and religious exercises began again. A speaker's platform was erected near the president's garden, and above it hung a large American flag. Two ministers preached sermons, and Edward T. Thurien of Philadelphia delivered an address. Thurien "expressed much thankfulness to President Lincoln and his administration for all that had been done for the colored race" and "urged those present to enlist and aid by all their power in crushing the rebellion, now that the colored people had been allowed to exercise arms." Thurien had formerly been a slave, and he "gave some interesting descriptions of the horrors of slavery" he had witnessed earlier in life.[25] According to one observer, an old man "with a voice like a gong" prayed in a deep voice and with his hands lifted up (alluding to the Old Testament Hebrew leader Joshua), "O Lord command the sun & moon to stand still while your Joshua Abraham Lincoln fights the battles of freedom." A woman then sang,

> Believers in that day
> They will rise and fly away
> Glad to hear the trumpet sound
> In that Morning
> Crying O Lord See How I long
> Glad to hear the trumpet sound
> In that morning.[26]

Several others delivered speeches until finally Pierre took the stand. He thanked Lincoln "for granting the use of the grounds and doing so much for the colored people. He said he knew there were many among those who have robbed God as well as men and women, and were now trying to break up this Government, who thought the bodies of the colored people ought now to be on a traitor's plantation. To-day they were permitted to assemble here, but yet many held they should yet be slaves to those who were helping Jeff Davis and his copperhead crew." As the sun began to set, the celebrants packed up "in a quiet and orderly manner" and prepared to return home. One Washington paper reported that a "handsome sum was realized for the banner." Pierre eventually had the banner made. It bore the words, "Whatever shall appear to be God's will, I will do," near Lincoln's signature. After the war, Pierre loaned the banner for local African American celebrations, such as one that celebrated emancipation in the District of Columbia and ratification of the Fifteenth Amendment in 1870.[27]

Lincoln's Democratic opponents were horrified by these social gatherings on the White House lawn, which they saw as an unwarranted expansion of rights for African Americans. The *Daily Milwaukee News* reported that, on a day set aside for "fasting, humiliation and prayer, the negroes of the District of Columbia were permitted, by the express assent of Mr. Lincoln, to hold a pic-nic upon the grounds surrounding the president's house." The editors reminded their readers that a similar event had taken place on Independence Day. "Up to that time no body of citizens had been allowed to assemble there for purposes of diversion—not even white Sabbath School children," they wrote. But now the black Baptists were "emboldened" by the success of the black Catholics on July 4 and "repeated their request for a jolification on the same grounds on fast day." The purpose of these picnics, concluded the editors, was "to praise the men who have elevated the negro to social equality with the white man."

After giving its own unfavorable view of the matter, the *News* reprinted two paragraphs from the *Washington Constitutional Union*. The "grand old trees" around the White House "were polluted by having swings attached to them whereby negro men could swing negro women," while the "sacred" grounds "were prostituted and disgraced by the erection of stands for negro merchants to vend fruits and cakes and drinks to negro customers." The editors lamented that "these negroes" received "the high approval and warm commendation of our president," while whites had never been given permission like this. "The public grounds were too sacred—of too high a character—in too close proximity to the residence of the august Abraham Lincoln for white men to use—their color would remind him too forcibly of the despotism he has erected on the ruins of the republic."[28]

These reports reveal how the Civil War had vastly different meanings for white and black Americans. Indeed, Attorney General Edward Bates took note of how differently these two constituencies treated the day of national humiliation and prayer. "It seems by this that the *white* and the black understand the Proclamation differently, and use the day for different and opposite purposes," he wrote in his diary after reading an article in the Washington *National Intelligencer* titled, "The Negroes' Jubilee." "The Whites humble in fasting and prayer, as well they may, in view of their great and many sins, which have called down God's vengeance, and has brought upon us this desolating war, and still continues it," he wrote. "But the Blacks rejoice exceedingly, over the results of the war, already accomplished in their favor, and exult in the hope of the continuance of the war, in all its desolations. And this is reasonable *in them*; for they are taught by those at the North, who, ostentatiously claim to be their only friends, that the war is waged solely for their emancipation, and for wiping out the blot of negro slavery, from this continent." Bates continued, "I do not believe that the negro[e]s desire that the Whites shall be reduced to slavery; but if, by the destructive processes of the war, their own personal freedom can be accomplished, we cannot expect them to reject that consummation, because, by the same processes, all the civil, social and political rights of white men may be destroyed."[29]

The black picnics at the White House in the summer of 1864 have been largely forgotten in the historical literature, but they still hold a special place in the memories of black Catholics in Washington, DC, as well as among the descendants of one of the organizers. In 2009, President Barack Obama's nominee for General Counsel of the Treasury Department testified before the Senate Committee on Finance that "Public service is in the blood of my family." He then recounted the story of "my grandmother's grandfather, Gabriel Coakley, [who] along with two other freed slaves . . . obtained permission from President Abraham Lincoln to hold a 'Strawberry Festival' on the front lawn of the White House on July 4, 1864. With these funds and others previously committed, Coakley founded Saint Augustine Catholic Church and School which recently celebrated its 150th Anniversary."[30]

10

"A TESTIMONIAL OF HER APPRECIATION"

Americans have sent gifts to presidents since George Washington first took office in 1789. Some of the most bizarre presents have become famous. In the summer of 1801, a group of Massachusetts Baptists sent Thomas Jefferson a 1,238-pound "Mammoth Cheese." The giant dairy product traveled from New England to Washington by boat, sled, and a wagon pulled by six horses. Accompanying the gift was an "Ode to the Mammoth Cheese," which included the lines, "No traitor to his country's cause" would ever "have a bite of thee between his jaws." For a year, Jefferson enjoyed cutting the cheese for guests at the White House. What was left of the stinky mass in 1803 was dumped into the Potomac River. Three decades later, a dairy farmer from New York sent Andrew Jackson an even larger cheese wheel, weighing in at 1,400 pounds.[1]

During his time in office, Abraham Lincoln also received some unusual gifts. In 1862, he politely declined a shipment of elephants from the King of Siam because, as Lincoln explained, "so generous an offer" could not "be made practically useful in the present condition of the United States." White Northerners sent him butter, fresh fruits, salmon, and other foods. One upstate New Yorker even sent a live "American Eagle" that had lost a foot in a trap. "But," the man assured him, "he is yet an Eagle and perhaps no more cripled [sic] than the Nation whose banner he represented; his wings are sound and will extend seven feet."[2] When the sculptor John Rogers sent Lincoln a statuette of his work, "Wounded Scout," which depicts a formerly enslaved man helping a wounded Union soldier, Lincoln replied that it "is very pretty and suggestive, and, I should think, excellent as a piece of art. Thank you for it."[3]

Throughout the war, African Americans wanted to express their gratitude to him as well. Countless free and enslaved black people included Lincoln in their nightly prayers. In Maryland, for example, a white woman observed that her slave named Jim "offers up a special prayer for Abraham Lincoln," while a black woman in New York told Lincoln that "the people of Color are praying day & night for your hands to be supported untill this great struggle proves victorious on the side of the Union." Hearing prayers said for "the Great Emancipator" could make an indelible mark on a young child's mind. Many years after the war, Booker T. Washington said his "first recollection of Abraham Lincoln" was waking up one morning on the dirt floor of his cabin to the sound of his mother "kneeling over my body earnestly praying that Abraham Lincoln might succeed and that one day she and her boy might be free."[4]

Some freedpeople sent Lincoln letters to communicate their appreciation. In April 1863, one South Carolinian who had escaped bondage and joined the Union Army wrote Lincoln that he "had the onner of righting to you these fue lines hoping that tha may find you in A most Perfic state of helte as it left me the saim." The soldier then added: "I only wish that I only cold have the Pleger of coming to Be hold you. with mine eyes[.] I am verry much longing to see you." Unfortunately, he never had the opportunity to meet his commander in chief. A year later, in March 1864, an escaped slave from Tennessee named Hannibal Cox sent Lincoln a poem. Cox had recently joined the Union Army, and several white soldiers taught him how to read and write. As a newly freed slave who was fighting for the Union and the liberation of his race, Cox wanted to share his patriotic fervor, as well as what he had learned, with the president. He copied a few lines of poetry out of a recent issue of *Harper's Weekly*, and sent them to Lincoln:

> Ho for the flag of the union. the Stripes and the Stars of light.—
> A million arms. Shall guard it. and may god defend the right.—
> Ay, brothers let us love it, and let Every heart be true.—
> And let Every arm be ready, for we have glorious work to do.—

Lincoln was apparently so moved by these gestures that he preserved both letters in his personal collection of papers.[5]

Some gifts were edible. In November 1864, a "self emancipated woman" from Natchez, Mississippi, shipped Lincoln something called "a nice *Liberty Cake*" to express her appreciation for what he had accomplished for slaves in the Confederacy.[6] Others expressed their gratitude in more public ways. Shortly before Christmas 1864, the *Chicago Tribune* reported that the black community of Chicago sent Lincoln a copy of John Rogers's statuette "Union Refugees."[7] In an even more public gesture, the black spiritualist Paschal B. Randolph dedicated the second edition of his book *Pre-Adamite Man* "To Honest Abraham Lincoln, President of the United States, as a testimonial of my gratitude for his efforts to save the nation, and widen the area of human freedom." Randolph had previously met with Lincoln and had asked for permission to dedicate the book to him. According to one news report, "Mr. Lincoln gave him an interview, and told him his field was educational, not that of the soldier, and suggested that he would be most useful as a teacher to his people in the South." Randolph welcomed this suggestion and moved to New Orleans where he helped found Lincoln Memorial High Grade and Normal School to train black teachers.[8]

Perhaps the first African American to personally deliver a gift to Lincoln was David Bustill Bowser, the famous artist from Philadelphia. Bowser traveled to Washington for the Odd Fellows anniversary celebration on October 9, 1863, at which he served as grand marshal. A few days later, on October 13, he presented Lincoln with a *carte de visite* of the flag he had painted for the Sixth US Colored Infantry. Lincoln must have been pleased with the imagery he saw. On the obverse, the goddess Liberty stands holding an American flag while beckoning a freedman to join the Union Army. In the background, an enslaved man applauds the new enlistee. Above this scene is a banner featuring the motto, "Freedom for All." The reverse of the flag features an American eagle.

No one else was present for their conversation, but Bowser later told an acquaintance that "Mr. Lincoln expressed much pleasure and gratification on the occasion." Upon reporting this story, the editors of the *Anglo-African* surmised that Lincoln did not feel "a tenth part of the joy that friend Bowser did in being permitted to present his artistic production to one who was so worthy of his highest regard." Bowser would go on to paint twenty-one portraits of the man his obituary called his "personal friend." According to Bowser family tradition, Lincoln personally sat for one of them.[9]

Other artists also wished to present their work to the president. For them, presenting a work of art was the highest expression of gratitude they could give, and it treated Lincoln as a patron. In the spring of 1864, Caroline Johnson, a black woman from Philadelphia who had worked as a nurse at wartime hospitals, decided to make a gift for Abraham and Mary Lincoln. According to the Philadelphia *Press*, "Mrs. Johnson has devoted much of her life to the manufacture of wax fruit, and her skill shows itself to be of a high order." Feeling "gratitude" to the president "for his proclamation of freedom," she spared no time or expense in crafting "a handsome pyramid of wax fruit" for him. She polished and then mounted it on a round table and surrounded it with an elaborate selection of seashells. Once she had perfected her design, she placed the entire display under a large piece of glass. On March 8, Johnson showed the piece to the editors of the *Press*, and they praised it for its beauty. "The gift will cost about $150—an expense to be borne entirely by Mrs. Johnson," reported the *Press*, "unless she may receive the co-operation of persons who feel an interest in showing to Mr. Lincoln how the colored people view his official conduct." Its estimated retail value was $350.[10]

Caroline Johnson obtained a letter of introduction to the president through an official in the Department of Agriculture named Isaac Newton. She must have been overjoyed when she learned that she would be received at the White House on Saturday, April 2. Lincoln normally greeted visitors at his office on Tuesdays and Fridays, so it was a special opportunity for her to meet the president at this time.

Mrs. Johnson and James Hamilton, a black Baptist minister, traveled from Philadelphia to Washington to present the gift to the Lincolns. On Friday, April 1, Newton sent the box containing the wax fruit to the White House with instructions that it should not be opened until Johnson came to present it. As an artist, it was important for her to set up the sculpture herself so that it would be properly displayed. The next day she went to the Executive Mansion at 1 p.m. to arrange the fruit on a table at the center of the library on the second floor.

The White House library was a large, oval-shaped sitting room in the Lincolns' private living quarters. President Millard Fillmore had installed bookshelves in the room in 1850, and every chief executive since had added books to the collection. The room was "chastely and not extravagantly furnished," reported the *New York Herald*, with green wallpaper and upholstered rocking chairs. Lincoln often stared out of the large, southward-facing windows at the unfinished Washington Monument, the Potomac River, and the Confederate state of Virginia in the distance. This room was not a public space. Indeed, it was reserved for family and friends. Often Lincoln came into the library in the early morning hours to think and to read before the busyness of the day set in. On Sundays he sat quietly on a sofa with his Bible. Sometimes, in the middle of an exhausting workday, he snuck into the library for a nap. One family friend recalled seeing him in there "in his stocking feet with one leg crossed over the other, the unshod foot slowly waving back and forth, as if in time to some inaudible music." On other occasions, he sat in a large armchair telling stories of frontiersmen and Indians to his two younger sons, Tad and Willie, and their friends. Lincoln's private secretary William O. Stoddard called it "a delightful retreat."[11] For Lincoln to invite an African American woman into this room, therefore, made a remarkable statement—it was something he had never done before. In fact, this may be the first time a person of color—other than a servant or member of the White House staff—was invited into the private living spaces of the first family.

The Washington correspondent of the Newark *Advertiser* reported on this "affair of considerable interest" in the presidential library. The reporter described how "Mrs. Caroline Johnson, a highly respected colored friend of Philadelphia," made "the formal presentation of a very choice collection of wax fruits to 'Abraham and Mary Lincoln,' . . . as a testimonial of her appreciation of the President's services in behalf of her oppressed race." Only a few people were present to witness this remarkable scene. The president stood next to Mrs. Johnson, while Mary Lincoln, Isaac Newton, and Reverend Hamilton all gathered nearby. Hamilton "touchingly alluded to the past sufferings of his people, to the rapid progress of their deliverance under the present Administration, and their hopes of the future." He asked the president and First Lady to accept the gift "as a specimen of the handiwork of a lady of color, and as an evidence of their confidence and esteem for their Chief who had brought them thus far out of the land of bondage." The minister then added, "Perhaps Mrs. Johnson would like to say a few words?"

Caroline Johnson was understandably nervous. She gazed down at the floor, fearing that she "had not a word to say." However, after a few moments, she placed her hand on her chest, feeling as though a fire was burning inside of her. "It burned and burned till it went all over me," she later recalled. "I think it was the Spirit." Her mind went to Isaiah 51, in which God promises everlasting comfort and salvation to the suffering. "Listen to me, you who pursue righteousness," wrote the Old Testament prophet, "look to the rock from which you were hewn. . . . Look to Abraham your father." With these words as her inspiration, Mrs. Johnson looked at Lincoln and said, "Mr. President, I believe God has hewn you out of a rock, for this great and mighty purpose. Many have been led away by bribes of gold, of silver, of presents; but you have stood firm, because God was with you, and if you are faithful to the end, he will be with you."

Lincoln was visibly moved by these words and he responded with a few emotional remarks, thanking her for "the beautiful present." He spoke briefly of "the difficulties" he had faced as president and attributed the "wondrous changes of the past three years to the ruling of an all-wise Providence." Choking back tears, Lincoln said, "You must not give me the praise—it belongs to God." After a few more words, Johnson, Hamilton, and Newton departed. It was a chilly day in Washington, DC, the temperature reaching only thirty-seven degrees by the time the three guests walked outside. Yet the cold weather hardly could have bothered them. They were overjoyed by their interaction with the president.

Mary Lincoln was delighted with the gift and planned to have it shipped home to Illinois.[12] Later that night, she showed it to Benjamin Brown French, the Commissioner of Public Buildings, who was at the White House for a levee. Following the reception, French wrote in his diary, "Mrs. Lincoln took me up into the Library to see a most beautiful arrangement of wax fruit, etc., made by a negro woman and presented to herself and Mr. Lincoln. She seemed to appreciate it very highly & to be exceedingly pleased with it."[13] Three days later, on April 5, Mary Lincoln sent a letter to Charles Sumner introducing Reverend Hamilton and Mrs. Johnson to him. She called them "very genteel & intelligent persons," and told the senator that Johnson had devoted much of the last three years to caring for sick and wounded Union soldiers.[14]

In the early 1870s, Mrs. Johnson's visit to the White House became part of a national debate over Lincoln's religious faith. When Lincoln's self-appointed bodyguard Ward Hill Lamon published a scandalous biography that depicted Lincoln as an infidel, the *Congregationalist* newspaper recounted Lincoln's conversation with Caroline Johnson as evidence that "Mr. Lincoln lived in the White House a life of Christian faith and works."[15] While it was an overstatement to claim that Lincoln lived "a life of Christian faith," his words to Mrs. Johnson were consistent with other statements he made about the role of Providence in the war. Clearly, the massive amounts of carnage and suffering were reshaping his understanding of the Bible and the will of God. As a young boy, Lincoln had learned a great deal about the Scriptures, memorizing substantial passages by heart. As he grew older, however, he began to exhibit some hostility toward both the Good Book and organized religion. As a teenager he mockingly parroted sermons he heard, gesturing with his hands to lampoon unsophisticated preachers. So well known was he for his irreverent views that when he ran for Congress in the 1840s, he was forced to publish a handbill defending himself against charges of infidelity. In his entire adult life Lincoln never joined a church. However, by the midpoint of the war he appears to have developed a deep and personal appreciation for the Bible.

At some point, probably in the last year of his life, Lincoln wrote out a tiny document now known as his "Meditation on the Divine Will." In it, Lincoln privately reflected upon how "the will of God prevails," even in a bloody conflict like the Civil War. Lincoln struggled to understand just what "God's purpose" might be in the war. Eventually he came to believe that God had his own plan— "something different from the purpose of either" the North or the South.[16] On April 4, 1864—just two days after he met with Mrs. Johnson—Lincoln expanded on these ideas in a public letter defending emancipation. "I claim not to have controlled events, but confess plainly that events have controlled me," he wrote. This statement was not posturing or false humility. In 1861 Lincoln had wanted to avoid the war, and he had pledged not to abolish slavery in the states where it already existed. For almost two years he had struggled to reunify the nation without freeing the slaves. But the Almighty had his own purposes. "God alone can claim it," Lincoln explained. Indeed, emancipation had been accomplished because of "the justice and goodness of God."[17]

Lincoln firmly believed that God's hand had been the prime mover in the process of emancipation. This is why he could, with genuine humility, tell Mrs. Johnson to give the praise to God. Moreover, his belief that the will of God would prevail gave Lincoln a sense of solace amid all the suffering of the war. Clearly God was using bloodshed to purify the nation of its sin—an argument Lincoln would eventually make in his second inaugural address. Americans now had no choice but to accept what God had wrought—that freedom for the enslaved would come through the chastisement of the nation. This would be a hard lesson for most Americans to accept, but it gave people of color like Mrs. Johnson a reason for hope. It also gave Lincoln hope that there was meaning and purpose in a seemingly endless war. Thus, in that quiet, private moment in the White House library, Lincoln was pleased to accept a beautiful gift from a grateful woman, but he wanted her to give honor where it was due.

During the summer of 1864, Lincoln continued to contemplate God's role in the devastation brought about by the rebellion. One day he met with his old friend Joshua Speed at the Soldier's Home on the outskirts of Washington. When Speed arrived, he found Lincoln sitting by a window, reading a Bible. "I am glad to see you profitably engaged," Speed said, perhaps with a hint of sarcasm. "Yes," replied Lincoln matter-of-factly, "I am profitably engaged." "Well," Speed continued, "if you have recovered from your skepticism, I am sorry to say that I have not." Lincoln stood up and placed his hand on Speed's shoulder. "You are wrong, Speed," he said. "Take all of this book upon reason that you can and the balance on faith, and you will live and die a happier and better man."[18]

About the same time that Lincoln was discussing the merits of the Scriptures with Speed, a group of black ministers from Baltimore decided to present a beautiful, ornate Bible to the president. On July 5, this "masterpiece of art and taste" went on display at Bethel Church, where people paid twenty-five cents to see it. Over the next few weeks, it could be seen at the Bible House on West Fayette Street.[19]

In July and August, several prominent white men from Baltimore wrote to Lincoln requesting that he meet with "a Committee of Colored men of this City" who wished to present him with "a very elegantly bound edition of the Bible, which they have prepared as an evidence of their regard & gratitude."[20] Lincoln finally met with the committee on Wednesday, September 7, "in the presence of a large crowd of spectators." The ministers in the delegation included Alexander Walker Wayman, a bishop in the African Methodist Episcopal Church who had been born free in Maryland in 1821; Samuel W. Chase, a prominent Presbyterian minister and grand master of the Colored Masonic Order; a minister named W. H. Brown; and a teacher named William H. Francis.

After Lincoln "individually welcomed" each of his guests, Reverend Chase made a short speech. "Mr. President," he began, "The loyal colored people of Baltimore have entrusted us with authority to present this Bible as a testimonial of their appreciation of your humane conduct towards the people of our race." Just as "all others of this nation are offering their tribute of respect to you," so too "we cannot omit suitable manifestation of ours." But Chase also wanted Lincoln to remember that black people had been loyal to the government even though they had not received full equality before the law. "Since our incorporation into the American family we have been true and loyal, and we are now ready to aid in defending the country, to be armed and trained in military matters, in order to assist in protecting and defending the star-spangled banner."

Chase's allusion to the Star-Spangled Banner recalled the enormous fifteen-star flag that had flown over Fort McHenry during the Battle of Baltimore in September 1814—exactly fifty years earlier. That flag served as a symbol of victory over tyranny in "the land of the free." Now the Union was in need of new defenders from Baltimore. In making his points, Chase echoed the words of other black visitors to the White House. He implicitly reminded Lincoln that a vast, disloyal white population resided in the slave states. In fact, there were many Confederate sympathizers in the loyal state of Maryland. But the black people of those states had remained steadfast for the Union. Lincoln could rely on them for support. They would be brave and dependable defenders of the Union.

Chase then turned to the reason for their visit. "Towards you, sir, our hearts will ever be warm with gratitude," he continued. "We come to present to you this copy of the Holy Scriptures, as a token of respect for your active participation in furtherance of the cause of the emancipation of our race." Chase knew that Lincoln's "great" act of emancipation would become "a matter of history," and he wanted the gratitude of the black community to be part of that story. "Hereafter, when our children shall ask what mean these tokens, they will be told of your worthy deeds, and will rise up and call you blessed," he said.

This remark carried even greater significance than Chase's earlier allusion to the Star-Spangled Banner. Indeed, most Americans at the time would have recognized that Chase was likening Lincoln to Christ. His words were drawn directly from two passages of Scripture. In Proverbs 31, words like these are used to describe a woman of noble character, while in the Gospel of Luke, the Virgin Mary states, "from henceforth all generations shall call me blessed" when she learns that she will bear the Messiah. Chase left little room to doubt how the black community of Baltimore viewed Abraham Lincoln.

Chase's historical and biblical allusions represented different types of salvation—one from British tyranny, the other from sin. Clearly these black leaders from Baltimore—who came with "authority" as representatives of the black community in their city—saw Lincoln as a savior to their nation and their race. And they wanted Lincoln to know that they were praying for him. Chase concluded: "The loyal colored people of this country everywhere will remember you at the Throne of Divine Grace. May the King Eternal, an all-wise Providence protect and keep you, and when you pass from this world to that of eternity, may you be borne to the bosom of your Saviour and your God."

Lincoln replied to Reverend Chase and the other ministers with a brief address. He told them that this "occasion would seem fitting for a lengthy response to the address which you have just made," but that he was not prepared to make one. He wished that he could promise to write them a letter to express his appreciation, but "experience taught me that business will not allow me to do so." Still, the president wanted to say something meaningful in this moment. "I can only now say, as I have often before said, it has always been a sentiment with me that all mankind should be free," he told them. "So far as able, within my sphere, I have always acted as I believed to be right and just; and I have done all I could for the good of mankind generally." These sentiments echoed words Lincoln had spoken to other black visitors to the White House, including the men who petitioned for the right to vote earlier that year. Lincoln truly desired all people of all colors everywhere to be free, but as president he did not believe he could simply do anything he wanted to attain that goal. He was bound by the Constitution—a document he had sworn to preserve, protect, and defend. Still, he would do all he could do within the Constitution's constraints to win freedom from bondage for as many people as possible.

Lincoln also wished to acknowledge the importance of the Bible. He spoke not simply of the physical gift that the ministers had given him, but of what Scripture meant for humanity. "In regard to this Great Book, I have but to say, it is the best gift God has given to man," he told the ministers. "All the good the Saviour gave to the world was communicated through this book. But for it we could not know right from wrong. All things most desirable for man's welfare, here and hereafter, are to be found portrayed in it." He then concluded, "To you I return my most sincere thanks for the very elegant copy of the great Book of God which you present."[21]

Lincoln rarely spoke of an afterlife, as he did in this moment (the "hereafter"). He must have been moved by Chase's words of prayer for Lincoln's soul—that God should protect him "when you pass from this world to that of eternity." In these extemporaneous remarks, Lincoln offered a glimpse into how his worldview was changing as a result of the war. No longer a "scoffer" of the Bible, he now found comfort in it—and hope that the suffering of this world would not be in vain. After this brief exchange, Lincoln laid the Bible on a nearby table and leafed through it. Then, as the four black men departed, he took "each of them by the hand as they passed out." As Reverend Wayman recalled, "We then shook his hand and bade him adieu, wishing him great success in his office, and re-election for another four years."[22]

The Bible was beautiful and ornate—a large pulpit edition bound in royal purple velvet and enclosed in a black walnut case. Affixed to the lid of the case was a silver plate featuring an engraving of the US Capitol and the words, "Holy Bible." The Good Book had originally been published by the American Bible Society in 1857 but had since been adorned with decorations and symbols to make it suitable for the president. The front cover featured elegant golden floral designs in two corners and an oval gold plate, nine inches in circumference, in the middle. At the top of the plate was an eagle with spread wings perched upon a shield. Thirty-three stars studded the sky beneath it, and another eagle sat on a globe to its left. In the middle of the scene stood Lincoln in a field removing shackles from the wrists of an enslaved man. The slave had dropped his rake on the ground and lifted his hands up toward the president. Below this scene was a banner with the word, "Emancipation." On the back cover of the Bible was a four-inch-by-two-inch gold plate that bore an inscription:

To
Abraham Lincoln
President of the United States
The Friend of Universal Freedom
From
the Loyal Coloured People of Baltimore
as a Token of Respect and Gratitude
Baltimore 4th July 1864

Tucked inside, near the front of the book, was a piece of silk with an inscription that praised Lincoln for his Emancipation Proclamation. That edict, the silk declared, "will hereafter be regarded as the most sublime State Paper of Modern Civilization." Moreover, the date that it was issued—January 1, 1863—"will always be to the Colored People of the United States, the most memorable day in the History of their race," for they will "look upon it, as the dawn of universal freedom, and the sure harbinger of their redemption, from the ignominy, and degradation which Slavery has heretofore fastened, alike upon the bond and free." So important was that day, the silk declared, that they "will date their rise and progress as a people, worthy of the rights, and privileges of Citizenship" from it.

The silk further proclaimed that "the Colored Men of America" owed gratitude to Lincoln for the "inestimable change in their condition and prospects." He had given them a "blessing" in his proclamation—something that would help them realize their hopes "as men and citizens." As such, this Bible was "the most appropriate token of our gratitude and affection" that they could give "to our Friend, the President of the United States." The silk closed by quoting the Golden Rule, which they said Lincoln had "so nobly followed—'Do unto others as ye would have others do unto you.'"[23]

The language of the silk was as meaningful as the words that Reverend Chase had spoken. It confirmed the Baltimoreans' gratitude for freedom while simultaneously letting Lincoln know that they wanted the full rights of citizenship. They knew that freedom from slavery would not be sufficient. Only with political rights, like the ballot, would African Americans be able to secure the freedom they had attained on January 1, 1863.

The Bible cost the black community of Baltimore $585.75 to produce—a significant amount of money at that time. The expense was covered by contributions from 272 women and 247 men. "Intrinsically valuable as this gift may be," wrote the editors of the Baltimore American, "it is of little account in comparison with the sentiments it represents or embodies. It will be properly appreciated by the great champion of emancipation; it will take its appropriate place in the history of his efforts towards the accomplishment of that grand consummation in which Maryland has taken a leading part. It will form one of the best and proudest memorials it has ever fallen to the lot of any public man to transmit to posterity."[24]

The artist Francis Carpenter, who spent six months at the White House working on a painting of Lincoln and the Emancipation Proclamation, noted, "No public testimonial of regard, it is safe to say, gave Mr. Lincoln more sincere pleasure during his entire public life, than that presented by the colored people of the city of Baltimore, in the summer of 1864, consisting of an elegant copy of the Holy Bible."²⁵ Lincoln's acceptance of this gift also offered encouragement to Christians throughout the North.²⁶

At some point after Lincoln's death, the Bible came into the possession of his son, Robert. Eventually Robert took it to Hildene, his summer home in Manchester, Vermont, where it largely disappeared from public memory. Then, about 1915, Dr. S. W. Crosthwait, a black leader in Nashville, began to wonder about the Bible's whereabouts. Upon learning that Robert Lincoln still had it in his possession, he wrote to Dr. Fayette McKenzie, the president of Fisk University, an historically black institution, urging him to approach Robert about donating the Bible to Fisk. Crosthwait believed that "this historic heirloom" would "do the most good to the greatest number" there because it would symbolize "the constant and sincere wish of the great President" that all African Americans gain an education. Moreover, he continued, "The very presence of this particular volume with its historic traditions and connections would be a perpetual source of inspiration to the colored people for higher thoughts and nobler deeds of citizenship." Crosthwait thought the Bible could be used during important holidays at the university, such as Emancipation Day, Lincoln's birthday, and Flag Day. Writing in the early years of the Jim Crow era, he predicted, "If the colored youth who are being educated were better informed in regard to Mr. Lincoln and his interpretation of the Word of God, they would be more hopeful, and therefore feel themselves to be in fact American citizens." Moreover, they would come to see Lincoln "as the best exemplar which the world has yet seen of American institutions . . . because he imbibed and lived up to the essential spirit of the doctrine of the Bible."

McKenzie took Crosthwait's advice and contacted Robert Lincoln in January 1916. Robert had planned to eventually donate the Bible to the Library of Congress, along with his father's papers, but McKenzie's request struck him "favorably" and he promised to consider it. On April 13, Robert told McKenzie that he intended "to send the Bible to you as you requested for I think that its interesting associations will be of more value in the custody of Fisk University than anywhere else that I can think of." He then informed McKenzie that he could expect to receive it by the end of May.

McKenzie was ecstatic. "I cannot express to you our appreciation of your generosity in promising Fisk University the Bible which belonged to your Father," he wrote to Robert on May 9. "We shall always treasure it as one of the great historic possessions of this historic institution." McKenzie pointed out that the Bible was only a few years older than Fisk, and he promised that the institution would receive it "in a proper and dignified manner." A few weeks later, McKenzie informed Robert that "the gratitude of Fisk University, and my own gratitude, for the gift of the volume once owned by President Lincoln, is too great for expression. I trust that the way we shall care for the volume will be the best evidence of our appreciation."

On June 4, 1916, Fisk University formally unveiled the Bible. The ceremony was an opportunity for black Americans to claim Lincoln as part of their own history, thus cementing their connection to him. Moreover, it would help all Americans to remember a history that had largely been forgotten—that Lincoln had been a personal friend to black men and women and had even welcomed them into the White House. McKenzie invited Robert Lincoln to participate in the event, but the president's son was unable to travel to Tennessee at that time. Dr. Crosthwait, the alumnus who had first had the idea to ask for the Bible, delivered remarks at the unveiling. He recounted Lincoln's impoverished upbringing and lack of formal education. These apparent deficiencies had actually proved to be advantageous, Crosthwait told the audience, for his mind did not get "polluted" and "confused with the theories and sophistries of mankind." Instead, what "made Lincoln great" was that he had "imbibed the principles of the Holy Scriptures." In the process, God had "chosen him to do a special work for a special people & for this nation."

Curiously, Crosthwait did not tell the story of the black ministers who gave the Bible to Lincoln. Instead, he related how Frederick Douglass had met with Lincoln several times during the war. He paraphrased what Douglass had said— that "Mr. Lincoln was one of the few white men he ever passed an hour with, who failed to remind him in some way before the interview terminated, that he was a negro." Crosthwait thought it remarkable that Lincoln "so valued the good judgment and friendship of Frederick Douglass the former slave." Why would an exalted national leader like Lincoln be willing to seek advice from a former slave? The answer was simple. "The truth found in this Book was the [missing word] element in Abraham Lincoln's education that made possible such a meeting of such men. He had been Providentially saved from the sophistries and fallacies & manmade theories of the churches, schools and other institutions of the time so that he was free to act according to the dictates of reason and a conscience quickened by the Spirit of God. All this came from the Bible." In other words, Lincoln's lack of formal education is what opened him up to listening to men like Douglass, a fellow self-made and self-educated man.[27]

Fisk University president Fayette McKenzie publicly celebrated the donation of the "sacred volume." In the *Fisk University News* he wrote, "The Lincoln Bible! No other volume could mean so much to Fisk University. Abraham Lincoln, the man whose pen proclaimed liberty to the slave, is reverenced by the colored people as no other American is." McKenzie predicted that the book "will be a permanent memorial, sacred in the eyes of every succeeding generation of students enrolled at Fisk University." Making it all the more special was that it had originally been "the gift of the colored people. Made sacred by his possession of it, by his touch and appreciation, it now comes back to the service of the colored people through a Negro University."[28]

The Bible made appearances at important events in the life of the university, such as a January 1, 1919, celebration of the Emancipation Proclamation. The formal part of the day took place in the chapel, where a picture of Lincoln had been hanging for years. Two girls sitting at the front of the sanctuary, dressed in white, served as the "custodians of the Bible," while two boys were its "guardians." The boys appeared at the back of the chapel and walked "with measured tread . . . bearing the Bible before them." One of the boys wore a military uniform "to denote Lincoln's great war work," while the other was dressed in civilian clothes "to denote the triumphs of liberty in peace." When the boys reached the front of the chapel the custodians rose to receive the Good Book, and the entire audience then stood up as well. The four students treated the Bible as carefully as if it were the Ark of the Covenant, placing it gently upon the table at the front. When they were finished, the audience sang "America," after which President McKenzie told the story of the Bible, reminding the audience that Lincoln's hands had touched it and that he had read from it "many times." The student body sat in rapt attention as McKenzie spoke. More songs were sung, the custodians opened the Bible for a scripture reading, a student read the Emancipation Proclamation, and African American educator Isaac Fisher (a disciple of Booker T. Washington) delivered an address on Lincoln as an emancipator.[29]

When not in use in the chapel, the Bible was initially stored in a vault on campus. Over the next few years, it appears to have been forgotten—perhaps following the departure of President McKenzie in 1925. Then, about 1931, Arthur A. Schomburg, the famous historian, collector, and then-curator of the Negro Collection at Fisk, made it his object to find the Bible and have it properly displayed. After locating the ornate book, he found "an old cigar glass case" in the university's oldest building. He cleaned and repaired the case and placed the Bible on display in the Negro Division of Literature and History, on the third floor of the university library. On a few rare occasions in the 1950s and 1960s, Fisk loaned the Bible to other institutions for exhibits around the country.[30]

In 2017, the Lincoln Bible returned to Washington, DC, for the grand opening of the Museum of the Bible. It probably had not been in the city since 1865. The museum's curators included it in an exhibit on slavery and the Bible. On one wall of the exhibit were words from Lincoln's second inaugural address.

Referring to Northerners and Southerners, he said: "Both read the same Bible, and pray to the same God." But Lincoln was not entirely accurate when he said this. On display near the Lincoln Bible was a Bible that had been published by slaveholders. This one omitted antislavery passages, such as the story of the Israelites' exodus from bondage in Egypt.[31] Clearly Southern slave owners did not want their chattels to hear the stories of Moses and Philemon. Thus, on display in the Museum of the Bible, the Baltimoreans' gift offered a powerful counter-story to the one that the proslavery Bible told. Even today, it continues to symbolize freedom from oppression.

Unlike most of the other gifts Lincoln received, the beautiful pulpit Bible has survived for more than a century and a half. Today, it is displayed in a glass case in the special collections room on the second floor of the John Hope and Aurelia E. Franklin Library at Fisk University (John Hope Franklin was an alumnus). It is altogether fitting and proper that it should be on display there, in a facility named for one of the greatest historians of the twentieth century. It is a testament to the admiration that the black community had for Lincoln in 1864, as he stood for reelection in one of the most consequential elections in American history. Although most black men were ineligible to vote, they were proud to make a lasting public statement of their support for the liberator of slaves.

INTERLUDE 4

City Point

On June 21, 1864, Lincoln arrived at City Point, Virginia—about 130 miles south of Washington—for a meeting with Union General Ulysses S. Grant. When Grant suggested that they "ride on and see the colored troops, who behaved so handsomely" in the attack on the works in front of Petersburg the previous week, Lincoln eagerly replied, "Oh, yes. I want to take a look at those boys." He had "read with the greatest delight" a War Department dispatch that described "how gallantly they behaved" and told Grant, "I was opposed on nearly every side when I first favored the raising of colored regiments; but they have proved their efficiency, and I am glad they have kept pace with the white troops in the recent assaults. When we wanted every able-bodied man who could be spared to go to the front, and my opposers kept objecting to the negroes, I used to tell them that at such times it was just as well to be a little color-blind."

Upon reaching the camp of the black troops of the Eighteenth Corps, one newspaperman reported that the soldiers "began to cheer, and the wildest demonstrations of joy were manifested along the lines." Some shouted, "Hurrah for the Liberator, Hurrah for the President." Grant's aide Horace Porter added that the scene "defies description." The black soldiers, he said, "beheld for the first time the liberator of their race—the man who by a stroke of his pen had struck the shackles from the limbs of their fellow-bondmen and proclaimed liberty to the enslaved." The enthusiasm of the black troops "now knew no limits," Porter added. "They cheered, laughed, cried, sang hymns of praise, and shouted in their negro dialect, 'God bress Massa Linkum!' 'De Lord save Fader Abraham!' 'De day ob jubilee am come, shuah.' They crowded about him and fondled his horse; some of them kissed his hands, while others ran off crying in triumph to their comrades that they had touched his clothes." Lincoln rode on his horse with his hat off and tears welling in his eyes. His "voice was so broken by emotion that he could scarcely articulate the words of thanks and congratulation which he tried to speak to the humble and devoted men through whose ranks he rode," wrote Porter. "The scene was affecting in the extreme, and no one could have witnessed it unmoved." Indeed, Assistant Secretary of War Charles A. Dana wrote later that day, "It was a memorable thing to behold the President, whose fortune it is to represent the principle of emancipation, passing bareheaded through the enthusiastic ranks of those negroes armed to defend the integrity of the American nation."[1]

Lincoln arrived back in Washington on June 23 "sunburnt and fagged but still refreshed and cheered," wrote John Hay in his diary. Everyone around him noticed how his mood had markedly improved. "The President was in very good spirits," observed Gideon Welles. "His journey has done him good, physically, and strengthened him mentally."[2]

These black soldiers had good reason to show such enthusiasm for Lincoln. They understood that their salvation ultimately depended upon victory in the field and Republican triumphs in the upcoming state and federal elections. They knew what white Southerners would do with them if the Confederacy won its independence. They also knew they had vicious enemies in the North, for they had undoubtedly read or heard Copperhead rhetoric during their time in uniform. They knew there were those in the North, such as one Ohio editor who opined that if "the negro [becomes] free, we will then have to grant them every right, social and political of the white man, or slaughter them. There is absolutely no end to the difficulties which must grow out of the Republican endeavor to equalize the white and black races."[3] Even if Lincoln was not the ideal candidate in every way, his reelection in November 1864 was preferable to life in a Confederate slaveholding republic—or with a Northern Democrat in the White House.

Unfortunately, Lincoln's chances looked bleak, for the summer of 1864 was an awful period for the Union.

11

"DOUGLASS, I HATE SLAVERY AS MUCH AS YOU DO"

In the weeks immediately preceding Lincoln's visit to the front, the Army of the Potomac lost nearly sixty thousand men killed, wounded, or missing during the Overland Campaign. By mid-summer, with Grant's troops entrenched around Petersburg and William Tecumseh Sherman stuck outside of Atlanta, Northerners' hopes for victory were quickly dissipating. On July 11 and 12, Confederate General Jubal Early even crossed the Potomac River and attacked Washington, DC. Wanting to see the fight, Lincoln went out to Fort Stevens, where he stood upon a parapet watching the Confederate onslaught. Standing nearby, helping the Union soldiers, was a local black woman named Elizabeth Thomas who owned much of the land that had been seized to construct Fort Stevens. Mrs. Thomas and Lincoln had interacted on several occasions since the beginning of the war. Seeing the president dangerously exposed, she exclaimed, "My God, make that fool get down off that hill and come in here." Within moments a Confederate bullet killed a Union soldier standing near the president. But if Elizabeth Thomas was horrified by the presence of Lincoln near the battle, others were awestruck. One African American in Washington wrote in his diary that Lincoln "road up and down the Lines all knight long whear the fedearl troops whear fighting." This man was so impressed by Lincoln's bravery that he concluded, "May the Hon Abraham Lincoln Name be recorded for ever ever on the Book of Fame he was as brave as man that ever been on the face of earth and all that he done he done it with Clear Conition [conscience] before his creator."[1]

Unfortunately, Union prospects continued to look abysmal throughout the summer of 1864. By August, Lincoln was convinced that he would lose the presidential election and that an incoming Democratic administration would undo all of the gains he had made toward freedom for the enslaved. Northern voters were tormented by the carnage on the battlefield, and many believed that Lincoln could not achieve peace with the Confederacy because he was unwilling to compromise on emancipation. "The people of the North are wild for Peace," wrote New York politician Thurlow Weed. "They are told that the President will only listen to terms of Peace on condition that Slavery be 'abandoned.'" The thought of continual war for the sake of black slaves demoralized many white voters.

During this period of political and military crisis, *New-York Tribune* editor Horace Greeley informed Lincoln that there were Confederate officials in Canada who were willing to negotiate for peace. While Lincoln doubted that they had any official authority from Jefferson Davis, Lincoln permitted Greeley to go to Niagara to meet with them. On July 9, he authorized Greeley to bring to Washington "any person anywhere professing to have any proposition of Jefferson Davis in writing, for peace, embracing the restoration of the Union and abandonment of slavery." All the while, Lincoln was confident that "nothing will come of" the mission.

As an emissary, Greeley was a disaster. He purposefully neglected to tell the Confederates of Lincoln's stipulation that terms of negotiation must include "abandonment of slavery" in the Confederacy. Eventually, on July 18, Greeley admitted to Lincoln that the Confederates were not actually "empowered" to negotiate. In response, Lincoln published a public letter—"To whom it may concern"—informing the Confederate emissaries that he would entertain "any proposition which embraces the restoration of peace, the integrity of the whole Union, and the abandonment of slavery, and which comes by and with an authority that can control the armies now at war against the United States." When the Confederates now learned about the prerequisite that Greeley had withheld from them, they wrongly concluded that Lincoln had been duplicitous.

Lincoln had a delicate situation on his hands. Many in the North believed that his terms of negotiation were too stringent, and that he should be willing to compromise on the slavery issue if it would mean peace. (Of course, Lincoln knew that Jefferson Davis would never be willing to negotiate for peace and would have to be defeated on the battlefield.) In response to the public outcry, Lincoln drafted a lawyerly public letter to a War Democrat and editor in Wisconsin named Charles D. Robinson. In the letter, Lincoln spoke of his commitment to preserving the Union and destroying slavery, but he closed with an ambiguous line: "If Jefferson Davis wishes, for himself, or for the benefit of his friends at the North, to know what I would do if he were to offer peace and re-union, saying nothing about slavery, let him try me."[2]

Now Lincoln had to decide whether to publish this letter.

While Lincoln was dealing with the Greeley fiasco, he also met with Union Army officer John Eaton for several conversations. Among the many subjects they discussed, Lincoln spoke of both his longing for peace and his desire to see slavery finally abolished. In one conversation he alluded to John Brown's 1859 raid on Harpers Ferry, indicating that he "was considering every possible means by which the Negro could be secured in his freedom." Lincoln confided in Eaton that he wanted to find a way to help slaves run away from their plantations and find security inside Union military lines.

Eaton mentioned that he had recently heard Frederick Douglass publicly criticize the president in a speech in Toledo, Ohio. To this, Lincoln asked Eaton whether Douglass knew of his March 13 letter to Louisiana governor Michael Hahn supporting limited black suffrage. Lincoln then asked Eaton if he thought Douglass might be persuaded to come back to the White House for a consultation.[3]

Arrangements were made for Douglass to again meet with Lincoln, and the famous orator arrived at the Executive Mansion on August 19. As Douglass waited in the reception room, he encountered a politician from Wisconsin who later told Lincoln about their brief conversation: "It was dark," he said. "There in a corner I saw a man quietly reading who possessed a remarkable physiognomy. I was rivetted to the spot. I stood & stared at him[.] He raised his flashing eyes & caught me in the act. I was compelled to speak. Said I, Are you the President. No, replied the stranger, I am Frederick Douglass."[4]

When Douglass entered Lincoln's office, he found the president in an "alarmed condition," for this was the period when Lincoln was most convinced that he would lose his bid for reelection. As Douglass later explained, "The country was struck with one of those bewilderments which dethrone reason for the moment. Everybody was thinking and dreaming of peace, and the impression had gone abroad that the President's anti-slavery policy was about the only thing which prevented a peaceful settlement with the Rebels." Lincoln felt immense pressure to modify his "To whom it may concern" letter, and the president wanted Douglass's advice for how to best handle this situation. Lincoln told Douglass that he "did not propose to take back" what he had said in that letter, but that he "wished to relieve the fears of his peace friends, by making it appear that the thing which they feared could not happen, and was wholly beyond his power." Lincoln then showed Douglass the draft of his letter to Charles D. Robinson (the one that ended, "let him try me") and asked his black guest whether he thought it should be published. Douglass answered resolutely, "Certainly not. It would be given a broader meaning than you intend to convey;

it would be taken as a complete surrender of your anti-slavery policy, and do you serious damage." Douglass then suggested that Lincoln have his surrogates respond to his Democratic opponents.[5]

Lincoln then turned the conversation to another vexing problem—one that he had discussed with Colonel Eaton. Believing that he would not be reelected, he wanted to devise a plan to free as many slaves as possible before March 1865, when the next president would be inaugurated. Douglass later recalled that Lincoln wanted "to make his Proclamation as effective as possible in the event of such a peace." Lincoln told him, "Douglass, I hate slavery as much as you do, and I want to see it abolished altogether." Later, in his autobiography, Douglass described their conversation in great detail:

> He said, in a regretful tone, "The slaves are not coming so rapidly and so numerously to us as I had hoped." I replied that the slaveholders knew how to keep such things from their slaves, and probably very few knew of his proclamation. "Well," he said, "I want you to set about devising some means of making them acquainted with it, and for bringing them into our lines." He spoke with great earnestness and much solicitude, and seemed troubled by the attitude of Mr. Greeley and by the growing impatience at the war that was being manifested throughout the North. He said he was being accused of protracting the war beyond its legitimate object and of failing to make peace when he might have done so to advantage. He was afraid of what might come of all these complaints, but was persuaded that no solid and lasting peace could come short of absolute submission on the part of the rebels, and he was not for giving them rest by futile conferences with unauthorized persons at Niagara Falls, or elsewhere. He saw the danger of premature peace, and, like a thoughtful and sagacious man as he was, wished to provide means of rendering such consummation as harmless as possible.

Douglass's interaction with Lincoln impressed him deeply, for he realized how thoroughly committed Lincoln was to emancipation. Their conversation reminded Douglass of something that had happened almost exactly two years earlier. In August 1862, Lincoln had published a public letter to Horace Greeley stating that his "paramount object in this struggle *is* to save the Union, and is *not* either to save or to destroy slavery." Douglass had been critical of that statement, for it made the president appear ambivalent about the moral issue of slavery. But Douglass did not know the full story behind the letter. He did not know that Lincoln had already decided to issue an emancipation edict, but that he was waiting for the politically prudent moment to do so. Nor did he know that Lincoln's object in writing that statement was to help prepare a white racist Northern public for emancipation.

Now, after meeting with Lincoln in August 1864, Douglass had a new understanding of the president's genuine commitment to emancipation. "What he said on this day showed a deeper moral conviction against slavery than I had ever seen before in anything spoken or written by him," Douglass later wrote. "I listened with the deepest interest and profoundest satisfaction, and, at his suggestion, agreed to undertake the organizing [of] a band of scouts, composed of colored men, whose business should be somewhat after the original plan of John Brown, to go into the rebel States, beyond the lines of our armies, and carry the news of emancipation, and urge the slaves to come within our boundaries."[6]

Partway through their meeting, a messenger twice announced that Governor William Buckingham of Connecticut had come to see the president. But Lincoln made Buckingham wait for thirty minutes in an adjoining room. "Tell the Governor to wait," said Lincoln, "I want to have a long talk with my friend Douglass." Their conversation took a full hour. For Douglass, this moment demonstrated Lincoln's "kindly disposition toward colored people."[7]

Immediately after the meeting, Douglass met with Eaton in a nearby home. The colonel found Douglass pacing back and forth in the parlor "in a state of extreme agitation." "I have just come from President Lincoln," Douglass excitedly told Eaton. "He treated me as a man; he did not let me feel for a moment that there was any difference in the color of our skins! The President is a most remarkable man. I am satisfied now that he is doing all that circumstances will permit him to do. He asked me a number of questions, which I am preparing to answer in writing." Douglass would later praise Lincoln's ability "to talk easily and freely to a negro without reminding him that he was a negro." News of the meeting also encouraged other African Americans. Army surgeon John H. Rapier wrote with tongue in cheek: "Did you ever hear such nonsense. The President of the US sending for a 'Nigger' to confer with him on the state of the Country."[8]

After returning home to Rochester, Douglass wrote Lincoln a letter outlining a plan to free the slaves. Douglass informed the president that he had "freely conversed with several trustworthy and Patriotic Colored men" and that they all concurred "in the wisdom and benevolence of the Idea, and some of them think it practicable."[9] Fortunately, nothing ever had to come of this desperate plan. On September 2, General Sherman captured the Confederate stronghold at Atlanta. From that point forward, Lincoln's reelection was essentially assured. Emancipation would remain a war aim, and passage of the Thirteenth Amendment would be a post-election priority for Lincoln and Congress. Nevertheless, Lincoln's meeting with Douglass is remarkably significant, for it confirms Lincoln's genuine personal commitment to emancipation. The plan Lincoln and

Douglass concocted together had nothing to do with winning the war—that is, with "military necessity." Rather, it had everything to do with freeing as many enslaved people as Lincoln could before he was out of office. This meeting, in short, demonstrated Lincoln's *moral commitment* to freedom.[10] If there was any doubt on this point, later that same day, Lincoln told several white guests, "There have been men who have proposed to me to return to slavery the black warriors of Port Hudson & Olustee to their masters to conciliate the South. I should be damned in time & in eternity for so doing. The world shall know that I will keep my faith to friends & enemies, come what will."[11] Freedom, for Lincoln, must be permanent.

Indeed, Lincoln sought to expand freedom any way he could, ardently supporting the push for emancipation in Maryland in 1864. As a loyal state, Maryland was exempt from the provisions of the Emancipation Proclamation. Consequently, Republicans who hoped to free the state's enslaved population had to do so through other means. In the spring of 1864, Maryland voters elected delegates to a constitutional convention to write a new antislavery constitution. In a private letter, Lincoln explained his support for the convention. "It needs not to be a secret, that I wish success to emancipation in Maryland," he wrote. "It would aid much to end the rebellion. Hence it is a matter of national consequence, in which every national man, may rightfully feel a deep interest."[12] A few days before the statewide referendum in October, Lincoln wrote a public letter to be read at a mass meeting in Baltimore. In it, he publicly endorsed the work of the convention: "I wish all men to be free," he wrote. "I wish the material prosperity of the already free which I feel sure the extinction of slavery would bring. I wish to see, in process of disappearing, that only thing which ever could bring this nation to civil war."[13] For Lincoln, emancipation in Maryland would accomplish several important things. First, it would be a moral good. Second, it would help bring about a quicker end to the war while simultaneously eradicating the very cause of the war.

Maryland voters ratified the new state constitution by a slim margin on October 12 and 13, and the governor declared that it would go into effect on the first day of November—one week before Lincoln would stand for reelection.[14] Lincoln rejoiced that it was "a big thing" that slavery would be forever abolished in the state.[15] On November 1, a large group of black Washingtonians assembled at the Fifteenth Street Presbyterian Church to celebrate emancipation in Maryland. The church was so crowded that several hundred people could not get in. On the outside, the church building was illuminated by a large number of torches that were fastened to a fence. Fireworks lit up the sky while the crowd listened to the band of the Third US Infantry. On the inside, hundreds of African Americans and "a sprinkling of whites" anxiously waited for the exercises to begin. John F. Cook Jr., one of the members of the black delegation who had met with Lincoln in August 1862, called the meeting to order. On Cook's motion, the gathering elected Rev. Henry Highland Garnet of New York to chair the meeting. Among the other officers elected was Anderson R. Abbott, the black Army surgeon who had attended a White House reception with Alexander T. Augusta earlier in the year. Sojourner Truth was among the speakers. It is likely that William Slade and Elizabeth Keckly were also present, although they were not mentioned in news reports.

The choir sang "My Country 'Tis of Thee, Sweet Land of Liberty," and a minister then offered a prayer of thanks to God. When Cook read the proclamation of the governor of Maryland which declared the state free, the crowd cheered wildly. Garnet then proposed that all present sing "Blow Ye Trumpets Blow," which has in its refrain, "The year of jubilee is come!" Everyone stood and sang enthusiastically.

From the pulpit, Garnet remarked on the wonderful sight he beheld: "respectable and intelligent people" gathered together to give thanks to God "for the blessings they had received." The black minister urged those present to "respect and reverence God" and to thank Him as "the instigator of this good and great work." He also encouraged them to be united in all things. "If we direct our energies and hearts under God we can accomplish everything, and push back the waves of oppression," he said.

Garnet implored African Americans "to stop finding fault with the President, for there was not a man living who could do better than the man in the executive chair." He knew that some whites and blacks had complained about Lincoln's seemingly slow path toward emancipation, but he thought that if those people "would pause for a moment, they would find but little cause of complaint. Who had given them cause of rejoicing there that evening but Abraham Lincoln." Garnet also praised the Union soldiers who had helped make emancipation a reality (the votes of white Union soldiers had provided the margin of victory in the referendum), and he proposed three cheers for Maryland and three cheers for Lincoln. The assemblage then adopted several resolutions congratulating the state of Maryland for this momentous achievement, praising the Lincoln administration and the military for what they had accomplished on behalf of "human liberty," and pledging their support for the Union.

Garnet called upon the congregation to sing "John Brown's Body," after which a collection was taken for the support of sick and wounded soldiers. After a few more remarks, the group decided to travel to the White House to serenade the president. Unfortunately for them, the hundreds of people who could not get into the church had already had the idea.[16] In a report titled "Light on a Dark Subject," journalist Noah Brooks described the scene at the White House. The hundreds of black revelers brought with them borrowed torches as well as transparencies that had been used at a recent Republican torchlight procession, some of which featured slogans and images about California, Indiana, and Massachusetts. The crowd seemed not to mind that these campaign transparencies celebrated electoral victories in other states. They approached the White House and with loud music and repeated cheers called upon the president to come out. It was late, but Lincoln stepped out upon the balcony, looked down, and said, "I have to guess, my friends, the object of this call, which has taken me quite by surprise this evening." One of the men in the crowd shouted up at him, "The emancipation of Maryland, sah." Upon hearing this, Lincoln made a short address: "It is no secret that I have wished, and still do wish, mankind everywhere to be free," he said. At this, the crowd erupted in applause and cries of, "God bless Abraham Lincoln." Lincoln continued: "And in the State of Maryland how great an advance has been made in this direction. It is difficult to realize that in that State, where human slavery existed for ages, ever since a period long before any here were born—by the action of her own citizens—the soil is made forever free." Now the cheering was long and loud. But even in victory, Lincoln would not gloat over his enemies:

> I have no feeling of triumph over those who were opposed to this measure and who voted against it, but I do believe that it will result in good to the white race as well as to those who have been made free by this act of emancipation, and I hope that the time will soon come when all will see that the perpetuation of freedom for all in Maryland is best for the interests of all, though some may thereby be made to suffer temporary pecuniary loss. And I hope that you, colored people, who have been emancipated, will use this great boon which has been given you to improve yourselves, both morally and intellectually; and now, good night.

Following the conclusion of Lincoln's remarks, the crowd cheered and "after some boggling about the order of march, the dark torchlighters gathered themselves up, and hurrahing, disappeared in the darkness."[17]

With the presidential election only one week away (November 8), it must have been gratifying to Lincoln to receive this sort of enthusiastic reception. Throughout the campaign he had endured substantial criticism from Radical Republicans and black abolitionists. Earlier in the year, members of his own party—including Secretary of the Treasury Salmon P. Chase and Union General John C. Fremont—had tried to supplant him as the Republican nominee. And abolitionists, including Frederick Douglass, were initially hesitant to support his re-nomination. In the spring of 1864, Douglass had written privately that the president's policies toward black soldiers "have worn my patience threadbare" while in June he publicly lamented that Lincoln appeared to live by the rule, "*Do evil by choice, right from necessity.*"[18] (This view would be dispelled by his meeting with Lincoln in August.)

Black soldiers' correspondence to Northern newspapers also, at times, expressed dissatisfaction with the president. In early September, one black cavalryman protested that he did "not in the least pretend to be a Lincolnite" since the president had acted so slowly to abolish slavery, had favored colonization, had offered bounties to slave owners in Kentucky for enlisting their slaves in the Army, and had not protected black Union soldiers from Confederate atrocities. Nevertheless, he would support Lincoln over the disloyal and proslavery Democratic Party because, "In this, as in many other things, Mr. Lincoln has shown his inefficiency as a statesman, and though we abhor him when we consider the many injustices he has allowed to be practiced on colored men, we cannot but think him a better object than George B. McClellan."[19]

By the fall, most Republicans and abolitionists had fallen into line. In late August, the Democrats met in Chicago and nominated Maj. Gen. George B. McClellan. Although Little Mac supported the war, he opposed emancipation. More problematic for the general, his party placed him on a platform that called the war a "failure" and gave him an antiwar running mate, Congressman George H. Pendleton of Ohio. When Union fortunes took a turn for the better in September, Northern morale soared and Radical Republicans fell into line. By October it was clear to all astute observers that Lincoln would win. As Douglass later explained, "When there was any shadow of a hope that a man of a more decidedly anti-slavery conviction and policy could be elected, I was not for Mr. Lincoln. But as soon as the Chicago convention, my mind was made up, and it is made still. All dates changed with the nomination of Mr. McClellan."[20]

Ironically, the Democrats used Douglass's 1863 visit to the White House to scare white voters into supporting McClellan. They repeatedly quoted from his speech in which he said that Lincoln greeted him "as one gentleman receive[s] another" to show that Lincoln and the Republican Party supported not only racial equality but also miscegenation (a term that was coined during the election). As one Pennsylvania paper reported, "Mr. Lincoln is as much an aider and abettor of the Abolitionists in this new policy of miscegenation as he has been in their policy of emancipation. He will go wherever they push him. Hear Frederick Douglass' account of his visit to the White House."[21] Another editor in Indiana crowed, "His policy of Emancipation is Miscegenation, and he acts out his doctrines. He received negroes on terms of equality at the White House. He recommended the United States Government to receive nigger ambassadors, and [he] associates with negroes, for proof of which read Frederic[k] Douglass' account of his visit to the White House." [22] At campaign rallies, Democrats boasted of their white supremacy. "Ours is a White Man's Government," proclaimed one campaign banner in Illinois. "Defile it not with Miscegenation."[23]

In order to minimize the racist attacks of the Democratic Party, Douglass largely kept a low profile during the campaign. Truth be told, the Republicans did not want prominent African Americans like Douglass out on the campaign trail anyway. As Douglass wrote privately, "the Republican committees do not wish to expose themselves to the charge of being the 'N—r' party. The Negro is the deformed child, which is put out of the room when company comes."[24]

Throughout the campaign, some African Americans never lost faith in Lincoln, despite their periodic frustrations with his administration's policies.[25] J. Sella Martin summed up the views of many when he said, "As a negro, I am for the man whose party and policy have given us a free capital, a confiscation law, and a proclamation of freedom, as against the man who, with honest enough intentions, expects to drive out the devils by Beelzebub."[26] In May 1864, a volunteer in the Fifty-Fifth Massachusetts wrote his cousin praising "our kind President [who] is making slow but sure efort to open up the way for us." He continued, "it is a glorious blesing and [a] great many others are engaged in this glorious under taking and al people of our color ought to be hapy and give our noble President al the praise that the tongue could ex press."[27] At the National Convention of Colored Men, held in Syracuse, New York, in October, John S. Rock, a lawyer from Boston, declared, "Lincoln is for Freedom and the Republic," while "McClellan, is for Despotism and Slavery."[28] Indeed, enslaved people in the states of the Confederacy understood that they were "free now according to law and President Lincoln's Proclamation." They also understood that a Democratic victory at the polls would undo all that had been gained during the war. Writing from North Carolina in early 1864, Abraham Galloway's wife, Martha A. Galloway, observed how the slaveholders "intend to elect McClellan President, and 'get all their niggers back again,' so they say."[29] In order to fight against McClellan's election, one disabled black soldier named George W. Jackson stayed up until 2 a.m. the morning of November 8 praying for Lincoln's reelection. Jackson prayed so loudly that he woke up his comrades in the middle of the night. The next morning an officer asked him who was going to be elected. "Masar Abraham Lincon," Jackson replied. When asked how he knew, he said, "why Captin god tolde me so . . . god bless Mr President."[30]

Lincoln's most unusual admirers during the campaign was a formerly enslaved Virginian. In the spring of 1862, William A. Jackson had escaped from the Confederate White House in Richmond, where Jefferson Davis had hired him as a carriage driver. Over the next few years, Jackson toured throughout the North, and also in England, giving speeches under the moniker "Jeff Davis' Coachman." At some point during his tour, Jackson went to Washington, DC, and met with Lincoln. Although no account of the meeting appears to survive, Jackson grew to become one of Lincoln's most ardent defenders. When the abolitionist Parker Pillsbury denounced Lincoln in May 1864 for being too slow on emancipation and black rights, Jackson took to the stage at a meeting of the American Anti-Slavery Society to defend the incumbent. Jackson declared that Lincoln "drives [the coach] just as fast as de people let him." At that, the crowd applauded. "Tell him to go faster, and he go," Jackson continued. "He work slow, but sure . . . and he is de best friend of de blackman." Jackson criticized Pillsbury for not doing "his duty" as a citizen by voting for the antislavery Lincoln. "I'se don't want anybody to talk about others not doing their duty, when they doesn't do it themselves," Jackson said to great laughter and applause. As for Jackson, "I'se a citizen. I'se going to vote for Mister Linkum next time." Jackson had worked the crowd brilliantly, and the audience thundered its approval. The next day, the New York *World*, a Democratic newspaper, headlined its coverage of the event, "Jeff Davis's Coachman to the Rescue of 'Old Abe.'"[31]

On November 8, 1864, Lincoln easily won reelection. Two nights later, on November 10, a large gathering of people met outside of the White House to serenade him. Lincoln and Seward both gave speeches. What was most remarkable, however, was that African Americans made up one-third of the audience. "But did you not notice the large proportion of negroes present?" asked one man who witnessed the scene. "The white men there would not have made up a very large assemblage." A journalist in Washington remarked, "Mr. Lincoln can be proud of the fact" that so many black people came out to congratulate him. "These men know very well who are their friends, and if McClellan was President they would make their plans for an emigration Northward [to Canada]." Optimistically, he added, "Four years more of an anti-slavery Administration will so change the position of the colored people of this entire region, and the feelings of the white inhabitants towards them. . . . The devilish anti-negro spirit is rapidly dying out, even in Northern towns."[32]

African Americans throughout the nation celebrated Lincoln's victory. An infantryman stationed on Morris Island, South Carolina, wrote home, "We are all glad to know that President Lincoln is re-elected. It gives us renewed hope and makes us eager to meet the foe," while a black convention in Xenia, Ohio, "hail[ed] with joy . . . the re-election of Abraham Lincoln."[33] Their faith was well placed. In a private conversation on November 17, Lincoln told a delegation of white visitors from Maryland that "the adoption of their free State constitution was a bigger thing" than Maryland's role in the presidential election, for presidential elections come every four years but "the adoption of the constitution, being a good thing, could not be undone."[34] In other words, making freedom permanent was more important to Lincoln than winning electoral votes.

12

"IN THE PRESENCE OF A FRIEND"

Isabella was unusually tall—five feet, eleven inches—with dark complexion, a low voice, and the remnants of the Dutch accent she had acquired in upstate New York. Born about 1797, she was one of ten or twelve children of her enslaved parents, but as a child she only knew one of her siblings. The rest had been kidnapped or sold off. At the age of nine, Isabella was sold away from her mother and father—the first of several times she would be merchandised. At the hands of her new owners, she endured physical, emotional, and sexual abuse that left scars on her body and soul. She finally attained freedom in 1826 by fleeing from her owner—one year before she would have become legally free under New York State law.[1]

Isabella breathed heavily one morning in 1826 as she approached the farm-house, where, only a year earlier, she had been enslaved. She had just learned that her five-year-old son Peter had been illegally sold to someone in Alabama. It was against New York law to sell a slave outside of the state, and young Isabella was determined to get him back. At the door, Isabella's former mistress scowled, "*Ugh! a fine* fuss to make about a little *nigger*! Why, have n't you as many of 'em left as you can see to take care of? A pity 'tis, the niggers are not all in Guinea!! Making such a halloo-balloo about the neighborhood; and all for a paltry nigger!!!"

"*I'll have my child again*," said Isabella firmly.

"Have *your child* again!" replied the white woman with contempt, thinking it would be absurd to retrieve him from the Deep South. "How can you get him? And what have you to support him with, if you could? Have you any money?"

"No," answered Isabella with a firm voice. "I have no money, but God has enough, or what's better! And I'll have my child again."

Although the door was closed to her, she would fight on. Isabella later said that in this moment she "felt so *tall within*—I felt as if the *power of a nation* was with me!" With nowhere left to turn, Isabella prayed to God for guidance.

It took a year, but with the assistance of local Quakers, Isabella successfully brought suit in court and had her son returned. When young Peter first saw his mother, he thought she was a "terrible monster," but eventually he said, "Well, you *do* look like my mother *used* to." When he finally came close, Isabella noticed how terribly her six-year-old boy had been beaten. His body bore scars and calluses from head to foot, and his back was badly torn. "Heavens! what is all *this*?" she asked. "Oh, Lord Jesus, look! see my poor child! Oh Lord, 'render unto them double' for all this! Oh my God! Pete, how *did* you bear it?" Peter replied that it "is nothing" and that he had seen others tortured far worse.[2]

The traumas of slavery made an indelible mark on Isabella's life. After experiencing a powerful conversion to Christianity, she changed her name to Sojourner Truth in 1843. For the rest of her life, she would travel throughout the North preaching the Gospel and advocating for abolitionism and women's rights. In 1851, at Akron, Ohio, she delivered her most famous speech, which may have included the line, "And ar'n't I a woman?" Seven years later, while speaking in Indiana, members of the audience suggested that she might be a man. Sojourner told the men "that her breasts had suckled many a white babe, to the exclusion of her own offspring; that some of those white babies had grown to man's estate; that, although they had suckled her colored breasts, they were, in her estimation, far more manly than they (her persecutors) appeared to be." At this point, she "disrobed her bosom" and asked the men "if they, too, wished to suck!"[3]

By the time the Civil War began, Sojourner Truth was living in an integrated community in Battle Creek, Michigan. She had become a national figure who had assumed the status of a legend. She was intelligent, tender, wise, quick-witted, sarcastic, devout, and filled with the Holy Spirit. She dressed in simple attire, a neat white cap, and plain gold-rimmed spectacles. But hidden within was a powerful persona. Some considered her a prophetess. "Her voice is strong, but flexible and penetrating," wrote one Englishman who met her during the war. "She has a wonderful fluency of utterance, and pours out with a volubility and force almost fanatical on religious subjects."[4] The most common adjective used by journalists to describe her was "remarkable."

In a nation filled with death, Truth seemed to defy mortality. One wartime newspaper estimated that "she is now between 80 and 90 years of age," while another stated that she was "a century old." A third called her "that old landmark of the past—the representative of the forever-gone age."[5] But when the war began, she was still in her sixties. And she was abounding with life. She told one acquaintance that her "natural age was nearly seventy, but that when the war broke out the Lord added twenty years to her life, so that she was now not quite fifty."[6] In truth, Sojourner had become an American elder—a person worthy of reverence and respect—a noble leader, a moral compass, a gifted storyteller, and an esteemed advisor to a non-literate people. Unlike elderly enslaved men and women who were too often seen as valueless in their old age (and were sometimes "turned out" by their owners and forced to fend for themselves when they were least capable of doing so), Sojourner had a peculiar dignity that was recognized by both black and white Americans. She was a maternal figure for the nation.[7]

Truth had the wisdom that comes with age. While she, like many abolitionists, wished that Lincoln would act more quickly to destroy slavery, she understood that things could not be changed immediately. "Oh, wait, chile! have patience!" she told one impatient abolitionist. "It takes a great while to turn about this great ship of state."[8]

In the spring of 1864, Sojourner decided to travel to Washington "to see the freedmen of my own race" and to meet the "first Antislavery President." "I never determined to do anything and failed," she said. She left Michigan with her twelve-year-old grandson in June. "It is difficult to comprehend the magnitude of her mission," opined the *Anglo-African*. "Her great heart throbs for all humanity." Along the way, she stopped in New York for several months to deliver lectures. In Boston, she met with Harriet Tubman, and the two women discussed their views of the president (Tubman was more critical of Lincoln). After this meeting, Truth continued on her way to Washington.[9]

In the nation's capital, someone advised Truth to call on Lincoln and Secretary of the Treasury Salmon P. Chase. "Oh! yes, I've thought of that," she replied. "Well, Sojourner, what are you going to say to President Lincoln? Just tell us." She straightened herself up to her full height, made a curtsy, and said, "Mr. Lincoln, I'm happy to see you, and give you my photograph. It's black, but it's got a white back to it. I shall be glad to get yours, with a greenback on it."[10] Over the years, historians have doubted the veracity of this story, wrongly thinking that Truth *actually said* these words to Lincoln when, in fact, she only said them as a joke *before* meeting him. Historians also wrongly thought it did not appear in the press until the final decades of the nineteenth century, but it first appeared as early as 1866. Finally, one leading authority on Sojourner Truth wrongly stated that Lincoln's portrait did not appear on greenback currency during the war, but, in fact, he was on the ten-dollar bill as early as 1861—just as Sojourner said.

On Saturday, October 29, Truth received an appointment to meet with the president. Mary Lincoln's seamstress Elizabeth Keckly may have helped to arrange the visit.[11] In a letter written less than three weeks after her meeting, Truth recalled arriving at the White House at about 8 a.m. with abolitionist Lucy Colman. About a dozen people were waiting to meet with Lincoln, including two black women. Truth "had a pleasant time while waiting" and "enjoyed" listening to the president interact with his other callers. By one account she had to wait upwards of three hours to be seen, but she does not seem to have minded. She noticed that the president "showed as much kindness and consideration to the colored persons as to the whites." One of the black women was sick and appeared to have been kicked out of her home because she could not afford to pay her rent. The president "listened to her with much attention, and replied with kindness and tenderness that he had given so much, he could give no more." But he told her where she could get help, and asked Lucy Colman to assist her, which she agreed to do.

Finally, it was Truth and Colman's turn. As they entered the office, Lincoln was seated at his desk between the windows. The two women walked up to him, and Colman said, "This is *Sojourner Truth*, who has come all the way from Michigan to see you." Lincoln stood up and "gave me his hand," and said, "I am glad to see you."

Sojourner was candid with Lincoln: "Mr. President, when you first took your seat, I feared you would be torn to pieces; for I likened you unto Daniel, who was thrown into the lions' den; for if the lions did not tear you to pieces, I knew it would be God that had saved you; and I said if he spared me, I would see you before the four years had expired. And He has done so, and I am now here to see you for myself." Lincoln must have smiled as he congratulated her on "having been spared."

Truth then paid Lincoln a high compliment, saying, "I appreciate you, for you are the best President who has ever taken the seat." Lincoln responded with typical humility, and also a sense that he knew events were beyond his control. "I expect you have reference to my having emancipated the slaves in my Proclamation," he began. Lincoln then mentioned the names of several of his predecessors, including George Washington, and said, "they were just as good, and would have done just as I have, if the time had come." Then, pointing out his office window at the Potomac, he added, "And if the people over the river had behaved themselves, I could not have done what I have. But they did not, and I was compelled to do these things." Truth replied, "I thank God you were the instrument selected by Him and the people to do these things."

Truth told Lincoln that she had never heard of him before he was a candidate for president. He smiled and said, "I had heard of you many times before that." (This last exchange was not part of Truth's original account of the meeting, written in November 1864. She told it to an audience in Detroit in 1869.) She presented Lincoln with a photograph, which she called "one of my shadows and songs, for which he thanked me, and said he would keep them as a remembrance." Lincoln then showed her the Bible that the black citizens of Baltimore had given him six weeks earlier. Truth said it was "beautiful beyond description," adding, "This is beautiful; and to think that the colored people have given this to the Head of the Government—and to think that Government once sanctioned laws that would not permit its people to learn enough to enable them to read that book! And for what? Let them answer who can."

Lincoln then wrote a note in Truth's "little book," which she called her "Book of Life." She noted with gratification that he used "the same hand that signed the death-warrant of *Slavery*" when he wrote: "For Aunty / Sojourner Truth / A. Lincoln / Oct. 29, 1864."

As she rose to leave, Lincoln "arose and took my hand, and said he would be pleased to have me call again." Truth later stated, "I felt that I was in the presence of a friend, and I now thank God from the bottom of my heart that I always have advocated this cause, and have done it openly and boldly; and now I shall feel still more in duty bound to do so."[12] After hearing about Truth's visit with Lincoln, Harriet Tubman stated that she wished she too had gone to the White House. Although Tubman had been critical of Lincoln's slow path toward emancipation, as well as the unequal treatment of black soldiers, she now conceded, "I'm sorry now I didn't see Mr. Lincoln and thank him."[13]

In December, Sojourner received a commission from the National Freedman's Relief Association to work as a counselor to former slaves at the Freedmen's Village in Arlington, Virginia. She later told a journalist that Lincoln "wanted me to see the colored people at Arlington Heights and Mason's Island, where they came running in and died like cattle" (there had been much disease in contraband camps during the war). Some observers found satisfaction in the irony that she was working "on Gen. Lee's estate in Virginia." There, she sought to teach freedpeople the values of neatness, good order, industriousness, and "how to live in freedom." She was once heard shouting, "Be clean! be clean! for cleanliness is godliness." Through her labor she quickly endeared herself to the Freedmen's Village's white Union officers. One acquaintance said that she was "a kind of female aide" to Captain George B. Carse, the village's superintendent.[14]

On Saturday, February 25, 1865, Truth sought to return to the White House for a reception being hosted by Mary Lincoln. Holding the arm of Captain Carse, she strode up to the White House door but was told by a policeman that he "wd. not allow her to go see the President." Captain Carse was livid. "If she is not good enough to enter, I am not," he declared. Standing nearby, Julia Wilbur, a Quaker who had come to Alexandria to work with black refugees, looked on in dismay. Truth turned to Wilbur and said, "Never mind honey. I don't mind it." Truth and Carse then left. That night, Wilbur wrote in her diary, "It did not occur to me until too late that I should have gone directly in & told the President. I would like to know what he wd. have said. I cannot think it was done by his orders."[15]

Several witnesses to this scene were outraged. Fred Tomkins, an English abolitionist, later described the beautiful music that wafted through the elegant White House rooms; "but the charm of sweet sounds was gone," he wrote, "when I saw the good old woman bent with grief, and the captain in disgust, leave the hall." Years later, Lucy Colman recalled that a British abolitionist named "Dr. Thompson"—she probably meant Fred Tomkins—"was very much surprised, and quite indignant" and said to Colman, "I would so like to take a colored person on my arm and enter the house." Colman replied, "I will arrange that; you shall." According to Colman, at the next public reception she introduced him to William Slade's daughter, Josephine, and Tomkins ushered her into the White House. Because she was beautiful, light-skinned, and holding the arm of an English abolitionist, wrote Colman, "the ushers did not detect her color, and so she passed in." Once inside, however, Mary Lincoln glared at Miss Slade. Colman remarked, "Color, in any degree, was a bar to the entrance."[16]

Colman's recollection—written almost thirty years later—gets a number of details wrong. She stated that Dr. Thompson (again, probably Tomkins) took Josephine Slade at the next public reception. It is more likely, however, that he took her inside that very day. A correspondent for a British newspaper (almost certainly Tomkins) wrote on February 25, 1865: "I had—shall I not say the honour?—of accompanying the first coloured lady ever admitted to these receptions. The lady referred to is a beautiful octoroon girl of 18 years of age, having the finest of black eyes and finely chiseled features. I must, however, add that she was not discerned as coloured." The correspondent stated that after the reception he accompanied the lady (Miss Slade) to the house of a friend, where he conversed with Sojourner Truth. "I must confess she is the most remarkable woman I ever met in my life," he wrote in awe. "Congressmen and senators have listened to her, and the President himself has received her several times to a private interview."[17]

Two days later, on Monday, February 27, Tomkins met with Lincoln and told him what had happened to Truth at the reception. Lincoln "expressed his sorrow, and said he had often seen her, that it should not occur again, and that she should see him the first opportunity: a promise which he kept by sending for her a few days afterward."[18]

It is not clear that this last statement was correct—that Truth met with Lincoln again at the White House; nor that he had seen her "often." But it is possible that Truth attended the White House reception following Lincoln's second inauguration on March 4. According to abolitionist Calvin Fairbank, Truth attended the reception and told the marshal she wanted to see Lincoln. "Well, the President is busy, I think, and you can't see him now," came the reply. "Yes, *I must see him. If he knew I was here he'd come down an' see me.*" The marshal went to the president who said, "I guarantee that she is Sojourner Truth. Bring her up here." According to Fairbank, "we approached near enough to catch the glimpses, and hear the words of greeting. 'SOJOURNER TRUTH! HOW GLAD I AM TO SEE YOU.'"[19]

It cannot be known with certainty that Truth met with Lincoln on the day of the second inauguration. The narrator of the story—Rev. Calvin Fairbank, a minister who spent nineteen years in prison and claimed to have received thirty-five thousand lashes for his work on the Underground Railroad—is notoriously unreliable. Nevertheless, his description of Lincoln's greeting is more plausible than those of some modern historians who have depicted Sojourner's interactions with Lincoln. Some have used their interactions to characterize Lincoln as a president who was unwilling to treat black women as equals. They do so because they rely too heavily on Colman's later recollections.

In her 1891 memoir, Lucy Colman recounted her visit to the White House with Sojourner. In it she depicted Lincoln as responding cruelly to the black soldier's wife and of sounding upset that he had been forced to free the slaves. She implausibly quoted Lincoln as saying to Truth, "I'm not an Abolitionist; I wouldn't free the slaves if I could save the Union in any other way—I'm obliged to do it." Colman was almost certainly paraphrasing Lincoln's August 1862 letter to Horace Greeley here—a carefully crafted document meant to shape public opinion to support emancipation *before* Lincoln issued the Emancipation Proclamation—not words Lincoln would have spoken to Truth in October 1864. Colman continued by saying that "Mr. Lincoln was not himself with this colored woman. . . . When we had done talking, which was some minutes, I knew he was not glad that the war had made him the emancipator of four million slaves." According to Colman, Lincoln only felt satisfaction about emancipation "when he realized that . . . his name would be immortal through the act." She concluded, "He believed in the white race, not in the colored, and did not want them put on an equality."[20]

The words Colman attributed to Lincoln conflict with things that we know he said around this time, including his private strategizing with Frederick Douglass to free as many slaves as possible in August 1864, and his public celebration of emancipation in Maryland three days after he met with Truth. To add to the absurdity, in her memoirs Colman depicted Lincoln's successor, Andrew Johnson, as offering greater respect to Sojourner when he met with her at the White House after Lincoln's death. Of even greater significance, Colman's hostility to Lincoln in 1891 conflicted with what she had written about the meeting at the time. In 1864—very soon after the visit—she published an anonymous squib describing the scene. In it, she admitted her hostility to Lincoln, saying that even if she were permitted to vote, "I could not have even promised to vote for him." Nevertheless, she continued, "our President received me and [Truth] with real politeness and a pleasing cordiality." Then, after describing Lincoln's "most awkward" appearance, she concluded, "What we want is resolute and determined action, and in that short interview with Mr. Lincoln I became convinced that, whatever may have been the former delinquencies of the President, he has now come to the conclusion to act." She concluded, "altogether the visit was quite satisfactory."[21]

Despite the inconsistencies and inaccuracies in Colman's later account of the meeting—and the highly implausible words she attributed to Lincoln—her memoir has had great influence among historians. Some modern writers have been persuaded by her conclusion that a white man like Lincoln could never have treated an unlettered black woman like Truth with dignity, respect, and "reverence." During the civil rights movement of the 1960s, one writer absurdly claimed that Truth "quietly and resolutely" staged "the first Sit-In" in American history. In 1995, another opined, "This was no social encounter between equals, nor even a political conclave; rather, it was a formal encounter, attendant upon his duties as he saw them and the equivalent of the modern-day photo opportunity." Truth's modern biographer Nell Irvin Painter similarly argued that Colman's later account offered the true "story behind the story" because it better reflected the "prevailing attitudes and scholarly appraisals of Lincoln's racial consciousness." Finally, Kate Masur uses a line from Colman's memoir—"Color, in any degree, was a bar to the entrance"—for the title of an article in which she argues that the Lincoln White House was not a particularly hospitable place for black people.[22]

Some writers have made a point to highlight Lincoln's use of the word "Aunty" when he signed Sojourner's Book of Life. Colman depicted Lincoln as a racist for calling Truth "aunty, as he would his washerwoman."[23] Two scholars, in fact, see Lincoln and Truth in conflict with one another throughout the entire meeting, arguing that "Lincoln may have intended a slight act of condescension by signing Truth's book 'For Aunty,'" but that ultimately, they conclude, "Truth outmaneuvered him even here."[24] Such analysis reads things into the historical record that simply are not there. Sojourner was not upset or offended by the appellation. She—of all people—knew what it was like to be insulted by white men and women, whether by her former mistress or by hostile white audiences. Lincoln's treatment of her was anything but disrespectful. He used the term "aunty" as a term of endearment, not one of paternalistic disrespect, in the same way that William Tecumseh Sherman's men affectionately called him "Uncle Billy" or Lincoln "Uncle Abe."[25]

The 1864 accounts by Truth and Colman are surely more reliable than Colman's reminiscence, as they align with the treatment that Lincoln is known to have given his black visitors—not what Painter calls the "scholarly appraisals of Lincoln's racial consciousness." In fact, Truth relished telling people about her visit with Lincoln. In April 1866, Julia Wilbur described a conversation with Truth in her diary: "She was in a talking mood & we were highly entertained. Sojourner hates rebels & Copperheads. Told us about her visit to President Lincoln &c."[26] There was no conflict between Truth and Lincoln. When Lincoln told her that he "was compelled to do these things," he was acknowledging his own human limitations—he was not "repudiat[ing] Truth's cause," as two scholars have alleged.[27] Just as he had told Caroline Johnson when she brought him the wax fruit display a few months earlier, God was to receive the praise, not him. Sojourner Truth understood what he meant, which is why she replied, "I thank God you were the instrument selected by Him and the people to do these things." It is little wonder that she concluded her account (dictated by her in November 1864) by saying, "I am proud to say that I never was treated with more kindness and cordiality than I was by that great and good man, *Abraham Lincoln*."[28]

13

"ALL THE PEOPLE . . . ARE INVITED"

A blanket of snow covered the streets and hills of Washington, DC, on Sunday, January 1, 1865, and boys and girls went out sledding and ice skating while their parents attended church. Cold winds blew down from the north, but the sun shone brightly in the sky, enabling people to enjoy their time outdoors. On Monday, January 2, the heads of the federal departments gave their employees a holiday, and receptions were held throughout the city to celebrate the New Year. Hundreds of people would throng to the White House to shake the hand of the president. However, the preparations for the reception this year were different than they had ever been before. The Washington *Daily Chronicle* carried a notice that "all the people present, of every creed, clime, color and sex are invited by the President to call upon him."[1]

Apparently heeding this invitation, several hundred black men and women decided to attend Lincoln's New Year's reception on January 2. While waiting outside of the building, most of the white visitors did not seem to mind their presence, "supposing they would confine themselves to the station assigned them by custom and bring up the rear of the president's visitors." But when the doors were opened the black visitors pressed forward "shoulder to shoulder with the whites." A raucous scene ensued. Many of the white attendees yelled out in disgust, "They are letting the negroes in" and "Put 'em out," while a rough-looking soldier growled, "Go to the kitchen, G—d d—n you." A small number of black people nevertheless entered the White House where they found Lincoln dressed in a black suit and wearing white gloves. When the first "colored woman presented herself, Mr. Lincoln shook hands with her and Mrs. Lincoln gave the invariable bow," reported the Washington correspondent for the *Boston Recorder*. But when a second appeared, "Mrs. Lincoln looked aghast; and when the third colored woman appeared, Mrs. Lincoln sent word to the door that no more colored persons could be admitted to mingle with the whites." Mary Lincoln stated that "if they would come at the conclusion of the levee, they should receive the same admittance." Ward Hill Lamon then immediately instructed the guards to remove any others who had entered and to not permit any more in until after the white visitors had all been greeted by the president.

A number of black Washingtonians decided to wait patiently until the doors were finally opened to them. One white attendee noticed them standing outside of the building for two hours, "watching earnestly." Some of them were "richly and gaily dressed," some stood in "tattered garments," and some wore "the most fanciful and grotesque costume." Among them were black soldiers and preachers. A white soldier in attendance noted that the assemblage included "colored people of all grades."

When the white visitors finally finished greeting President Lincoln and the First Lady, the black callers "summoned up courage, and began timidly to approach the door," pressing forward "eagerly." Upon seeing Lincoln, wrote one observer, "the feelings of the poor creatures overcame them." By now Lincoln was tired, having shaken hundreds of hands over the previous two hours, "but here his nerves rallied at the unwonted sight, and he welcomed this motley crowd with a heartiness that made them wild with exceeding joy." The black visitors laughed and cried at the sight of their president, and through their tears exulted, "God bless you!" "God bless Abraham Lincoln," and "God bress Massa Linkum!" One white observer noted that Lincoln "has within him a great heart, that feels for his brother man of whatever hue or condition. May the hopes of this down-trodden people soon be realized, and may Abraham Lincoln live to see every yoke broken, and every American citizen rejoicing in the boon of liberty!" Sadly, outside of the White House, young men could be heard "cursing the President for this act."[2]

Radical Republicans and abolitionists regretted that the black attendees were required to wait until the end of the reception to enter. One white attendee, W. J. Pond, deplored having to witness this treatment of his fellow Americans. "Guards were speedily placed around the spacious portico, with crossed bayonets, and if one chanced to get in at the entrance door, he was quickly ejected," Pond reported to William Lloyd Garrison's *Liberator*. Pond knew there were many whites who thought that black people had no business at the White House, but from his perspective, "Had the simple boon of shaking hands with the President been extended to the colored people, it certainly would not have grieved *me*, even though I had found myself in the crowd in close proximity to some of them." Pond reflected on the ways he and other white Americans interacted with African Americans in everyday life—as bootblacks, waiters, and carriage drivers. Considering the close proximity in which white and black people routinely lived their lives, Pond did not think that their presence at a New Year's reception "ought to offend or injure anybody." Should any white attendees feel themselves "aggrieved" by the presence of black visitors, *they* would "certainly have the right to retire, and seek more congenial relations where they could find them."

Pond reminded the readers of the *Liberator* that Lincoln had recently received the black ministers from Baltimore. For Pond, these sorts of moments with the president were important ways to integrate African Americans into mainstream society. "To have allowed them a common privilege would have greatly gratified them, and would have done them more substantial good than a great many declarations to the effect that one 'thinks them the worst abused people in the world,'" he wrote in an apparent allusion to Lincoln's statement to the black delegation in August 1862. "More than this, it would have had the excellent effect to hurt the feelings of a certain class, who, thus far, as I judge, have not had their feelings injured half enough in this manner to do them any good, but just enough to stir up within them the demon of colorphobia, and thus to reveal the innate vulgarity of their character."[3] In other words, welcoming loyal black citizens into the White House would put disloyal Northern Democrats and Southern traitors in their proper place.

In fact, Democrats were outraged when they read about these happenings at the White House, and they heaped scorn upon the president for his racial egalitarianism. "Are not such scenes at the White House disgusting?" asked the editors of the *Illinois State Register* in Lincoln's hometown of Springfield. "When will the white people of this country awake to the sense of shame that the dominant party is bringing upon us by the practical establishment of the social equality of the negro?" Similarly, a Missouri paper mocked "the performances of negroes who come to call on their great father."[4]

This important moment has received some attention in recent years. Historian Kate Masur writes, "The paper attributed the invitation to 'the President' himself, but there is no evidence that Lincoln was behind it; the source may well have been the paper's editor, John Forney, a Lincoln ally who was often somewhat more progressive on matters of emancipation and race than the president." But historian Michael Burlingame counters, "By the same token, there is no evidence to prove that Lincoln was *not* behind the invitation. It is quite telling that a newspaper *known as his administration's organ* announced that the president himself invited *people of all colors* to attend the reception."[5] It is possible that Forney issued the invitation without Lincoln's foreknowledge or approval, but it seems much more likely that the *Chronicle* was simply communicating Lincoln's wish that all people of all colors be invited to ring in the New Year with him.

INTERLUDE 5

The House Chamber

The spring of 1865 was a time of celebration for black Americans and their white allies. Passage of the Thirteenth Amendment in Congress on January 31 marked the beginning of a constitutional revolution that would forever end race-based slavery in the United States. Among the spectators in the packed galleries of the House of Representatives that day were Henry Highland Garnet and "many a black brother and sister." Garnet later stated with satisfaction, "Oh, it was quite a pepper and salt mixture."[1]

In honor of this achievement, Lincoln urged congressional leaders to invite Garnet to deliver a sermon in the House of Representatives chamber on Sunday, February 12 (Lincoln's birthday). That morning the floor and galleries were overflowing with spectators. Soldiers, civilians, government officials, men, women, and children—black and white—filled up the seats that were usually occupied by members of Congress. The galleries, too, were filled with people, most of whom were black. A choir from Garnet's church (which included Dr. Anderson R. Abbott, in uniform) sang several hymns, including "All Hail the Power of Jesus' Name" and "Arise, My Soul, Shake Off Thy Fears." From the Speaker's rostrum at the front of the House chamber, Garnet preached a sermon based on Matthew 23:4. "For they bind heavy burdens and grievous to be borne, and lay them on men's shoulders," he intoned, "but they themselves will not move them with one of their fingers." He told the story of his upbringing in slavery. "The first sounds that startled my ear, and sent a shudder through my soul, were the cracking of the whip, and the clanking of chains," he said. The minister then celebrated emancipation, but called on Congress to bring about equality and justice for all men, including the right to vote.

African Americans in the nation's capital were moved by this occurrence, seeing it as a sign of the changing times. "But a short while ago . . . no colored persons were permitted within the precincts of the Houses of Congress, except as servants," wrote a correspondent to the *Anglo-African*. But now they could "enter there at will" to watch the proceedings. This writer was also pleased to inform his readers that he had recently attended a reception at the White House where he had "the privilege and pleasure . . . to grasp by the hand the Chief Magistrate of the nation." Never in "the good old days of slaveholding Democracy," this correspondent wrote with satisfaction, would "the habituants of the White House . . . in their wildest fancies, dreamed of the possibility, even, of a colored face entering within its sacred portals except as a servant or a slave."[2] How quickly things had changed in the previous four years.

White Washingtonians were equally impressed by Garnet's sermon in the House chamber, and what it represented. "That the world moves can be no longer doubted," wrote journalist Lois Bryan Adams, "for what less than a revolution could have brought about what has now been witnessed by all Washington—a spectacle of a black man preaching against slavery from the Speaker's desk in the House of Representatives at the Capitol." Even the mixed-race audience, Adams noted, "in such a place was a novel and wonderful sight, even in these days of wonders." Perhaps one day soon, she hoped, "mind and soul, and not the color of his skin, shall mark the measure of a man."[3]

"I'VE COME
TO PROPOSE
SOMETHING TO YOU"

When Frederick Douglass first met with Lincoln in August 1863, he explained how frustrating it was that worthy black soldiers were not permitted to rise through the ranks. At that meeting Lincoln had pledged to commission any black officer that the War Department sent him, but these were few in number. In 1865, a prominent black leader came to meet with Lincoln to discuss a radical new idea—not simply commissioning black officers, but forming a black Army that would be led by black officers as well as sympathetic whites.

Born free to a free black seamstress and a plantation slave in Charles Town, Virginia (now West Virginia), in 1812, Martin R. Delany would go on to become, in the words of a contemporary, "one of the great men of this age." In the 1820s, Delany's mother moved to western Pennsylvania to avoid punishment for teaching him how to read. In 1843 he founded a newspaper, the *Mystery*, which he edited until 1847, when he joined Frederick Douglass as an editor of the *North Star*. Two years later Delany was admitted to Harvard Medical School, but several months after matriculating he was dismissed on account of his race. In 1856 Delany moved to Canada, where he practiced medicine. All the while, Delany was an advocate of black emigration, and in 1859 he traveled to the Niger Valley in West Africa in hopes of establishing a settlement for African Americans.[1]

In the spring of 1863, several men sent letters of introduction to President Lincoln on Delany's behalf, telling the president that Delany was "a reliable man" and "a man of energy and intelligence." Should Lincoln decide to entrust federal colonization funds to Delany, they urged, it "will be faithfully and legitimately applied." But Lincoln was moving away from support for colonization by this time, and nothing came of these overtures. Instead, Delany turned his attention to the recruitment of black volunteers for the Union Army—including his own son, who fought with the Fifty-Fourth Massachusetts. In December 1863 Delany sent a letter to Secretary of War Edwin M. Stanton urging that the most effective way to recruit black soldiers would be through "intelligent competent black men . . . because knowing and being of that people as a race, they can command such influence as is required to accomplish the object." Delany asked for authority to supervise the recruitment of black soldiers in the seceded states, although Stanton does not appear to have responded to the letter.[2]

Delany finally received an audience with Lincoln in February 1865. In 1868, Delany published a lengthy account of the meeting, which he recalled as taking place on February 9. This date seems unlikely, however, because during the meeting Delany heard cannons boom outside of the White House in celebration of the capture of Charleston; but Charleston did not surrender to Union authorities until February 18. It is likely that Delany and Lincoln actually met on February 21, as that is a date that cannons roared in the national capital to celebrate the capture of the Confederate stronghold.[3]

Delany was fifty-two years old when he met with Lincoln. One newspaper described him as "a negro, having no 'visible admixture' of white blood. He is black—black as the blackest—large, heavy set, vigorous, with a bald, sleek head, which shines like a newly polished boot." Another said that his face "shone like black Italian marble."[4] Henry Highland Garnet tried to persuade Delany not to meet with Lincoln, allegedly telling him, "So many of our men have called upon him of late, all expecting something, and coming away dissatisfied, some of them openly complaining, that I am fearful he has come to the conclusion to receive no more black visitors." But Delany was determined to meet with the president, and Garnet was wrong about how Lincoln would respond to an African American caller.

Delany professed that his intention was "to ask nothing of the president, but to offer him something for the government." In other words, he had an idea he wanted Lincoln to hear and consider. On that cold day in February, Delany walked into Lincoln's White House office and was introduced to the president. Lincoln offered Delany "a generous grasp and shake of the hand [that] brought me to a seat in front of him." Delany would never forget his first impression of the commander in chief. "No one could mistake the fact that an able and master spirit was before me," he wrote almost twenty years later. "Serious without sadness, and pleasant withal, he was soon seated, placing himself at ease, the better to give me a patient audience." Lincoln opened the conversation by asking, "What can I do for you, sir?"

"Nothing, Mr. President," Delany replied, "but I've come to propose something to you, which I think will be beneficial to the nation in this critical hour of her peril." Delany later recalled that he would "never forget" the "inquiring look" on Lincoln's face when he said these words. Lincoln, a man who could normally conceal his emotions when he wanted to, was unable to do so in this moment. He was so used to having visitors ask him for things that he was unprepared for Delany's answer of an offer rather than a request.

With words that conveyed respect for his visitor, Lincoln urged Delany to proceed, saying, "Go on, sir." Delany paused for a moment and then reminded the president of the ways that African Americans were helping to subdue the rebellion. Yet they were facing "heartless and almost relentless prejudice" from within the military. They did not all receive equal pay, and they had little opportunity for advancement in the ranks. Delany believed that Lincoln and his advisors ought to do something "to check this growing feeling against the slave, else nothing that we could do would avail. And if such were not expedited, all might be lost," he warned. Black soldiers had done their duty "faithfully and well," he continued, and they ought to be recognized for their service.

To this, Lincoln readily assented. Delany then reminded Lincoln that the armies had placed black people in positions "of confidence"—as pickets, scouts, and guides to lead the Union armies through hostile terrain—and that in these roles, African Americans had served the United States to great effect. It followed, Delany argued, "that if you can find them of higher qualifications, they may, with equal credit, fill higher more important trusts."

"*Certainly*," Lincoln replied emphatically. "And what do you propose to do?"

Delany answered that he knew there was "too much prejudice among the whites for the soldiers to serve under a black commander, or the officers to be willing to associate with him." This was a "fact" which could not be denied or ignored. But the United States could induce Southern black men to join the Union Army by offering them the opportunity to serve under black officers.

Lincoln looked at Delany "earnestly yet anxiously" and asked, "How will you remedy the great difficulty you have just now so justly described, about the objections of white soldiers to colored commanders, and officers to colored associates?"

Delany replied that he had the "remedy" to this problem, and that it would "complete the prestige of the Union army":

I propose, sir, an army of blacks, commanded entirely by black officers, except such whites as may volunteer to serve; this army to penetrate through the heart of the South, and make conquests, with the banner of Emancipation unfurled, proclaiming freedom as they go, sustaining and protecting it by arming the emancipated, taking them as fresh troops, and leaving a few veterans among the new freemen, when occasion requires, keeping this banner unfurled until every slave is free, according to the letter of your proclamation. I would also take from those already in the service all that are competent for commission[ed] officers, and establish at once in the South a camp of instructions.

Delany predicted that in three months they could have an army of forty thousand African Americans "in motion, the presence of which anywhere would itself be a power irresistible." The sight of this army, he continued, would "give confidence to the slaves, and retain them to the Union, stop foreign intervention, and speedily bring the war to a close."

By now Lincoln was excited. For four years his paramount goal had been to preserve the Union and to end the bloody killing on the battlefield. Perhaps such an idea could help speed up that day when the fighting would cease.

"This," he said, "is the very thing I have been looking and hoping for; but nobody offered it. I have thought it over and over again. I have talked about it; I hoped and prayed for it; but till now it never has been proposed. White men couldn't do this, because they are doing all in that direction now that they can; but we find, for various reasons, it does not meet the case under consideration. The blacks should go to the interior, and the whites be kept on the frontiers."

"Yes, sir," Delany replied; "they would require but little, as they could subsist on the country as they went along."

"Certainly," said Lincoln; "a few light artillery, with the cavalry, would comprise your principal advance, because all the siege work would be on the frontiers and waters, done by the white division of the army. Won't this be a grand thing?" he said with a joyous expression on his face. But just as quickly Lincoln became more subdued. He continued: "When I issued my Emancipation Proclamation, I had this thing in contemplation. I then gave them a chance by prohibiting any interference on the part of the army; but they did not embrace it." According to Delany, Lincoln made this last remark "rather sadly, accompanying the word with an emphatic gesture." Just as Lincoln had said to Douglass a few months earlier, in August 1864, he wished that more slaves had seized the opportunity to free themselves and to join the Union Army. Delany replied by pointing out that the slaves "could not read your proclamation, nor could they know anything about it, only, when they did hear, to know that they were free."

The two men continued talking about Lincoln's policies when, suddenly, Lincoln asked, "Will you take command?"

Delany, possibly taken aback, replied, "If there be none better qualified than I am, sir, by that time I will. While it is my desire to serve, as black men we shall have to prepare ourselves, as we have had no opportunities of experience and practice in the service as officers."

"That matters but little, comparatively," Lincoln replied, "as some of the finest officers we have never studied the tactics till they entered the army as subordinates." Moreover, Lincoln continued, "the tactics are easily learned, especially among your people. It is the head that we now require most—men of plans and executive ability."

"I thank you, Mr. President," said Delany, "for the—"

"No—not at all," Lincoln interrupted.

Delany then reached into his pocket. "I will show you some letters of introduction, sir," he began.

But Lincoln cut him off. "Not now," said the president. "I know all about you. I see nothing now to be done but to give you a line of introduction to the secretary of war." At that moment the two men heard cannon fire booming in the distance. "Stanton is firing! listen! he is in his glory! noble man!" Lincoln said.

"What is it, Mr. President?" asked Delany.

"The firing!"

"What is it about, sir?"

"Why, don't you know? Haven't you heard the news? Charleston is ours!" Lincoln then wrote something out at the table and handed it to Delany. It was a letter of introduction to Secretary Stanton instructing him, "Do not fail to have an interview with this most extraordinary and intelligent black man."

While some of the language in this recollection seems unlikely—with the war so close to concluding, it seems doubtful that Lincoln would have worried about foreign intervention or thought it necessary to equip an entirely new army—Lincoln nevertheless did commission Delany a major in the Union Army on February 27. Delany thus became the highest-ranking black commissioned field officer (unlike Alexander T. Augusta, who was a surgeon).[5]

15

"A SACRED EFFORT"

On March 4, 1865, African Americans played a central part of the pageantry of Lincoln's second inauguration. Rain and hail had fallen from the sky for two days before the inauguration, and the streets had turned to sludge. But that did not dampen the spirits of the thousands who came out to celebrate Lincoln's swearing in. "The mud was deep, and prancing horses splashed it upon each other and upon the people," wrote Lois Bryan Adams, "but nobody seemed to care." Thousands of people tramped through the muck on Pennsylvania Avenue as they made their way to the Capitol building. Flags hung on buildings everywhere one looked, although they were dripping from the rain. Soldiers, fire companies, and civic organizations formed a procession for the president. Among the marchers were members of a regiment of US Colored Troops and a large company of black Odd Fellows. One parade float, pulled by four horses and decked out with flags, featured a "fanciful" structure called the Temple of Liberty. As one observer described it, "Within this temple, as one of its pillars, stands a black man. He is at the rear end of the edifice, but the tallest man in it, and the only one standing." Clearly for the Republican organizers of this event, African Americans were to be welcomed into the body politic. One Iowan who watched the procession wrote that she watched "black troops and white!—Yes, Africa! Four years ago, down-trodden, now uprisen, Free." Many years later, an ex-slave claimed that he attended the inaugural ceremony and "shook hands with [Lincoln] in Washington." A reporter for the *Times* of London remarked that "at least half the multitude were colored people" dressed "in festive reds, blues, and yellows, and very gaudy colors."[1]

In his speech, Lincoln reminded the audience that enslaved people made up one-eighth of the nation's population, and that "these slaves constituted a peculiar and powerful interest. All knew," Lincoln said, "that this interest was, somehow, the cause of the war." This line was a far cry from what Lincoln had told the black delegation in August 1862. Back then, he had blamed black people for the war, telling them that *they* were the cause and that white Americans suffered because of their presence in the United States. Now Lincoln placed the responsibility squarely on the white population of the entire nation, not only Southern slave owners, for white Northerners had been complicit in the national transgression of human bondage. And the penalty for this sin was death. Hundreds of thousands of dead.

Quoting the Gospel of Matthew, Lincoln wanted his audience to contemplate the reality that God gave "to both North and South, this terrible war, as the woe due to those by whom the offence came." It was natural that all Americans might wish for "this mighty scourge of war" to "speedily pass away," but they must be willing to accept the punishment that God had ordained for them, even if it meant that the war continue "until all the wealth piled by the bond-man's two hundred and fifty years of unrequited toil shall be sunk, and until every drop of blood drawn with the lash, shall be paid by another drawn with the sword." From this point, Lincoln arrived at his majestic conclusion. If both Northern and Southern whites could understand that they bore the guilt of sin that had brought on this war, then perhaps they could forgive one another: "With malice toward none; with charity for all; with firmness in the right, as God gives us to see the right, let us strive on to finish the work we are in; to bind up the nation's wounds; to care for him who shall have borne the battle, and for his widow, and his orphan—to do all which may achieve and cherish a just, and a lasting peace, among ourselves, and with all nations."[2]

The white members of the audience stood quietly as Lincoln delivered the speech, while the black men and women exulted "bress de Lord" as an almost call-and-response reply to each sentence.[3] This reaction was telling. That they could chant "bless the Lord" as though they were at a church service reveals that they heard deep truths in the president's speech. Perhaps they were pleased not to be blamed for the war, as they had been by Lincoln in 1862. Perhaps, too, they saw something different in the war than white Americans saw. Just as with the White House a picnic on a day of fasting in August 1864, the war and its carnage had different meanings for white and black Americans. To be sure, both groups had suffered tremendously, but one group had hope for a new sense of justice that had eluded them for two and a half centuries. They hoped that they, too, would be treated as citizens with all of the rights and responsibilities that citizenship entailed.

Standing toward the front of the audience that day was Frederick Douglass. Joining him was Louise Dorsey, a former slave who was married to a successful Philadelphia businessman. The famous black orator and his companion took a position near the Capitol, as Douglass recollected, "where I could see the Presidential procession as it came upon the east portico, and where I could hear and see all that took place." They were so close, in fact, that Douglass made eye contact with Vice President Andrew Johnson, who was drunk. Lincoln apparently noticed Douglass in the audience and pointed him out to Johnson. Johnson was not pleased to see them, and Douglass could recognize the "bitter contempt and aversion" in his eyes. He turned to Mrs. Dorsey and said, "Whatever Andrew Johnson may be, he is certainly no friend of our race." But this experience did not dampen Douglass's enthusiasm. Douglass later remarked that Lincoln's speech "sounded more like a sermon than a state paper."[4]

Following the inauguration, the Lincolns prepared to welcome thousands of guests into their home for a reception. At the White House, Elizabeth Keckly was busy dressing Mrs. Lincoln for the occasion. When the president entered the room, Keckly congratulated him. He reached out and "grasped my outstretched hand warmly, and held it while he spoke," she later recalled. Lincoln thanked Keckly for her well wishes and remarked on the difficult road ahead.[5] Meanwhile, Frederick Douglass and Mrs. Dorsey made their way to the White House for the reception. It had taken Douglass some time to find someone "my own color" who would be willing to accompany him. Everyone he asked was worried that they would be turned away, and they did not want to deal with such an indignity. But Douglass was willing to take the risk. As he later explained, the passage of the Thirteenth Amendment and the heroism of black soldiers impelled him to believe that "it was not too great an assumption for a colored man to offer his congratulations to the President with those of other citizens." Moreover, "if the colored man would have his rights, he must take them."

As Douglass and Mrs. Dorsey walked slowly toward the White House, the great orator thought to himself, "I had for some time looked upon myself as a man, but now in this multitude of the elite of the land, I felt myself a man among men." Unfortunately, his confidence would soon be shaken. At the White House door, two policemen took him "rudely by the arm and ordered me to stand back, for their directions were to admit no persons of my color." Douglass would not submit to this affront and told the officers that this must be a mistake, "for no such order could have emanated from President Lincoln; and that if he knew I was at the door he would desire my admission." As a line started to build, the policemen suddenly "assumed an air of politeness" and offered to escort Douglass in. He followed them, but soon realized that it was a ruse—they were walking him to a window that had been turned into a temporary exit! Douglass exclaimed, "You have deceived me. I shall not go out of this building till I see President Lincoln." At that moment, Douglass saw someone he recognized and said, "Be so kind as to say to Mr. Lincoln that Frederick Douglass is detained by officers at the door." Before long, Douglass and Mrs. Dorsey were permitted to roam freely, and they made their way into the East Room. Lincoln stood there greeting visitors, head-and-shoulders above most of the crowd. When he saw Douglass, he bellowed, "Here comes my friend Douglass." Lincoln then took Douglass by the hand and said, "I am glad to see you. I saw you in the crowd to-day, listening to my inaugural address; how did you like it?"

Douglass was taken aback by this question and replied, "Mr. Lincoln, I must not detain you with my poor opinion, when there are thousands waiting to shake hands with you."

"No, no," rejoined Lincoln, "you must stop a little, Douglass; there is no man in the country whose opinion I value more than yours. I want to know what you think of it?"

At this, Douglass said, "Mr. Lincoln, that was a sacred effort."

"I am glad you liked it!" said Lincoln. Douglass then walked on, beaming on the inside. The great abolitionist later learned that there had been "no orders from Mr. Lincoln, or from any one else" to exclude African Americans from the festivities. The policemen "were simply complying with an old custom," which Douglass rightly identified as an "outgrowth of slavery." Later, when reflecting on this moment, he wrote, "I have found in my experience that the way to break down an unreasonable custom, is to contradict it in practice" for "there can be nothing blameworthy in people thus equal meeting each other on the plane of civil or social rights." In fact, others did follow his example that day. The *Baltimore Sun* and Philadelphia *Press* both reported that "many colored persons" attended the White House reception.[6]

After leaving the White House, Douglass went to a friend's home, where he saw Elizabeth Keckly. Keckly observed that he "was very proud of the manner in which Mr. Lincoln received him" as he "related the incident with great pleasure to myself and others." Two days later, on Monday, March 6, Keckly spent much of the day helping Mary Lincoln prepare for the inaugural ball. When Lincoln came into the room, Keckly told him "how much Mr. Douglass had been pleased on the night he was presented to Mr. Lincoln."

Mary turned to her husband and asked, "Father, why was not Mr. Douglass introduced to me?"

"I do not know," replied the president. "I thought he was presented."

"But he was not."

"It must have been an oversight then, mother; I am sorry you did not meet him."[7]

Unfortunately, someone associated with Lincoln's inauguration decided to bar African Americans from the Second Inaugural Ball, which took place at the Patent Office Building (now the Smithsonian's National Portrait Gallery) on the evening of March 6.[8] It is unclear who made this decision.

Shortly after the inauguration, Lincoln sent a message to the home where Douglass was staying, inviting him to tea at the Soldiers' Home. Regrettably, Douglass had a speaking engagement on the evening of the invitation, and he made it "one of the rules of my conduct in life never to break an engagement, if possible to keep it." He therefore turned down the invitation. Many years later, Douglass wrote, "I have often regretted that I did not make this an exception to my general rule. Could I have known that no such opportunity would come to me again, I should have justified myself in disappointing a large audience for the sake of such a visit with Abraham Lincoln."[9]

Douglass's three meetings with Lincoln transformed the way he thought about the sixteenth president. Years later, he wrote in an autobiography, "I have often said elsewhere what I wish to repeat here, that Mr. Lincoln was not only a great President, but a GREAT MAN—too great to be small in anything. In his company I was never in any way reminded of my humble origin, or of my unpopular color."[10] Douglass attributed the genuine nature of Lincoln's interactions with African Americans to his humble upbringing. In his famous speech at the "Emancipation" statue dedication at Lincoln Park in Washington, DC, in 1876, Douglass argued that his early life "among the lowly" and the difficult labor he performed as a boy and young man "linked [him] in brotherly sympathy with the sons of toil in every loyal part of the Republic."[11]

16

"SHE IS MY EQUAL, AND THE EQUAL OF ALL OTHERS"

As President Lincoln traveled throughout Washington, DC, during the war years, he often encountered ex-slaves who had fled to the nation's capital to escape from bondage. Black refugees from Virginia and Maryland flooded into the city after slavery was abolished there in April 1862, and by the end of the war, the black population in Washington had risen to forty thousand. Many of these refugees lived in squalor and destitution, yet they bore a steady resolve. "It is wonderful to see with what uncomplaining patience their sufferings are borne," wrote journalist Lois Bryan Adams. "Scarcely ever is one seen on the street begging, and it is only by going to their miserable huts and shanties that their nakedness and starvation are found out." Many of these freedpeople hoped that Lincoln could help them meet their needs. One poor old woman who had escaped from the Confederacy with three helpless grandchildren, but who had left her husband and children behind, was overheard on the street in April 1865 telling her grandson that she "reckoned Massa Lincoln would set daddy free now, and the Lor' would send him right up to Washington." Lincoln often did what he could to help these poor suffering souls. When Elizabeth Keckly formed the Contraband Relief Association in 1862, Lincoln and the First Lady both "made frequent contributions."[1]

Lincoln's empathy was rooted in the poverty of his youth. One black child whose father worked as a waiter at the White House later recalled that Lincoln "was kind to everybody. . . . He was a poor man who learned to work hard as a boy. He knew all about life and the struggles of the unfortunate. That was why he sympathized with us colored folks, and we loved him."[2]

Sometimes Lincoln gave charity directly to suffering people. On August 11, 1863—the day after his first meeting with Frederick Douglass—Lincoln wrote out a five-dollar check from his account at Riggs Bank and gave it to a "Colored man, with one leg." Little is known about the background of this remarkable event. All that we know of the man comes from the banker's granddaughter, who later claimed that he "was a fine looking man with a beard that was turning gray and he always stood on H Street between the Old Freeman House and St. John's Church," across Lafayette Square from the White House. Mr. Riggs, Lincoln's banker, apparently "gave him something every morning as he passed along there on foot from his house to the bank."[3] Perhaps Lincoln and Riggs talked about the man on occasion when they were conducting business. It is also likely that Lincoln saw him standing on the street corner day after day. One way or the other, Lincoln felt compelled to offer him a modest amount of money to alleviate his suffering. This small act of compassion, coming from the president, must have meant a great deal to that old man, whoever he was.

Lincoln also cared for the members of the White House staff, even after they no longer worked for him. He treated his black staff like "people," recalled one White House servant—something that earlier servants would rarely have experienced. The servants, in turn, loved Lincoln for his kindness and consideration.[4] Elizabeth Keckly later told a reporter that Lincoln was as considerate of her "as he was of any of the white people about the White House."[5] To be sure, early in his presidency, Lincoln was not willing to buck the traditions of the White House. He dismissed his dark-skinned servant, William H. Johnson, whom he had brought with him from Illinois, because the light-skinned White House staff treated Johnson badly. But Lincoln then worked hard to find Johnson other employment. He wrote several letters of recommendation to heads of federal departments, calling Johnson "honest, faithful, sober, industrious and handy as a servant." Eventually Johnson found work with the Treasury Department.

A mere three years later, in January 1864, Johnson lay dying of smallpox, which he almost certainly contracted while caring for Lincoln following his trip to Gettysburg in November 1863. On January 11, a journalist found Lincoln counting greenbacks. When the newspaperman asked what he was doing, Lincoln replied, "This, sir, is something out of my usual line; but a President of the United States has a multiplicity of duties not specified in the Constitution or acts of Congress. This is one of them. This money belongs to a poor negro who is a porter in one of the Departments [the Treasury], and who is at present very bad with the small pox." Lincoln told the reporter, "He did not catch it from me, however; at least I think not. He is now in hospital, and could not draw his pay because he could not sign his name. I have been at considerable trouble to overcome the difficulty and get it for him, and have at length succeeded in cutting red tape. . . . I am now dividing the money and putting by a portion labeled, in an envelope, with my own hands, according to his wish." The reporter wrote, "No one who witnessed the transaction could fail to appreciate the goodness of heart which would prompt a man who is borne down by the weight of cares unparalleled in the world's history, to turn aside for a time from them to succor one of the humblest of his fellow creatures in sickness and sorrow."

Sadly, Johnson died from the illness. He had borrowed $150 from the First National Bank of Washington, and Lincoln had served as a cosigner. One day shortly after Johnson's death, the bank's cashier, William J. Huntington, mentioned the outstanding debt to Lincoln. "Oh, yes," replied Lincoln with emotion, "William is gone. I bought a coffin for the poor fellow, and have had to help his family." Huntington said he would forgive the loan, but Lincoln would have none of it. "No you don't," said the president. "I endorsed the notes, and am bound to pay them; and it is your duty to make me pay them." The banker replied that forgiving the debt could be a "charitable" action on the part of the bank, but Lincoln again said no. "Well, Mr. Lincoln," said Huntington, "I will tell you how we can arrange this. The loan to William was a joint one between you and the bank. You stand half of the loss, and I will cancel the other." Lincoln considered this option for a moment and then replied, "Mr. Huntington, that sounds fair, but it is insidious; you are going to get ahead of me; you are going to give me the smallest note to pay. There must be a fair divide over poor William. Reckon up the interest on both notes, and chop the whole right straight through the middle, so that my half shall be as big as yours. That's the way we will fix it." Huntington agreed to do this, saying, "After this, Mr. President, you can never deny that you *indorse* the negro." "That's a fact!" Lincoln said with a smile, "but I don't intend to deny it."[6]

Shortly after William H. Johnson's death, Lincoln helped his former barber, Solomon James Johnson, find employment as a messenger in the Treasury Department, in February 1864. Lincoln appears to have met with Solomon Johnson again about a year later, on March 15, 1865, for he gave Johnson a note informing the secretary of the Treasury that "I shall be glad" if Johnson "could get a little promotion." Johnson would go on (after Lincoln's death) to become the first black clerk working for the federal government.[7] Earlier in the war, Lincoln had also helped a twenty-one-year-old waiter and White House barber named Samuel Williams land a position in the Treasury Department.[8]

Lincoln's concern for his former staff is noteworthy. Some scholars have criticized him for using the pejorative term "boy" in his letters of recommendation for William H. Johnson, Solomon James Johnson, and Samuel Williams, but there is a far greater significance to these episodes.[9] Most presidents would not have been overly concerned with the welfare of African American servants—especially when considering the concerns facing Lincoln as a wartime commander in chief. Despite all of the burdens of the war, Lincoln took time to meet with these former servants and to hand them letters of recommendation. He also encouraged his Cabinet secretaries to hire them within their departments. One acquaintance of Solomon Johnson's wrote in November 1864, "He has for a long time shaved the President who I have reason to believe is also interested in his success." Indeed, Lincoln was. John E. Washington wrote in 1942, "I think Lincoln's constant interest in William Johnson shows us, even more than do some of his greatest public deeds and much heralded acts, the great heart of this man." After bringing Johnson from Illinois to Washington, and then being compelled to dismiss him, Lincoln "thereafter never ceased to be interested in him, but continued to assist him in every manner possible."[10] In fact, one of the most famous stories of the Lincoln presidency is of the headstone he is said to have purchased for William H. Johnson and placed at Arlington National Cemetery, bearing the word "Citizen."[11]

Despite all of the burdens that were pressing in upon him, Lincoln paid careful attention to his surroundings. One evening, at the end of a long day of work, he sat by a window in the White House and looked out on the streets below. As he had for several days now, he saw an elderly black man standing outside with a basket. He called for his valet, William Slade, to come over. As the president's usher and valet, Slade was the third highest ranked member of the White House domestic staff, behind only the steward and stewardess. Described in the historical record as being "of medium height, olive in complexion, with light eyes and straight chestnut-brown hair," Slade had great responsibility in the Executive Mansion, managing the other servants and attending to the president's needs—even helping Lincoln dress in the morning and prepare for bed at night. "William," Lincoln asked, "who is that old colored man outside with an empty basket on his arm? I have noticed him for some days, as he comes regularly, and leaves with the empty basket. Go downstairs, get him and bring him up here to see me." Slade went to find the man, and within a few minutes, the basket-bearing gentleman was standing before the president. He tried to say, "Good evening," but was so nervous that he could not utter a sound. Lincoln broke the ice. "Well, Uncle," he said with compassion in his voice, "I've seen you coming here for several days with your empty basket and then in a few minutes you go away. I've waited to see if you would come again and if you did I intended to send for you to learn your story. What can I do for you?"

"Thank you, sir," replied the man, who was now feeling more at ease. "You know, Mr. Lincoln, I heard that you had the Constitution here and how it has *provisions* in it. Well, as we are hungry and have nothing to eat in my house, I just thought I'd come around and get mine." Lincoln laughed when he heard the man's misunderstanding of the word "provisions," and instructed Slade to take him to the kitchen and fill his basket. The man bowed to Lincoln as he left the room, all the while thanking God and the president for this new provision he was about to receive.[12]

Outside of the White House, Lincoln also showed kindness toward African Americans he encountered. In May 1862, he visited a Washington hospital where a white nurse introduced him to three black cooks who were preparing food for sick and wounded soldiers. At least one of the cooks was a former slave from Kentucky. Lincoln greeted them in "a kindly tone," recalled the nurse. "How do you do, Lucy?" he said to the first. The nurse then remarked that he stuck out his "long hand in recognition of the woman's services." Next Lincoln gave the two black men a "hearty grip" and asked them, "How do you do, Garner? how do you do, Brown?" The president left the room and the three black cooks stood there with "shining faces" that testified to their "amazement and joy for all time." But soon, sadly, the nurse noticed what the convalescing Union officers thought of this scene. They expressed a "feeling of intense disapprobation and disgust" and claimed that it was a "mean, contemptible trick" for her "to introduce those d— niggers to the President."[13] Fortunately, the president paid the soldiers' racist views no mind. He treated the black cooks the same way that he did the white soldiers at the hospital. He was grateful for their service to the nation, and he did not alter his behavior toward them simply because white soldiers were staring in disbelief.

Lincoln interacted with innumerable African Americans as he traversed the city of Washington during the war years. In April 1863, while driving around some of the encampments of black refugees with Mary Lincoln and journalist Noah Brooks, the president and his party happened upon a large number of shanties and small tents scattered over a hillside. "As if by magic," Brooks wrote, "the entire population of blacks and yellows swarmed out" to see the president. They shouted, "Hurrah for Massa Linkum!" with great excitement. Mrs. Lincoln smiled at the many children who crowded by their carriage and asked her husband how many of "those piccaninnies" might be named *Abraham Lincoln*. Lincoln joked, "Let's see; this is April, 1863. I should say that of all those babies, under two years of age, perhaps two thirds have been named for me."[14]

On a number of occasions, the Lincolns stopped at the Contraband Camp on Seventh Street, near present-day Howard University, when they traveled to and from their retreat at the Soldiers' Home. On Christmas Day, 1862, Mary Lincoln visited the camp, bringing with her forty-five turkeys, apples, cranberries and "other good things."[15] On one Saturday morning, President Lincoln and the First Lady went there, wanting to hear the ex-slaves sing. Upon their arrival, Uncle Ben, an illiterate slave preacher, opened the meeting with a prayer of blessing upon the president. When he finished, the contrabands stood up and sang, "My Country 'Tis of Thee." Lincoln took off his hat and joined in.

After this first song was complete, the commander of the camp called to Mary Dines, a refugee from Maryland, and asked her what pieces she and the other contrabands were prepared to sing. Mary's knees trembled as she "stumbled in front of the people" and began singing "Nobody Knows What Trouble I See, But Jesus." She later recalled that "the thought of singing before the President nearly killed" her. She sang the first verse by herself, constantly glancing over at Lincoln. Then the rest of the contrabands joined in. They sang for an hour, and Mary saw the president wipe tears away from his eyes. The singers seemed to forget that the president was there, and they "began to shout and yell, but he didn't laugh at them." Mary "believed that the Holy Ghost was working on him." The final piece they sang was "John Brown's Body," and Lincoln "joined in the chorus and sang as loud as anyone there." *Glory, Glory, Hallelujah! His soul goes marching on!* Mary thought the president had "a sweet voice, and it sounded so sad, when he tried to follow her with the first tune, he really choked up once or twice."

Lincoln returned to the contraband camp on another wet, dreary day, and said to the young runaway slave, "Well, Mary, what can the people sing for me today? I've been thinking about you all since I left here and am not feeling so well. I just want them to sing some more good old hymns for me again. Tell Uncle Ben to pray a good old-fashioned prayer." Uncle Ben offered a fervent appeal to God to "send down His loving kindness and blessings on the colored people's friend." The gathering then sang seven songs, with Lincoln joining in each one. Mary recalled that Lincoln "was so tenderhearted that he filled-up when he went over to bid the real old folks good-by[e]." Lincoln bowed his head during the closing prayer, and Mary said "he was no President when he came to camp. He just stood and sang and prayed just like all the rest of the people."[16]

Mary Dines's recollection depicted Lincoln as interacting with 'the least of these' in a humble and genuine manner. While her recollection was recorded many years after the Civil War, it aligns with contemporary reports of Lincoln's interactions with black men and women on the streets of Washington, DC. Another remarkable story comes from the pen of Lincoln's private secretary, William O. Stoddard, who kept a detailed record of his experiences in the White House. In one brief note, Stoddard described a chance encounter between the president and a black woman outside of the Executive Mansion in August 1862. Nothing is known of the woman, but she was likely an ex-slave who had fled to Washington during the war. While Stoddard's account features some condescending perceptions, it also captures the excitement of an ordinary black woman who met the commander in chief—and the humility of a president who treated all people with grace.

It was a sweltering summer morning in Washington, and the heat seemed to increase as one got nearer to the White House. The air was dense and humid, and the intense summer sun hit pedestrians "with peculiar power." Stoddard watched Lincoln as he walked back to the White House from the War Department. The president stopped just beyond one of the gates and took off his signature top hat to mop his forehead with a handkerchief. At that moment, a black woman approached the president. Stoddard described her as "an uncommonly black black woman! she is, and she stands right in his path, looking up into his face." She was extremely overweight. Wrote Stoddard: "She is not in a starved condition, by any means. She might weigh three hundred, and every pound of her is aware that she is looking into the face of the greatest man in the world." Lincoln smiled and laughed as he reached out his hand to her. In response, she laughed too, but she was speechless. "Perhaps she was never before sure that Abraham Lincoln was a reality, a human being—that is, apparently human," Stoddard surmised. "Her eyes roll wonderfully, and her smile is all over her face, and it takes elsewhere the semblance of an embodied chuckle; but all the words she ever knew have gone a wool-gathering." Lincoln said to her, "You look happy. Reckon you must be." She still could not speak. "Gurgle—chuckle—all over the big black woman, as her hand timidly meets his. Lincoln did "the shaking and lets go." She then turned to walk away "without an articulate syllable, and so almost bursting with pride and delight that she stuffs the corners of her check apron into her mouth."[17] Stoddard's bigoted account contrasts sharply with Lincoln's kind demeanor toward the woman. Watching from afar, the private secretary could not help but record the scene with a sense of condescension toward her. Lincoln, by contrast, treated her with dignity and respect—even offering a handshake, just as he would a foreign dignitary or congressman who came to meet with him in his office.

Lincoln's interactions with these poor men and women of color are touching reminders of his empathy and ability to connect with people who came from life circumstances quite different from his own. Since the mid-1850s, he had argued that even enslaved women deserved the rights contained in the Declaration of Independence. In "her natural right to eat the bread she earns with her own hands without asking leave of any one else, she is my equal, and the equal of all others," he had told a white audience in Springfield, Illinois, in 1857.[18] This was a remarkable statement for a white, male politician to make in the Midwest in the 1850s, for, by using a hypothetical black woman as his example, he was telling a racist, misogynist audience that *all people* had value and worth and were included in the sacred words of the Declaration. Now, in these private moments, he practiced what he had been preaching. He treated all comers as equals and connected with them on an emotional level in ways that no white person likely ever had. It is difficult to imagine many other presidents or politicians behaving in this way toward what Christ called "the least of these." Certainly no president before Lincoln had ever done so.

One final, touching moment took place on Lincoln's last full day alive, as the Civil War was coming to a dramatic close. The capture of Richmond in early April 1865 was greeted with "the wildest excitement" in Washington, DC. Throngs of people celebrated, formed impromptu parades, played music, sang, and danced in the streets. White and black revelers alike mingled in the jubilation. Journalist Lois Bryan Adams noted, "The streets were everywhere crowded with happy-looking black faces."[19] And yet there were still difficult times ahead for the newly freed. A story survives of a former slave from Richmond named Nancy Bushrod who escaped from slavery and settled around Washington, DC, during the Civil War. Nancy's husband, Tom, joined the Union Army, and she was left all alone to care for her twin boys and baby girl. At some point in late 1864 or early 1865 Tom stopped sending her money, and the family fell on hard times. Unfortunately, Nancy was unable to find work as a domestic because there had been such an influx of black women into the city over the previous three years. In a state of despair, she resolved on April 14, 1865, to visit the White House and see if President Lincoln could help her get her husband's pay. She had not eaten for two days and "was faint from her five-mile walk" by the time she reached the White House. But she was determined.

As Nancy approached the Executive Mansion, a guard at the gate gruffly asked her, "Business with the President?" She answered grimly, "Befo' Gawd, yes." One guard whispered to another, "Let her pass—they'll stop her farther on." Nancy took a deep breath and stepped onward. As expected, however, she was stopped again at the main entrance to the building. "No further, madam," a soldier told her. "Against orders." But Nancy would not be thwarted. According to one account, "In a flash she darted under his arm and went straight to the guard at the farther door."

When Nancy got to the next guard she implored, "Fo' Gawd's sake, please lemme see Mistah Linkun." The guard replied, "Madam, the President is busy; he can not see you." At this rebuff, Nancy's grief must have been apparent for all to see. She may have even let out a cry of despair. But then something amazing happened. As she later described it, "All of a sudden de do' open, an' Mistah Linkun hissef stood lookin' at me. I knowed him, fo' dar wuz a whimsy smile on his blessed face, an' he wuz a sayin', deep an' soft-like, 'There is time for all who need me. Let the good woman come in.'"

Lincoln listened to Nancy's story and then replied, "You are entitled to your soldier-husband's pay. Come this time to-morrow, and the papers will be signed and ready for you." She was in utter disbelief. As she turned to leave, he called her back. "My good woman," Lincoln added, "perhaps you'll see many a day when all the food in the house is a single loaf of bread. Even so, give every child a slice, and *send your children off to school*." With that, Lincoln gave her a bow and went back to a table piled high with papers. In this moment Nancy felt "like I wuz a natch-ral born lady." As she later told it, "Honey, I couldn't open my mouf to tell him how I'se gwine 'membah him fo'evah fer dem words, an' I couldn't see him kase de tears wuz fallin'." Although rain was soaking her body during her five-mile walk home, "Lincoln's kindness enveloped her like sunshine," states an early account of this story, "and the words, 'Send your children off to school,' crystallized into purpose."

Unfortunately, when Nancy returned to the White House on April 15, things had changed. Crowds blocked Pennsylvania Avenue so that she could not get near the entrance. A large policeman of Scottish descent, struggling to hold back tears, told her, "Ye dinna ken the President's deid? Woman, whaur ye livin'?" Nancy clung to a nearby lamppost and pledged, "Befo' Gawd I swear it, I'se gwine ter fin' wuk, I'se gwine ter make Mistah Linkun's words come true. I'se gwine ter sen' my chillun off ter school!" Over time, Nancy followed through on giving her children an education.

Upon hearing this story many years later, one white woman remarked that Lincoln "Always [had] time for all who needed him. That's why the common people stood by him loyally, even in his darkest days." Another agreed, "And on that very last day of his life, with a nation's problems weighing him down, he had time to help a poor colored woman."[20]

It is unclear whether the story of Nancy Bushrod is true. Searches of census and military service records at the National Archives, as well as slavery records at the Library of Virginia, have been unable to confirm her existence. It is quite possible that the story is apocryphal—either fabricated by white racial egalitarians who wished to portray Lincoln in a positive light, or concocted by paternalistic whites who wanted a useful morality tale for black citizens in the early twentieth century. But the story may be true. Lincoln met with ordinary men and women like Nancy Bushrod throughout the war years. In October 1864, Sojourner Truth had watched him interact with two black women who were in similarly dire situations, and he did what he could to provide a solution to their problems. Indeed, the story reflects the well-documented treatment that Lincoln gave to black visitors to the White House, whether male or female, during his time as president. Of equal importance, it accurately captures the admiration that many African Americans had for Lincoln during the last four years of his life.

INTERLUDE 6

Richmond

By the time the Civil War came to a close, African Americans had developed an extraordinary fondness for Father Abraham. When Lincoln visited Richmond on April 4, 1865, he was greeted by an enthusiastic crowd of former slaves shouting, "Hallelujah!" "Glory! Glory! Glory!" "Bress de Lord! Bress de Lord!" "Hurrah! Hurrah! President Linkum hab come!" "Thank you, dear Jesus, for this sight of the great conqueror," and "Thank you, Master Lincoln." Former slaves gathered around the president, singing, crying, and smiling. Some wore rags, some were barefoot, and others were clothed in pieces of old Union and Confederate uniforms. A black orderly with the Twenty-Ninth Connecticut Volunteers approached an ex-slave woman and told her, "Madam, there is the man that made you free." She replied, "Is that President Lincoln?" When he confirmed that it was, the woman clasped her hands and said, "Glory to God. Give Him the praise for his goodness" and "shouted till her voice failed her." Another older black woman who had just been released from a slave jail enthusiastically cried, "I know that I am free, for I have seen Father Abraham and felt him." When some in the exuberant crowd knelt before the president, he reportedly replied, "Don't kneel to me. That is not right. You must kneel to God only, and thank him for the liberty you will hereafter enjoy."[1]

Lincoln made his way through the crowd, walking uphill toward the Virginia statehouse. At one point when he became weary, he took a moment to sit and rest. An elderly black man dressed in little more than rags, and "with tears of joy rolling down his cheeks," approached him and took off his hat. "May de good Lord bress and keep you safe, Massa President Linkum," he said. In response, Lincoln removed his stovepipe hat and "bowed in silence." This act, wrote

Boston journalist Charles C. Coffin, "upset the forms, laws, customs, and ceremonies of centuries," for in this moment the president showed a solemn sign of respect to a former bondsman as no American president likely ever had done before. Indeed, the scene caused "unspeakable contempt" among Southern whites, observed Coffin, for they knew it was "a death-shock to chivalry, and a mortal wound to caste." As Coffin concluded, "Abraham Lincoln was walking their streets; and, worst of all, that plain, honest-hearted man was recognizing the 'niggers' as human beings by returning their salutations!"[2]

To the ex-slaves who saw him, Lincoln was like a messiah making a triumphal entry into their city. Coffin noted "their demonstrations of pleasure, the shouting, dancing, the thanksgiving to God, the mention of the name of Jesus—as if President Lincoln were next to the son of God in their affections." One black soldier later wrote, "I never saw so many colored people in all my life, women and children of all sizes running after Father, or Master Abraham, as they called him. To see the colored people, one would think they had all gone crazy." But perhaps most remarkable was the ease with which Lincoln mingled with the exuberant crowd. He "walked in silence" among Richmond's white and black residents, wrote one observer. "It was a man of the people among the people. It was a great deliverer among the delivered. No wonder tears came to his eyes when he looked on the poor colored people who were once slaves, and heard the blessings uttered from thankful hearts and thanksgiving to God and Jesus."[3]

Outside of the Virginia State Capitol—the site where the Confederate Congress had met—Lincoln addressed a large crowd that primarily consisted of former slaves. According to one report, he said,

> My poor friends, you are free—free as air. You can cast off the name of slave and trample upon it; it will come to you no more. Liberty is your birthright. God gave it to you as he gave it to others, and it is a sin that you have been deprived of it for so many years. But you must try to deserve this priceless boon. Let the world see that you merit it, and are able to maintain it by your good works. Don't let your joy carry you into excesses. Learn the laws and obey them; obey God's commandments and thank him for giving you liberty, for to him you owe all things. There, now, let me pass on; I have but little time to spare. I want to see the capital, and must return at once to Washington to secure to you that liberty which you seem to prize so highly.

A black witness to the scene heard, "Now you Colored people are free, as free as I am. God made you free and if those who are your superiors are not able to recognize that you are free, we will have to take the sword and musket and again teach them that you are free. You are as free as I am, having the same rights of liberty, life and the pursuit of happiness." The culmination of Lincoln's long effort was finally coming to fruition—the rights embodied in the Declaration of Independence would now be applied to all people, black as well as white. At the end of the day, as Lincoln boarded a vessel to depart, an older black woman shouted, "Don't drown, Massa Abe, for God's sake!"[4]

A few days later, when Lincoln and several guests toured Petersburg, several black waiters from the *River Queen* asked to go with the presidential party to see the fallen Confederate stronghold. The Marquis de Chambrun reported, "The President, who was blinded by no prejudices against race or color, and who had not what can be termed false dignity, allowed them to sit quietly with us." As in Richmond, former slaves flocked to the president as he walked around Petersburg. Elizabeth Keckly, who was present on the trip, also recorded a friendly conversation that Lincoln had with a local black boy who managed to enter the president's train car.[5]

On April 9, Robert E. Lee finally surrendered to Ulysses S. Grant at Appomattox Court House, Virginia, effectively sounding the death knell of the Confederacy. In the Deep South, newly freed slaves rejoiced enthusiastically upon learning this news, just as if Lincoln was there with them. In Charleston, South Carolina, a crowd of several thousand white and black Americans gathered at Zion's Church to hear speeches by several white abolitionists (including William Lloyd Garrison and Massachusetts Senator Henry Wilson), as well as Maj. Martin R. Delany of the 104th US Colored Troops. The crowd cheered the various speakers, but, according to one white attendee, "it remained for 'old Abe's' name to elicit the wildest and nois[i]est enthusiasm, every one sprung to their feet when our honored President was named as the 'great Emancipator' and hats and 'kerchiefs, swung to the wildest cheers!"[6]

"THE GREAT GUIDING HAND THAT NOW LAY PARALYZED IN DEATH"

Lincoln delivered his last public address on April 11, 1865. In it, he declared that he supported conferring the elective franchise on "the colored man" who was either "very intelligent" or to "those who serve our cause as soldiers." If a person shared in the responsibility of citizenship by fighting for the nation, then he deserved to exercise the privileges of citizenship as well.[1] Elizabeth Keckly watched this speech from inside the White House, just a few paces away from the president. She recalled that Lincoln's face was pale but that his "soul flash[ed] through his eyes." Standing there, she had an awful thought and whispered to a friend, "What an easy matter would it be to kill the President, as he stands there! He could be shot down from the crowd, and no one would be able to tell who fired the shot."[2] Keckly's fears would soon be realized. Standing below the White House portico that night, John Wilkes Booth angrily declared, "That means nigger citizenship. Now, by God! I'll put him through."[3] It is no understatement to say that Abraham Lincoln was killed for being the first president to publicly advocate for the expansion of citizenship rights to African Americans. Union General Winfield Scott Hancock captured this idea when he issued an "appeal to the colored people" of Washington, DC, on April 24, 1865, saying, "Your President has been murdered! He has fallen by the assassin, and without a moment's warning, simply and solely because he was your friend and the friend of our country. Had he been unfaithful to you and to the great cause of human freedom he might have lived."[4]

It is little wonder that black Americans felt the keenest sense of loss when Lincoln died only ten days after his triumphal entry in Richmond. Reflecting on this moment many years later, a black Union Army veteran wrote, "Our faith was almost staggered, that faith which had sustained us in so many battles, was now staggering under a blow which was severer than any battles, the death of our Immortal leader."[5] None captured this sorrow better than Secretary of the Navy Gideon Welles, who noted in his diary that he saw "several hundred colored people, mostly women and children, weeping and wailing their loss" on Pennsylvania Avenue outside of the White House on April 15. "This crowd did not appear to diminish through the whole of that cold, wet day," he continued, "they seemed not to know what was to be their fate since their great benefactor was dead, and their hopeless grief affected me more than almost anything else, though strong and brave men wept when I met them."[6] Journalist Jane Swisshelm observed, "Then the presence of the thousands of Freed-people who regarded Abraham Lincoln as their Moses, adds to the impressiveness of the scene. With tears and lamentations they lean their faces against the iron fence around the Presidential Mansion, and groan with a feeling akin to despair lest now, that their friend is gone, they shall be returned to their old masters. Old men and women lament, and pray, and ask in such a hopeless way what their fate is to be."[7]

Not far from the White House an anguished black woman wailed, "My good President! My good President! I would rather have died myself! I would rather have given the babe from my bosom! Oh, Jesus! Oh, Jesus!" Another wrung her hands and cried, "O, they have killed him—the best friend we ever had." Young black men pledged to exact revenge. "If the North would just leave *us* to finish this war!" declared one. "They have done enough, just let them leave the rebels to us!" Some African Americans in the Washington suburbs fasted from meals so that they could afford to purchase black crepe to hang from their doors and windows. One black woman sadly declared that she "would put black on her house if it took the last cent in her pocket." Jane Swisshelm reported that "it is touching to see, on every little negro hut in the suburbs, some respectful testimonial of sorrow." A Washington family that could not afford to purchase black cloth simply hung a black skirt over their door. Others hung any bits of wool or cotton they had. Upon seeing these meager decorations, Swisshelm asked, "Was ever [a] mortal so wept by the poor?"[8]

From his post at the L'Ouverture Hospital in Alexandria, Virginia, Rev. Chauncey Leonard—the former emigrationist who had met with Lincoln at the White House in November 1862—wrote, "As soldiers in the US service we mourn the loss of our Noble Chief Magistrate." Leonard captured the hope that Lincoln inspired in his black constituents—that a vast political improvement was on the horizon at the end of the Civil War. "We have looked to him as our earthly Pilot to guide us through this National storm, and plant us securely on the Platform of Liberty and Equal Political right," he wrote, "but God in his wise Providence has removed him. Brave men weep for him who is no more." Upon visiting the hospital, Julia Wilbur observed that the black soldiers convalescing there "all feel so deeply. They cannot express their feelings any more than we can. We all feel that we have lost; personally have lost a friend."[9] At the Freedmen's Village in Arlington, Sojourner Truth led a memorial service for the martyred president she had come to see as a friend.[10] In Baltimore, Bishop Daniel Payne announced Lincoln's death to the attendees at the forty-eighth annual conference of the African Methodist Episcopal (AME) Church. The delegates then adopted resolutions deploring the "cowardly assassination" of "the great and good Abraham Lincoln." Sadly, Payne's Wilberforce University in Ohio was burned to the ground by an arsonist that very same night.[11]

Flags outside the White House now flew at half-mast, weighted down with black crepe. "Spring has been trying to smile," wrote journalist Lois Bryan Adams, "but it seems like an effort without heart in it." The bright beauty of the season "seems only mockery beside all these mourning badges and drooping, crepe-wreathed banners." The White House became a place of grieving. So recently it had been a site of "gay and brilliant throngs of levees and reception days," but now a pall hung about it with "the gloom and loneliness of the sepulcher," Adams continued. "All the columns of the great portico are shrouded in black from the roof to the ground, and from end to end of the broad front are looped the emblems of mourning for its late beloved and honored occupant."[12]

William Slade had the sad and unenviable duty of preparing Lincoln's body for the upcoming funeral train and burial. Before departing for Springfield, Lincoln's corpse lay in the East Room where mourners came to pay their final respects. Any color barriers that may have existed in 1861 were completely torn down—at least for this brief period of mourning. It is what Lincoln would have wanted. One contemporary observer remarked that among the twenty-five thousand weeping people who shuffled past the open coffin, "Every class, race and condition of society was represented in the throng of mourners, and the sad tears and farewells of whites and blacks were mingled by the coffin of him to whom humanity was everywhere the same."[13] Congressman George W. Julian of Indiana wrote in his diary, "The negroes appeared finely in the procession, and the President's hold on them is wonderful, and indeed on the whole country, including even those who regarded his death as a providential means of saving the country. He was a plain man of the people, indeed *one* of them, and hence their devotion to him."[14] Julia Wilbur similarly noted, "Colored people were mixed all the way through & I heard nothing said that was out of place, all wore an air of seriousness, & no loud words were heard."[15] One such mourner was a black woman who noted that George Washington "went in for liberty," and she "love[d] him for it; but he didn't see things clear through 'em as Lincoln did. Lincoln didn't stop with white folks, but kept straight ahead and took us too."[16] Also among the mourners who filed past the open coffin was Anderson R. Abbott, the black Army surgeon who had visited the White House with Alexander T. Augusta in February 1864, and Richard H. Parker, the black minister from Norfolk who had come to ask for the right to vote. As Abbott stood there gazing upon "the pale, cold face of the President," he thought of "the loss to the negro race in their nascent life of freedom" and of "the great guiding hand that now lay paralyzed in death."[17]

While the bereaved gazed upon Lincoln's open casket in the East Room, Mary Lincoln sat upstairs, too overcome with grief to attend her husband's funeral. There, two African American women did their best to comfort her. "Mrs. Slade & Mrs. Keckley have been with Mrs. Lincoln nearly all the time since the murder, not as servants but as friends," wrote Julia Wilbur in her diary on April 20. "Both colored women; & Mrs. Lincoln said she chose them because her husband was appreciated by the colored race; they (the colored people) understood him."[18]

At Henry Highland Garnet's Fifteenth Street Presbyterian Church, Lincoln was eulogized as "emancipator, benefactor, friend and leader."[19] When his body was taken to the Capitol on April 19, the Twenty-Second US Colored Infantry led the procession (they had taken the lead position by accident and, due to the crowds, were unable to reposition themselves). These men had cheered for the president at City Point on June 21, 1864. Now they marched in his funeral. In a few short hours they would be on their way to Maryland in pursuit of John Wilkes Booth. An officer in the regiment wrote in his diary, "Our regt marched splendidly."[20]

Thousands of mourners lined the streets, and four thousand African Americans brought up the rear of the procession. Members of black fraternal organizations and various denominations marched together. Among them were people who had met with Lincoln at the White House, like Bishop Payne and Rev. Alexander W. Wayman, who chartered a train from Baltimore that morning.[21] "There were no truer mourners when all were sad, than the poor colored people who crowded the streets, joined the procession and exhibited their feelings and anxiety for the man whom they regarded as a benefactor and father," wrote Navy Secretary Welles in his diary. "Women, as well as men, with their little children thronged the streets, concernment and trouble and distress depicted on their countenances and in their bearing. The vacant holiday expression had given way to real grief."[22] Exactly four years earlier, Lincoln had traveled to the

Capitol building and shaken hands with Nicholas Biddle, the black man who had been badly wounded while passing through Baltimore. When his body left Washington on April 21 for the funeral train back to Illinois, two regiments of US Colored Troops were part of the escort to the depot. "They stood with arms reversed, heads bowed, all weeping like children at the loss of a father," wrote one observer.[23]

African Americans throughout the North openly expressed their agony when news arrived of Lincoln's untimely death. Many felt as though they had lost their best friend. "We, as a people, feel more than all others that we are bereaved. We had learned to love Mr. Lincoln," declared the pastor of the AME Church in Troy, New York. "We looked up to him as our saviour, our deliverer." When Lincoln's funeral train passed through Baltimore, African American crowds "were convulsed with a grief they could not control, and sobs, cries, and tears told how deeply they mourned their deliverer." Bishops Payne and Wayman led the "colored portion" of the funeral procession in the city. In Philadelphia, three hundred thousand people filed past Lincoln's body to pay their respects. The open coffin rested near the Liberty Bell at Independence Hall, where four years earlier he had said that he would rather be assassinated than to sacrifice the principles of the Declaration of Independence. A homemade wreath sat on a pedestal near the coffin. It had been presented by an elderly black woman, who told a guard that "it was all she had to give." The lines to see Lincoln's body were "liberally sprinkled" with black men and women. Emilie Davis, a free woman of color, tried for three consecutive days to see Lincoln's body. On April 22, she remarked that Lincoln's "was the gravits [gravest?] funneral i ever saw." The next day she tried twice to see his body, "but could not for the crowd." Finally, on April 24, she "got to see him after waiting" for several hours. It was, she said, "a sight worth seeing."[24]

In New York, the city council issued an order forbidding African Americans from participating in the funeral procession. Black minister J. Sella Martin was outraged, arguing that Lincoln had "lifted" black people "by the most solemn official acts to the dignity of citizens and defenders of the union." They therefore ought to be "allowed the honor of following his remains to the grave." Secretary of War Edwin M. Stanton fumed that "no discrimination respecting color should be exercised in admitting persons to the funeral procession." Some five thousand black people had planned to participate, but only about two hundred wound up marching in the procession. They carried banners saying, "Abraham Lincoln, our Emancipator" and "To Millions of Bondsmen He Liberty Gave." One black woman cried out, "He died for me! He was crucified for me! God bless him!" while another mourned, "We have lost our Moses."[25]

A few days later, the funeral train chugged its way to the Midwest. At Cleveland, Ohio, black Masons, Odd Fellows, and members of the Colored Equal Rights League all participated in a procession. The Odd Fellows carried a banner that stated, "We mourn for Abraham Lincoln, the True Friend of Liberty." At Indianapolis, Mattie Jackson, a former slave, went to see "his dear dead face," for, she wrote, "I could not feel convinced of his death until I gazed upon his remains, and heard the last roll of the muffled drum and the farewell boom of the cannon. I was then convinced that though we were left to the tender mercies of God, we were without a leader." Jackson was one of thousands of Indianans to see Lincoln's body. One estimate stated that 150 people walked past Lincoln's coffin to pay their respects every minute from 9 a.m. until night, including "black people and white, indiscriminately associated." A group of black Masons carried a copy of the Emancipation Proclamation as well as banners that said, "*Colored Men, always Loyal,*" "*Lincoln, Martyr of Liberty,*" "*He Lives in our Memories,*" and "*Slavery is Dead.*"[26] Lincoln, no doubt, would have been proud to see such intermingling of the races.

The final funeral took place in Lincoln's adopted hometown of Springfield. There, a local black minister, Henry Brown, who had done odd jobs for the Lincolns before the war, led Lincoln's horse, Old Bob, in the procession. Lincoln's old friend and barber, William de Fleurville, joined the other black men and women of Springfield at the rear. Nine years later, a beautiful tomb would be dedicated at Oak Ridge Cemetery for Lincoln. Veterans contributed $27,682 toward the erection of the monument, $8,000 of which came from black soldiers.[27]

Ex-slaves and black Union soldiers in the South had real reason to fear. In New Orleans, an ex-Confederate told a group of mourners, "You will soon be back with your masters under the lash, where you ought to be, damn you."[28] Some ex-slaves in Virginia worried that they would "have to be slaves again." A woman at Fort Monroe in Virginia lamented, "They killed our best friend." Similarly, a black soldier in Natchez, Mississippi, wrote in fear, "*Slavery is not dead,*" while another stationed in North Carolina believed that "trouble and destitution, as well as hatred and revenge, await our poor people in these Southern States" so that they will feel as though they were "under slavery's cruel power still."[29]

Former slaves throughout the South reacted "like children bereaved of an only and beloved parent" and left "*fatherless,*" wrote a *New-York Tribune* correspondent. Indeed, for many African Americans (as for many whites) it felt like losing a member of the family. "Let us go to our homes, and write upon the records of our family Bible the name of Abraham Lincoln," declared George W.

Le Vere, the black minister who had met with Lincoln in November 1863. "And leave it to be handed down to our children, and to their children's children." Some saw Lincoln as a Christ figure. "Lincoln died for we, Christ died for we, and me believe him de same mans," declared one freedman in Hilton Head, South Carolina.[30] Some thought he was omnipresent.[31] Others equated him with the nation. One grieving woman in Charleston wailed, "O Lord! O Lord! Massa Sam's dead! Massa Sam's dead! O Lord! Massa Sam's dead!" When asked who Massa Sam was, she replied, "Uncle Sam! . . . Mr. Lincum!" In that same city, black schoolgirls approached their teacher "weeping bitterly and begged to be taken out of their classes." Their teacher noted that former slaves in the city "express their sorrow and sense of loss in many cases, with sobs and loud lamentations!" Just as Welles had noticed in Washington, this observer in South Carolina wrote, "The colored people are frightened and apprehensive. They feel a personal loss, and fear the result of it to themselves!" According to another teacher for freedpeople in Charleston, a white man who had rejoiced at Lincoln's death "would have been torn in pieces by the colored people, if he hadn't been rescued by the guard."[32] In New Orleans, ten thousand black men and women marched through the streets, and for thirty days they wore mourning bands on their left arms.[33]

The white observers who recorded these scenes captured a moment that had never before occurred in American history—throngs of African American men, women, and children openly grieving the death of an American president. Never before had black people had a reason to grieve, for no other president had concerned himself with their plight in the ways that Lincoln had. Black Americans—in both the North and the South—had come to understand Lincoln to be *their* president, and some had come to see the White House as *their* people's house, too. In meeting with him and sending him letters, they had exercised *their* First Amendment right to petition the government for a redress of grievances. Thus, ex-slaves in Petersburg, Virginia, could resolve, "That in the death of our beloved President, Abraham Lincoln, we have lost a Patriot, a Statesman, and Philanthropist, whose loss we sincerely deplore and that he, in the natural goodness of his heart, proclaimed freedom to the slave, we trust in God, that his successor, President Andrew Johnson may also use his influence in according to us that equally sacred right—the elective franchise."[34] How disappointed these freedmen and women would become.

Despite the uncertainty that came with Lincoln's death, however, many African Americans felt a tremendous amount of hope for the future. One black sailor rejoiced at the advancement he saw in members of his race. "Surely in four years great changes have taken place," he wrote in May 1865. "From the President's proclamation of the 1st of January [1863] up to the present, our progress has been onward and upward." This soldier noted that John S. Rock of Boston had become the first African American admitted to the bar of the US Supreme Court, that Henry Highland Garnet had preached before Congress, and that Martin R. Delany had received a commission in the Union Army. "Four years ago, a colored man would not be allowed in the Capitol unless he had a dust-pan and broom in his hand. The idea of a colored lawyer speaking in the Supreme Court, would have been preposterous, or a colored minister preaching in those halls, entirely out of the question. A colored major in the regular Army would have been hooted at, as it would be placing him on too much of an equality." Then, reflecting upon the recently deceased Lincoln, this soldier concluded: "These, and various other great advantages, too numerous for comment, have been brought about by this glorious man."[35]

EPILOGUE

"Emphatically the Black Man's President"

In the immediate postwar period, most African Americans revered Lincoln as a savior for their race. In a eulogy delivered at the Cooper Union in New York City on June 1, 1865, Frederick Douglass declared that "no people or class of people in this country, have a better reason for lamenting the death of Abraham Lincoln, and for desiring to honor and perpetuate his memory, than have the colored people." To be sure, Lincoln had been "unsurpassed in his devotion, to the welfare of the white race," but when compared to his predecessors, Lincoln was "emphatically the black man's President: the first to show any respect for their rights as men" (this was a clear allusion to Chief Justice Taney's decision in *Dred Scott*, which stated that African Americans had "no rights which the white man was bound to respect"). Indeed, although Lincoln did not always act in the best interest of the "colored people," they nevertheless "fully believed in Abraham Lincoln" and "firmly trusted in him." This was not blind allegiance, Douglass maintained, but based on their understanding of the man and his mission. Indeed, this was like trust in God. Alluding to the Old Testament passage Job 13:15—in which the suffering Job says, "Though he slay me, yet will I trust in him"—Douglass stated, "Even though he sometimes smote them, and wounded them severely, yet they firmly trusted in him." In drawing this parallel between Lincoln and God, Lincoln became more than a Moses—he was a messiah.

"It was my privilege to know Abraham Lincoln and to know him well," Douglass told the enraptured crowd. Douglass recounted how he had met the president, and how Lincoln had always treated him as an equal. He recalled how, less than a year earlier, in August 1864, Lincoln had made the governor of Connecticut wait for "a full hour" because Lincoln "want[ed] to have a long talk with my friend Douglass." In conversation with black men and women, Douglass said, Lincoln spoke "without any thing like condecension [*sic*], and without in anywise reminding him of the unpopularity of his color." In this way, Lincoln was "the first American President, who thus rose above the prejudices of his times, and country." When Douglass and the other black men and women met to mourn Lincoln that evening in Manhattan, Douglass declared that "we speak here to night not merely as colored men, but as men among men, and as American citizens—having the same interest in the welfare[,] permanence and prosperity, of the country—that any other class of citizens may be supposed to have." Douglass hoped that the vote for black men would soon be on the horizon. And Lincoln had set the example. According to Douglass, Lincoln "came to look upon the Blackman as an American citizen."[1]

Sojourner Truth also recollected her meeting with Lincoln with great pride. At an Emancipation celebration in 1868 she told a large gathering in Battle Creek, Michigan, of her experience. A newspaper correspondent reported that "good old Sojourner Truth" was "now 92 years of age" (she was actually about seventy-one). In her speech, Truth gave an "exceedingly interesting" account of when she held the Bible from the Baltimore ministers and told Lincoln, "Mr. Lincoln, I think it is a great thing to have de Word of God up to de head of de nation." "Yes," replied Lincoln with a twinkle in his eye. "I think so too." She then went on to offer reasons why people should vote for Ulysses S. Grant in the upcoming presidential election.[2]

Black leaders hoped that Lincoln's public support for black suffrage at the end of his life would encourage other Republicans to follow his example. In a speech following the New Orleans Massacre of 1866, Paschal B. Randolph implored Republican leaders not to "desert us" to the violence of ex-Confederates. Randolph argued that if Republicans did not give black men the vote, "the enemy will triumph." He made similar arguments to those that had been made by the delegations of black Southern men who had met with Lincoln in 1864, asking, "Have you ever found a negro traitor?" The crowd responded enthusiastically, "No! No!" Randolph then continued, "The dead Lincoln, had he lived, would to-day give us the right of manhood." Then, to the sound of cheering, he sang out, "We are coming, Father Abraham, five hundred thousand more." Lincoln had pointed the way and now the Republican Party needed to fulfill his support of black political rights. Only with the ballot could black people protect themselves from illegal violence. "I am here to say," Randolph said, "stand by those millions of loyal hearts that stood by you when the Union flag was trailed in the dust."[3]

Black men and women throughout the country sought to commemorate Lincoln's life and legacy. Some did it privately. In Texas shortly after the war, a white teacher noted that even when poor black families were "wanting the bare necessities of life," they still found a few pennies to purchase a picture of Lincoln that they would hang on the walls of their cabins. When she asked one ex-slave why the picture was there, the answer came, "He freed us, and I like him, so I have it there."⁴ The artist Thomas Eakins captured this in a postwar painting in which an older black man teaches a young boy to dance, while a portrait of Abraham and Tad Lincoln hangs on the wall in the background.⁵ During an autumn visit to Lincoln's tomb in Springfield, Paschal B. Randolph wept tears that fell "like rain upon the sod" and knelt down to place "tear-wet flowers, at the shrine of the man whose pen had stricken the shackles from nearly five millions of people."⁶

Despite their widespread mourning, ex-slaves found much to celebrate in the immediate postwar period. On a day of fasting and humiliation in June 1865 in commemoration of Lincoln's death, Philadelphia diarist Sidney George Fisher met several groups of African Americans "on the road in gay attire and happy smiling faces." He was struck that they "regarded it as a holiday." He asked one of them, "Well, boys, where are you going?"

"Going to meeting Sir."

"But why do you go?"

"Cause this thanksgiving day sir."

"It is indeed. Well, what are you going to give thanks for."

"For our liberties sir," said both men, smiling.⁷

July 4, 1865, seemed to be the first national birthday for which African Americans had much to celebrate. In San Francisco, the "colored people were out in force and were loudly cheered, and seemed to feel a new era had dawned upon their long oppressed race."⁸ That same day, black women in Augusta, Georgia, carried a banner in a parade that read, "Abraham Lincoln the Father of Our Liberties and Savior of His Country." In Washington, a young black orator proclaimed this the "first Fourth of July of the colored people." In fact, thousands of African Americans gathered on the White House grounds that day for the first time "that the colored people have attempted any celebration of a national character." "The city . . . did not celebrate," wrote Lois Bryan Adams, "but its adopted citizens [meaning black refugees] did, and I was there to see it." Eloquent speakers discoursed. Celebrants wore patriotic badges and carried banners. A band played beautiful music, as girls and boys drank cold lemonade and played with red, white, and blue streamers. In front of the speaker's stand was a large portrait of Lincoln featuring the words, "With malice toward none, / With charity for all."[9]

If black Americans believed that the White House grounds would now always be open to them, and that they had found a friend and ally in Andrew Johnson—as they had in Lincoln—they would be sorely disappointed. At Lincoln's funeral in April 1865, one elderly black man wondered aloud, "Do you think Mr. Johnson will hold fast to what he [Lincoln] did, or will he forget us, and send us back to the hell we was in?"[10] How soon a tragic answer would come. In April 1865, Johnson had an interview at the White House with John Mercer Langston, and in June he treated a black delegation from Richmond in a cordial manner. But the new occupant of the White House very quickly proved an ungracious host for black visitors. When he reviewed Henry McNeal Turner's First US Colored Infantry outside of the White House in the autumn of 1865, he gave some remarks to the effect that only if black Americans became industrious, virtuous and intelligent, "perhaps the two races can live in this country together, but we need not try to . . . alter the laws of nature & of God." Standing in the crowd and listening with disgust, Julia Wilbur interpreted the president to mean, "if you will be submissive & work for us as formerly, & be very humble we will let you stay in this country, but you are niggers, an inferior race & you need not think you will ever be equal to the white race."[11]

In August 1865, the American Baptist Missionary Convention held its annual meeting at a church in Alexandria, Virginia. On the fifth day of the meeting the ministers decided to form a delegation to call upon the president—much as they had done with Lincoln two years earlier, on August 21, 1863. They wished to present Johnson "with an address relative to our rights" and to assure him "of our sympathy and prayers." Among the ministers were men who had been at the meeting with Lincoln—Leonard A. Grimes, Edmund Kelly, Sampson White, and William E. Walker. Also joining them was Chaplain Chauncey Leonard.

At 9 a.m. on Friday, August 25, fourteen delegates made their way into Washington while the rest of the ministers gathered at the convention to pray for them. What a difference from their earlier meeting with Lincoln. At first Johnson greeted them "cordially" and shook their hands, thanking them "for our interest manifested in him." But the meeting quickly soured. When one or two of the delegates pressed Johnson on matters related to racial equality before the law, the president accused them of building "an argument upon false premises" and of having an "overleaning northern proclivity." Johnson admitted that equality "was in the future, and how it was to be brought about was yet undecided." Taking ten steps backward, he surmised that the best way for black people to achieve equality might be found in colonization. Edmund Kelly concluded that

Johnson's "want of faith in the immutability and ultimate triumph of right over wrong prevents him from giving the colored people a fair chance in the race." Kelly and the other ministers prayed that Johnson would convert to Christianity so that his eyes might be opened to a better way. Of course, Kelly could not help comparing his two meetings with presidents. "In some respects, our interviews with the lamented Lincoln, and the second meeting with Mr. Johnson presented a comparison, and in others a contrast," he wrote a few days later. When they met with Lincoln, "we were introduced standing, and then all invited to seats by the President, who conversed freely, the good President leading off." Johnson, by contrast, was rude and defensive, and never offered them a seat.[12]

African Americans came to the White House for the New Year's reception on January 1, 1866, but they were not admitted until the end of the event. Johnson appears to have gone upstairs before they entered and therefore did not greet them.[13] When Frederick Douglass and several other black leaders met with Johnson on February 7, 1866, to discuss the right to vote, Johnson treated his black guests with rudeness and condescension. Unlike Lincoln, Johnson had no interest in enfranchising black men. After Douglass and the others departed, Johnson called them "those d—d sons of b—s" and said that Douglass was "just like any nigger" and "would sooner cut a white man's throat than not." This unfortunate experience caused Douglass to reflect on the kindness he had received from Lincoln during the war. A week later, on February 13, Douglass delivered a speech in Washington in which he reminded his audience of "the great privilege" he had "to know Abraham Lincoln; and to get near to him." Based on Douglass's "conversations with him," he "believed that had Mr. Lincoln been living to-day, he would have stood with those who stand foremost, and gone with those who go farthest, in the cause of equal and universal suffrage."[14] It was Douglass's personal interactions with Lincoln that gave him such confidence.

Johnson met with Paschal B. Randolph in July 1866, and left his black visitor with a favorable impression.[15] However, over time, African Americans came to believe that they were no longer welcome at the White House. To be sure, a black delegation from Philadelphia received a warmer reception from President Grant in 1872 than Douglass had received from Johnson. Johnson and Grant also both met with Sojourner Truth. But African Americans stopped attending social functions at the Executive Mansion, as they had done during the last fifteen months of the Lincoln presidency. One evening before a levee in 1869, a White House usher entered the second-floor library and asked First Lady Julia Dent Grant, "Madam, if any colored people call, are they to be admitted?" Mrs. Grant thought for a moment and then replied, "This is my reception day. Admit all who call." Reflecting on this moment more than two decades later, she wrote in her memoirs, "No colored people called, however, nor did they at any time during General Grant's two terms of office." Mrs. Grant figured that they did not come because they were "modest and not aggressive," but, in fact, the police had not permitted them to pass through the White House gates.[16] The precedents that had been set during Lincoln's time in office—meeting with African Americans to discuss political matters, and welcoming them at social functions—were quickly discontinued. In 1881, shortly before the inauguration of James A. Garfield, a black Baptist minister in South Carolina observed, "Many of our people are looking to the incoming administration for great things. While I am very favorably impressed with the good designs of the government, yet I don't think we ought to fix up ourselves to be knocking so much at the doors of the White House, but rather at the doors of the school house and church."[17]

By the early twentieth century, most Americans had forgotten about Lincoln's welcoming of black Americans at the Executive Mansion. White Southerners were outraged in 1901 when they read in the papers that Teddy Roosevelt invited Booker T. Washington to dine with him at the White House. "The people of the north and south are not ready for social equality with the negro," crowed the governor of South Carolina. Others castigated Roosevelt for his "unprecedented . . . mistake." Residents of Richmond, Virginia, ostentatiously hissed at his portrait, while the governor of Georgia proclaimed, "No self-respecting southern man can ally himself with the president after what has occurred." The *Baltimore Sun* blasted the president's actions under the headline: "The Black Man to be Put on Top of the White Man," implying that Roosevelt's gesture would degrade the entire white race, just as many whites had viewed Lincoln's hospitality toward African Americans during the Civil War. So loud was the condemnation from "down in Dixie," that the *Topeka Daily Herald* headlined its story, "The New Rebellion in the South."[18]

Despite the failures and disappointments of Reconstruction and the rise of Jim Crow, African Americans longed to honor the martyred president. When Lincoln's tomb was dedicated in Springfield, Illinois, in 1874, Bishop Alexander W. Wayman offered a prayer of thanksgiving "for the privilege we enjoy of assembling at this place at this time, to show . . . our appreciation of one that once occupied a conspicuous position in our world, but has passed away to the spirit world."[19] Black veterans in Missouri pooled their money to establish a school for African Americans in Jefferson City called Lincoln Institute (now Lincoln University), while Paschal B. Randolph helped found the Lincoln Memorial High Grade and Normal School for the training of black teachers in New Orleans. Near Charleston, South Carolina, Richard H. Cain helped establish the black community of Lincolnville. Meanwhile, African Methodist Episcopal congregants in Raleigh, North Carolina, attended Lincoln Church. Some believed that Lincoln's birthday should be made a national holiday. In 1866, a veteran of the Twenty-Fourth US Colored Troops wrote to President Johnson and Secretary of War Edwin Stanton asking permission for black veterans in Delaware "to turn under armes on the 12th of Februeary to Silabrat of our Well belovid Mr Aberham Lincoln birth day."[20]

Others wanted permanent, public displays of their affection. On April 20, 1865, Maj. Martin R. Delany urged in a public letter that each black American contribute at least one cent to build a national monument "to the memory of President Lincoln, the Father of American Liberty." Such an act, Delany said, would be "a just and appropriate tribute of respect and lasting gratitude from the colored people of the United States." And at such a low cost, every black person could contribute, with "parents paying for every child." Five days later, the National Lincoln Monument Association was organized in Washington, DC. Among its officers were at least ten men who had met with Abraham Lincoln during the war—Bishop Daniel A. Payne, who met with Lincoln in April 1862; John F. Cook Jr., a member of the black delegation of August 1862; Robert Smalls, the South Carolinian who escaped slavery and met with Lincoln in August 1862; Leonard A. Grimes and Alfred Boulden, two of the black Baptist ministers who met with Lincoln in August 1863; Abraham H. Galloway, the fugitive slave from North Carolina who asked for the vote in April 1864; Alexander W. Wayman and Samuel W. Chase, two of the black ministers who gave Lincoln the Bible in September 1864; and Frederick Douglass and Martin Delany. On July 4, 1865, the Monument Association held a large celebration in Washington, DC, where local churches carried banners. The Fifteenth Street Presbyterian Church's banner had been painted by David B. Bowser, the black artist who had met with Lincoln in October 1863. It featured a portrait of Lincoln and the words, "With malice toward none, / With charity for all."[21]

Ironically, a monument to Lincoln from the black community came not from these leaders, but from a former Virginia slave who was now living in Marietta, Ohio. Charlotte Scott was struck down with grief when she learned of Lincoln's assassination in April 1865. She immediately handed five dollars to her former enslaver, telling him, "The colored people have lost their best friend on earth. Mr. Lincoln was our best friend and I will give five dollars of my wages toward erecting a monument to his memory." Word of her remarkable gesture made it into the newspapers, and soon other African Americans made similar contributions. Together, they raised roughly $20,000 for the project.[22]

By the time Mrs. Scott's statue was dedicated in Washington, DC, in 1876, much of the hope of the early postwar period had dissipated. Reconstruction had been an utter disappointment for freedpeople, whose rights had been continually and violently abridged by whites who acted in both private capacities and as government officials. The American people, it seemed, needed a reminder of the importance and relevance of Lincoln's legacy.

April 14, 1876—the eleventh anniversary of Lincoln's assassination—was set for the unveiling of the Freedmen's Memorial in Lincoln Park. Serving on the committee of arrangements were a number of prominent black leaders, including Frederick Douglass, John Mercer Langston, John F. Cook, Blanche K. Bruce, Henry McNeal Turner, and Pinckney Pinchback. Sitting in the audience were members of Congress and the Supreme Court, President Ulysses S. Grant and his Cabinet, and Charlotte Scott. The president would pull the cord to unveil the statue.

Members of twenty black civic organizations from Baltimore and Washington paraded for nearly two hours through the streets of Washington prior to the unveiling. At the ceremony, a young black woman named Henrietta Cordelia Ray read a poem she had written titled "Lincoln," that offered the statue as "a loving tribute" to the "Emancipator, hero, martyr, friend!" And though it had been eleven years since the tragic night at Ford's Theatre, she wrote, "We see thee still, responsive to our gaze, / As ever to thy country's solemn needs." In the following weeks, the *People's Advocate*, a newly established black newspaper in Alexandria, offered new subscribers a photograph of the Lincoln statue, which it called "a work of art . . . unsurpassed for beauty and grandeur."[23]

In his dedicatory speech, Frederick Douglass reminded the audience of why they were there that day—"to express, as best we may, by appropriate forms and ceremonies, our grateful sense of the vast, high, and preeminent services rendered to ourselves, to our race, to our country, and to the whole world by Abraham Lincoln." But, Douglass continued, Lincoln "was not, in the fullest sense of the word, either our man or our model. In his interests, in his associations, in his habits of thought, and in his prejudices, he was a white man." In fact, rather than see Lincoln as *emphatically the black man's president*, Douglass said, "He was preeminently the white man's President, entirely devoted to the welfare of white men." Lincoln was not a radical abolitionist, but merely an opponent to the extension of slavery. He was slow to bring freedom to the slaves, instead prioritizing the restoration of the Union. He even had pledged in his first inaugural address to enforce the Fugitive Slave Act of 1850. "You are the children of Abraham Lincoln," Douglass told the white members of his audience. "We are at best only his stepchildren; children by adoption, children by force of circumstances and necessity."

Throughout the war Lincoln's actions had often sorely disappointed black men and women. Douglass alluded to Lincoln's infamous colonization meeting with the black delegation in August 1862, reminding his audience of "when he strangely told us that we were the cause of the war," and "when he still more strangely told us that we were to leave the land in which we were born." Yet, Douglass declared, "Our faith in him was often taxed and strained to the uttermost, but it never failed." He continued:

> I have said that President Lincoln was a white man, and shared the prejudices common to his countrymen towards the colored race. Looking back to his times and to the condition of his country, we are compelled to admit that this unfriendly feeling on his part may be safely set down as one element of his wonderful success in organizing the loyal American people for the tremendous conflict before them, and bringing them safely through that conflict. His great mission was to accomplish two things: first, to save his country from dismemberment and ruin; and, second, to free his country from the great crime of slavery. To do one or the other, or both, he must have the earnest sympathy and the powerful cooperation of his loyal fellow-countrymen. Without this primary and essential condition to success his efforts must have been vain and utterly fruitless. Had he put the abolition of slavery before the salvation of the Union, he would have inevitably driven from him a powerful class of the American people and rendered resistance to rebellion impossible. Viewed from the genuine abolition ground, Mr. Lincoln seemed tardy, cold, dull, and indifferent; but measuring him by the sentiment of his country, a sentiment he was bound as a statesman to consult, he was swift, zealous, radical, and determined.

Here was a reasoned assessment of Lincoln's statesmanship—one that recognized the political realities Lincoln faced as commander in chief during the Civil War. Lincoln had longed to push the nation forward toward universal freedom, but he could not do so until he had convinced the American people of the rightness of his cause. In the end, Douglass could not help but recognize the monumental nature of Lincoln's accomplishments. In the face of opposition from all sides, Lincoln had persevered. He was limited in the options he could take; yet he found a way to free the slaves. Douglass, in short, was publicly acknowledging that Lincoln had been right in his approach, and that he (Douglass) had been unfair in his wartime criticisms. Thus, Douglass concluded, "infinite wisdom has seldom sent any man into the world better fitted for his mission than Abraham Lincoln."[24]

Over the ensuing decades, the statue in Lincoln Park became a site of black political activism in the District of Columbia. Almost every April between 1876 and 1900, black Washingtonians marched past the statue, or held meetings and celebrations there, in honor of Emancipation Day in the District. On some occasions they took their parade routes miles out of the way just to pay homage to what the *Washington Bee* called "the Charlotte Scott Emancipation statue in Lincoln Park." (In the 1990s the statue became the focal point of another black woman's attempt to make April 16 a holiday in the District of Columbia—something finally accomplished in 2005.)[25]

By the late nineteenth century, Charlotte Scott had become an important symbol of black freedom and activism. When she died in 1891, the Washington *Evening Star* opined that her "name, at one time, was doubtless upon the lips of every man and woman in the United States and is now read by the thousands who annually visit the Lincoln statue at Lincoln Park."[26] In an Emancipation Day speech in Marietta, Ohio, in 1893, Governor William McKinley recommended erecting a monument to her memory. The future president pledged "a handsome subscription" toward the cause.[27] But a monument to her was not needed—for she already had one. The *Washington Bee* observed that "the letters on the Charlotte Scott, Lincoln Emancipation statue on Capitol hill" were "indelibly carved in the hearts of the people." Indeed, on Lincoln's birthday in 1914, Mrs. Helen A. Davis, a prominent woman of color in Washington, declared at a meeting of the Dunbar Literary Society: "Charlotte Scott needs no monument erected to her memory; his monument is hers; she has been given full honor, as will be seen in the inscription on the monument."[28]

Although Charlotte Scott never met the sixteenth president, her legacy became intertwined with his. Like many—if not most—African Americans who lived through the Civil War, she felt like she had lost a personal friend when John Wilkes Booth committed his terrible deed at Ford's Theatre in April 1865. For decades after her death, her "friendship" with Lincoln would live on in the hearts of those who remembered her selfless five-dollar gesture. In many ways, she came to personify the relationship that had developed between Abraham Lincoln and African Americans during the war.

In 1945, a young African American boy named Henry Burke attended an Emancipation Day celebration in his hometown of Marietta, Ohio. It was a beautiful autumn day at the Washington County Fairgrounds, and he was one of only a few children who were allowed to skip school for the occasion. Only five years old, Burke could not "really grasp the importance of the event," he wrote many years later, "but one thin memory" stayed with him for the rest of his life. As he stood there among the large assembly, Burke saw a tall, well-dressed man stand up to give a speech. For the next few minutes this "very black" gentleman talked about Charlotte Scott. "Now, I would be stretching it if I told you I can remember every word of his speech," Burke recollected in 2011, "but I can recall these words: 'Lincoln's friend.'" Over the course of his long life, Burke came to imagine Charlotte Scott as Lincoln's "very special friend." In a way, she was, even though they never met on earth. And for Burke, the Freedmen's Memorial in Washington, DC, was "a monument to that friendship."[29]

APPENDIX

Unconfirmed Meetings

A misreading of Benjamin Quarles's classic book *The Negro in the Civil War* (1953) has led some historians to erroneously conclude that J. Sella Martin, William C. Nell, Robert Morris, and William Wells Brown visited Lincoln. A myth has also arisen that Lincoln's friend and barber William de Fleurville visited the White House, with some scholars stating that he made several visits to see his old friend in Washington, DC. This myth is based on a misreading of a touching letter that Fleurville sent to Lincoln in 1863.[1]

An unpublished biography of Henry McNeal Turner claims that Lincoln called Turner to the White House after the minister wrote to him. To date, the editors of the Papers of Abraham Lincoln project have not located any correspondence between the two men. The biography contains a 266-word statement of what Turner allegedly said at the meeting, including that "Frederick Douglass and myself were the first to call on you, and ask that the black man have the chance to fight for his country and freedom." The language attributed to Turner does not align with what we know of Lincoln's other meetings with African Americans. Moreover, Douglass did not meet with Lincoln until August 1863, so he could not have personally urged Lincoln to arm black soldiers.[2]

Curiously, another mythical meeting involving Frederick Douglass has also gained some currency. Pinckney Benton Stewart Pinchback had been recruiting black soldiers in Louisiana since 1862, but he was frustrated that he could not receive a commission to lead them. In September 1863, he resigned from the Army, telling Union General Nathaniel P. Banks that "nearly all" of the white officers in his regiment were "Inimical to me, and I can foresee nothing but dissatisfaction and discontent which will make my position verry disagreable

Indeed." In the spring of 1865, Pinchback decided to travel to Washington to seek a redress of his grievances from the president. Sadly, John Wilkes Booth reached Lincoln first, rendering Pinchback's trip "useless."

Over time, Pinchback's story evolved. In the myth that developed, he participated in a heated meeting with Lincoln and Frederick Douglass. Pinchback's biographer writes, "Figures like P. B. S. Pinchback inspire legends, and one of them is that Pinchback did indeed visit Abraham Lincoln, in the company of none other than Frederick Douglass." According to the story, the two black men "expressed dissatisfaction" that the Emancipation Proclamation only freed slaves in areas under Confederate control. Lincoln turned to Douglass and said, "Mr. Douglass, for the sake of your people, I wish you and I could sit in this chair [the presidency] together." In response, a visibly irritated Pinchback retorted, "Excuse me, Mr. President, I've got to go vomit." (According to the tale, Douglass and Pinchback had gotten drunk together the night before.) Pinchback's biographer points out that "such undocumented legends depict Pinchback as a scoundrel," adding, "It is likely that Pinchback never did see Lincoln."[3] In fact, the story is a complete fabrication. Douglass proudly described his three visits with Lincoln, and he never recounted anything like this in any of his speeches or autobiographical writings. Moreover, by the spring of 1865, no African American would have been complaining about the reach of the Emancipation Proclamation, as the Thirteenth Amendment had passed through Congress in January of that year.

Historian Michael Burlingame plausibly speculates that Lincoln may have met with Henry Highland Garnet in 1861.[4] To date no concrete evidence for such a meeting has been located.

NOTES

PREFACE

1. At the time of this writing (June 2021) the San Francisco School Board has delayed any action on the renaming plan.

2. Scott A. Sandage and Jonathan W. White, "What Frederick Douglass Had to Say About Monuments," *Smithsonian Magazine* (June 30, 2020).

3. Philip S. Foner and Yuval Taylor, eds., *Frederick Douglass: Selected Speeches and Writings* (Chicago: Lawrence Hill Books, 1999), 624 (hereafter *Douglass Speeches*).

4. "Opinion of W. E. B. Du Bois," *Crisis* 24 (July 1922): 103; Lerone Bennett Jr., "Was Abe Lincoln a White Supremacist," *Ebony* 23 (February 1968): 35–38, 40, 42.

5. Matt Maguire, "The Debate over Abraham Lincoln and Self-Emancipation in American Hip-Hop," *The Lincoln Forum Bulletin* 46 (Fall 2019): 4–5.

6. Nikole Hannah-Jones, "Our Democracy's Founding Ideals were False When They Were Written. Black Americans have Fought to Make Them True," *New York Times Magazine* (August 14, 2019).

7. Harold Holzer, *Emancipating Lincoln: The Proclamation in Text, Context, and Memory* (Cambridge, MA: Harvard University Press, 2012), 81; Michael Burlingame, *Abraham Lincoln: A Life*, 2 vols. (Baltimore: Johns Hopkins University Press, 2008, 2:471 (hereafter *AL-AL*); Benjamin Quarles, *Lincoln and the Negro* (New York: Oxford University Press, 1962), 151 (hereafter *LATN*).

8. James M. McPherson, *The Negro's Civil War: How American Negroes Felt and Acted During the War for the Union* (New York: Pantheon, 1965), 50 (hereafter *Negro's Civil War*).

9. James B. Conroy, *Lincoln's White House: The People's House in Wartime* (Lanham, MD: Rowman & Littlefield, 2016), 40, 153, 180, 200, 229–30 (hereafter *Lincoln's*

White House); John E. Washington, *They Knew Lincoln* (New York: E. P. Dutton, 1942), 105, 108–9, 124 (hereafter *They Knew Lincoln*); Julia Taft Bayne, *Tad Lincoln's Father* (Boston: Little, Brown and Co., 1931), 78–79; Jean Lee Cole, ed., *Freedom's Witness: The Civil War Correspondence of Henry McNeal Turner* (Morgantown: University of West Virginia Press, 2013), 74, 83–84, 88–93 (hereafter *Freedom's Witness*). Following Willie's death in 1862, Tad played with William Slade's children at the Slade home on Massachusetts Avenue.

10. New York *Anglo-African*, October 10, 1863 (hereafter *NYAA*); Boston *Traveler*, January 14, 1865; Julia Wilbur Diary, Haverford College, Quaker and Special Collections (transcriptions by Alexandria Archaeology), January 2, 1865 (hereafter Wilbur Diary).

11. Michael Burlingame, ed., *Inside the White House in War Times: Memoirs and Reports of Lincoln's Secretary, William O. Stoddard* (Lincoln: University of Nebraska Press, 2000), 172–73 (hereafter *Stoddard*).

12. John David Smith, *Lincoln and the US Colored Troops* (Carbondale: Southern Illinois University Press, 2013), 92–93.

13. *New York Daily Herald*, March 29, 1865.

14. Some also entered the building just to look around. For an account that was likely written by William J. Wilson, see *NYAA*, September 26, 1863.

15. *Dred Scott v. Sandford*, 60 US 393 at 407 (1857).

16. Michael Burlingame, "African Americans at White House Receptions during Lincoln's Administration," *Journal of the Abraham Lincoln Association* 41 (Summer 2020): 61 (hereafter "Receptions").

17. Millersburg (OH) *Holmes County Farmer*, March 26, 1863.

18. Bloomsburg (PA) *Star of the North*, December 21, 1864.

19. *Lincoln's White House*, 200.

20. "Receptions," 63.

21. Joseph George Jr., "Philadelphians Greet Their President-Elect—1861," *Pennsylvania History* 29 (October 1962): 387–88; *AL-AL*, 2:23.

22. *NYAA*, November 5, 1864.

23. James Oliver Horton and Lois E. Horton, *In Hope of Liberty: Culture, Community, and Protest Among Northern Free Blacks, 1700–1860* (New York: Oxford University Press, 1997), 62, 221; David W. Blight, *Race and Reunion: The Civil War in American Memory* (Cambridge, MA: Harvard University Press, 2001), 126.

24. See, for example, Matilda Carter, WPA (Works Progress Administration) interview, January 4, 1937. Carter was a refugee in Hampton, Virginia, and may have seen Lincoln when he visited the area in 1862 or 1865.

25. Elizabeth Keckley, *Behind the Scenes; Or, Thirty Years a Slave, and Four Years in the White House* (New York: G. W. Carleton, 1868), 153–55, 158, 203, 364–68 (hereafter *Behind the Scenes*).

26. Philip S. Foner, *The Life and Writings of Frederick Douglass*, 5 vols. (New York: International Publishers, 1952), 4:174; *LATN*, 247; *They Knew Lincoln*, 105–17;

Natalie Sweet, "A Representative 'of Our People': The Agency of William Slade, Leader in the African American Community and Usher to Abraham Lincoln," *Journal of the Abraham Lincoln Association* 34 (Summer 2013): 21–41; *Canonsburg* (PA) *Weekly Notes*, March 5, 1891; *Freedom's Witness*, 66, 108.

27. James Weldon Johnson, "Fifty Years," in Alice Moore Dunbar-Nelson, ed., *The Dunbar Speaker and Entertainer* (Naperville, IL: J. L. Nichols, 1920), 270.

28. James Oliver Horton and Lois E. Horton, *The Man and the Martyr: Abraham Lincoln in African American History and Memory* (Gettysburg, PA: Gettysburg College, 2006), 25 (hereafter *Man and Martyr*).

29. Kate Masur, *An Example for All the Land: Emancipation and the Struggle over Equality in Washington, DC* (Chapel Hill: University of North Carolina Press, 2010), 104–5; Kate Masur, "Color Was a Bar to the Entrance: African American Activism and the Question of Social Equality in Lincoln's White House," *American Quarterly* 69 (March 2017): 1–22 (hereafter "Color Was a Bar").

30. Washington, DC, *Evening Star*, June 10, 1863 (hereafter *ES*).

31. Quoted in Michael Burlingame, "President Lincoln's Meetings with African Americans," *Journal of the Abraham Lincoln Association* 41 (Winter 2021): 40 (hereafter "Meetings").

32. *AL-AL*, 2:830.

33. "Transcript: Read Michelle Obama's full speech from the 2016 DNC," WashingtonPost.com (July 26, 2016).

34. Clarence Lusane, *The Black History of the White House* (San Francisco: City Lights Books, 2011), 103–30; Seale, *President's House*, 1:5, 38, 50–68, 99–102, 121–22, 134–35, 177, 181, 194, 212, 257–58, 282, 315.

35. William Dusinberre, *Slavemaster President: The Double Career of James Polk* (New York: Oxford University Press, 2003), 11–21.

36. Seale, *President's House*, 1:337.

37. David McCullough, *John Adams* (New York: Simon & Schuster, 2001), 519.

38. James B. Conroy, *Jefferson's White House: Monticello on the Potomac* (Lanham, MD: Rowman & Littlefield, 2019), 50.

39. John Stauffer, *Giants: The Parallel Lives of Frederick Douglass and Abraham Lincoln* (New York: Twelve, 2008), 289.

40. Seale, *President's House*, 1:179, 2:653.

41. Daniel Alexander Payne, *Recollections of Seventy Years* (Nashville: A.M.E. Sunday School Union, 1888), 148.

42. Lusane, *Black History*, 154–56, 163–65; William J. Simmons, *Men of Mark: Eminent, Progressive and Rising* (Cleveland: Geo. M. Rewell, 1887), 794–97 (hereafter *Men of Mark*).

43. *Pittsburgh Post*, January 10, 1861.

44. *Nashville Union and American*, February 28, 1861.

CHAPTER 1

1. Roy P. Basler et al., eds., *The Collected Works of Abraham Lincoln*, 9 vols. (New Brunswick, NJ: Rutgers University Press, 1953–1955), 1:260 (hereafter *CWL*).

2. Allen C. Guelzo, *Abraham Lincoln: Redeemer President* (Grand Rapids, MI: William B. Eerdmans, 1999), 127.

3. *CWL*, 1:228–29.

4. *CWL*, 2:320.

5. Online edition of *AL-AL*, Knox College Lincoln Studies Center website, chap. 1, n49.

6. Burlingame, *Inner World*, 21–22; Thomas B. Searight, *The Old Pike: A History of the National Road, with Incidents, Accidents, and Anecdotes Thereon* (Uniontown, PA: T. B. Searight, 1894), 109.

7. *CWL*, 4:61.

8. *LATN*, 17.

9. Louis A. Warren, *Lincoln's Youth: Indiana Years, 1816–1830* (Indianapolis: Indiana Historical Society, 1991), 173–86; Ralph Clayton, *Cash for Blood: The Baltimore to New Orleans Domestic Slave Trade* (Bowie, MD: Heritage Books, 2002), 644–45; Don E. Fehrenbacher and Virginia Fehrenbacher, eds., *Recollected Words of Abraham Lincoln* (Sanford: Stanford University Press, 1996), 131 (hereafter *Recollected Words*).

10. *Recollected Words*, 457.

11. William H. Herndon and Jesse W. Weik, *Herndon's Lincoln*, eds. Douglas L. Wilson and Rodney O. Davis (Urbana: University of Illinois Press, 2006), 60; Isaac N. Arnold, *The Life of Abraham Lincoln* (Chicago: Jansen, McClurg, & Co., 1884), 31.

12. *CWL*, 4:63–64; Herndon and Weik, *Herndon's Lincoln*, 424; Douglas L. Wilson and Rodney O. Davis, eds., *Herndon's Informants: Letters, Interviews, and Statements about Abraham Lincoln* (Urbana: University of Illinois Press, 1998), 615. Other spurious testimony about Lincoln's time in New Orleans also survives. See Lincoln to Alexander H. Stephens, January 19, 1860, Gilbert A. Tracy, ed., *Uncollected Letters of Abraham Lincoln* (Boston: Houghton Mifflin, 1917), 128; *CWL*, 8:460.

13. Arnold, *Life of Lincoln*, 31.

14. *Recollected Words*, 61; Burlingame, *Inner World*, 22–23.

15. Illinois const., art. 6, sec. 1 (1818); Richard E. Hart, "Springfield's African Americans as Part of the Lincoln Community," *Journal of the Abraham Lincoln Association* 20 (Winter 1999): 35–54.

16. Allen C. Guelzo, *Lincoln and Douglas: The Debates that Defined America* (New York: Simon and Schuster, 2008), 10–11, 83; Mark E. Neely Jr., *Lincoln and the Triumph of the Nation: Constitutional Conflict in the American Civil War* (Chapel Hill: University of North Carolina Press, 2011), 113–18; *An Act to prevent immigration of free negroes into this state*, act of February 12, 1853, in *General Laws of the State of Illinois, Passed by the Eighteenth General Assembly, Convened January 3, 1853* (Springfield: Lanphier & Walker, 1853), 57–60.

17. Carl Adams, "Lincoln's First Freed Slave: A Review of *Bailey v. Cromwell*, 1841," *Journal of the Illinois State Historical Society* 101 (Fall-Winter 2008): 235–59.

18. Wilson and Davis, *Herndon's Informants*, 379–80; Charles M. Segal, "Lincoln, Benjamin Jonas and the Black Code," *Journal of the Illinois State Historical Society* 46 (Autumn 1953): 277–82.

19. Charles R. McKirdy, *Apostate Lincoln: The Matson Slave Case* (Jackson: University of Mississippi Press, 2011); Roger D. Billings Jr., "Abraham Lincoln and the Duty of Zealous Representation: The Matson Slave Case," *Connecticut Public Interest Law Journal* 14 (Spring-Summer 2015): 179–206; Guy C. Fraker, *Lincoln's Ladder to the Presidency: The Eighth Judicial Circuit* (Carbondale: Southern Illinois University Press, 2012), 49–53; *AL-AL*, 1:252.

20. *AL-AL*, 1:256; Hart, "Springfield's African Americans," 44; Lowell H. Harrison, *Lincoln of Kentucky* (Lexington: University Press of Kentucky, 2000), 82; William H. Townsend, *Lincoln and the Bluegrass: Slavery and Civil War in Kentucky* (University of Kentucky Press, 1955), 73.

21. Hart, "Springfield's African Americans," 46–47; *They Knew Lincoln*, 190–93; *CWL*, 2:159 and 3:518; Brian Dirck, *Lincoln the Lawyer* (Urbana: University of Illinois Press, 2007), 149, 207; *LATN*, 26.

22. *CWL*, 1:74–76, 4:65; *AL-AL*, 1:122–23, 141–42.

23. *AL-AL*, 1:124, 154–55, 160, 232; *LATN*, 39–40, 204.

24. Chris DeRose, *Congressman Lincoln: The Making of America's Greatest President* (New York: Threshold, 2013), 79–82, 110–15; Solomon Northup, *Twelve Years A Slave* (New York: Miller, Orton, & Mulligan, 1855), 41–43; *Journal of the House of Representatives of the United States*, 30th Cong., 1st sess., pp. 250–52; *AL-AL*, 1:259, 286; *CWL*, 2:253; Jeff Forret, *Williams' Gang: A Notorious Slave Trader and His Cargo of Black Convicts* (New York: Cambridge University Press, 2020), 249–52.

25. Carol Wilson, *Freedom at Risk: The Kidnapping of Free Blacks in America, 1790–1865* (Lexington: University Press of Kentucky, 1994); Richard Bell, *Stolen: Five Free Boys Kidnapped into Slavery and Their Astonishing Odyssey Home* (New York: Simon & Schuster, 2019).

26. Don E. Fehrenbacher, *The Slaveholding Republic: An Account of the United States Government's Relations to Slavery* (New York: Oxford University Press, 2001), 51–52, 67, 82.

27. John G. Nicolay and John Hay, *Abraham Lincoln: A History*, 10 vols. (New York: Century, 1890), 1:286–87.

28. Lincoln, "A bill for an act to abolish slavery in the District of Columbia, by the consent of the free white people of said District, and with compensation to owners," January 10, 1849, and James Q. Howard, "Biographical Notes" (May 1860), Abraham Lincoln Papers, Manuscript Division, Library of Congress (hereafter Lincoln Papers); *Congressional Globe*, 30th Cong., 2nd sess., p. 212; *CWL*, 2:20–22; DeRose, *Congressman Lincoln*, 226–27.

29. *AL-AL*, 1:292; *Congressional Globe*, 37th Cong. 2nd sess., pp. 1518–19.

30. *CWL*, 3:145–46; Guelzo, *Lincoln and Douglas*, xxv, 191–200.

31. Matthew Norman, "The Other Lincoln-Douglas Debate: The Race Issue in a Comparative Context," *Journal of the Abraham Lincoln Association* 31 (Winter 2010): 1–21; *Liberator*, July 13, 1860.

32. *CWL*, 3:177–78; Lucas Morel, "America Wasn't Founded on White Supremacy," *The American Mind* (October 17, 2019).

33. Jonathan W. White, *Lincoln on Law, Leadership, and Life* (Naperville, IL: Sourcebooks, 2015), 25, 49–50.

34. *CWL*, 3:312.

35. *CWL*, 2:398–410; Alexander Keyssar, *The Right to Vote: The Contested History of Democracy in the United States* (New York: Basic Books, 2000), 328–29.

36. *CWL*, 2:464.

37. *AL-AL*, 1:428.

38. *CWL*, 4:263–64.

39. *Charleston* (SC) *Mercury*, March 5, 1861; *Baltimore Sun*, March 6–7, 1861.

40. *AL-AL*, 1:380, 396.

41. Donald Yacovone, ed., *Freedom's Journey: African American Voices of the Civil War* (Chicago: Lawrence Hill, 2004), 253; George, "Philadelphians Greet Their President-Elect," 390; Thomas Wentworth Higginson, *Army Life in a Black Regiment* (1869; reprint, New York: W. W. Norton, 1984), 46, 55; Matthew J. Clavin, *Aiming for Pensacola: Fugitive Slaves on the Atlantic and Southern Frontiers* (Cambridge, MA: Harvard University Press, 2015), 149–50, 160.

42. Jonathan W. White, *Abraham Lincoln and Treason in the Civil War: The Trials of John Merryman* (Baton Rouge: Louisiana State University Press, 2011), chap. 1; John David Hoptak, "Nick Biddle: A Forgotten Hero of the Civil War," *Pennsylvania Heritage* 36 (Spring 2010): 6–13; John David Hoptak, ed., *Dear Ma: The Civil War Letters of Curtis Clay Pollock: First Defender and First Lieutenant, 48th Pennsylvania Infantry* (Mechanicsburg, PA: Sunbury, 2017), 18; Heber S. Thompson, *The First Defenders* (1910), 14–15, 151–52; James M. Guthrie, *Camp-Fires of the Afro-American; or, The Colored Man as a Patriot* (Philadelphia: Afro-American, 1899), 265.

INTERLUDE 1

1. Ernest Duvergier de Hauranne, *A Frenchman in Lincoln's America*, 2 vols., trans. and ed. Ralph H. Bowen (Chicago: R. R. Donnelley & Sons, 1975), 2:349; Lois Bryan Adams, *Letter from Washington, 1863–1865*, ed. Evelyn Leasher (Detroit: Wayne State University Press, 1999), 223–26 (hereafter *Letter from Washington*).

2. *Stoddard*, 5; David Herbert Donald, *Lincoln at Home: Two Glimpses of Abraham Lincoln's Family Life* (New York: Simon & Schuster, 2000), 24–25, 31.

3. *Daily Nashville Patriot*, July 26, 1860; *Lincoln's White House*, 16–17; *Stoddard*, 6; *CWL*, 2:404–8.

4. John Russell Young, "John Hay, Secretary of State," *Munsey's Magazine* 20 (November 1898): 246; *Stoddard*, 57, 151.

5. New York *World*, May 20, 1865; *Lincoln's White House*, 17; *Northumberland County Democrat*, May 3, 1861; *Stoddard*, 11–13, 145, 183; William E. Gienapp and Erica L. Gienapp, eds., *The Civil War Diary of Gideon Welles, Lincoln's Secretary of the Navy: The Original Manuscript Edition* (Urbana: University of Illinois Press, 2014), 216, 242–43 (hereafter *Welles Diary*); *LATN*, 119.

6. *AL-AL*, 1:360–61.

7. *AL-AL*, 1:361; Michael Burlingame and John R. Turner Ettlinger, eds., *Inside Lincoln's White House: The Complete Civil War Diary of John Hay* (Carbondale: Southern Illinois University Press, 1997), 69 (hereafter *Hay Diary*).

CHAPTER 2

1. *CWL*, 4:156.

2. Elizabeth Zoe Vicary, "Payne, Daniel Alexander," in John A. Garraty and Mark C. Carnes, eds., *American National Biography*, 24 vols. (New York: Oxford University Press, 1999), 17:170; "Payne, Daniel Alexander," in Dumas Malone, ed., *Dictionary of American Biography, Vol. VII: Mills – Platner* (New York: Charles Scribner's Sons, 1934), 324–25; *Men of Mark*, 1078–85.

3. Daniel Alexander Payne, *Welcome to the Ransomed, or, Duties of the Colored Inhabitants of the District of Columbia* (Baltimore: Bull & Tuttle, 1862).

4. Payne, *Recollections of Seventy Years*, 145–48; Philadelphia *Christian Recorder*, April 26, 1862 (hereafter *CR*).

5. Mitch Kachun, *Festivals of Freedom: Memory and Meaning in African American Emancipation Celebrations, 1808–1915* (Amherst: University of Massachusetts Press, 2003), 101; John Hope Franklin, *The Emancipation Proclamation* (New York: Doubleday, 1963), 18, 100.

6. *CWL*, 5:169, 192.

7. *LATN*, 141.

8. Payne, *Recollections of Seventy Years*, 145; *LATN*, 104–6.

9. Melvin R. Williams, "A Blueprint for Change: The Black Community in Washington, DC, 1860–1870," *Records of the Columbia Historical Society* 71/72 (1971–1972): 366, 368; Alexander Crummell and J. D. Johnson to Caleb B. Smith, May 16, 1862, National Archives (hereafter NARA) microfilm M160 (Records of the Office of the Secretary of the Interior Relating to the Suppression of the African Slave Trade and Negro Colonization, 1854–1872), reel 8.

10. *An Act for the Release of certain Persons held to Service or Labor in the District of Columbia*, act of April 16, 1862, in 12 Stat. 376–78; *An Act to suppress Insurrection, to punish Treason and Rebellion, to seize and confiscate the Property of Rebels, and for other Purposes*, act of July 17, 1862, in 12 Stat. 589–92.

11. Sarah J. Hale, ed., *Liberia; or, Mr. Peyton's Experiments* (New York: Harper & Brothers, 1853), 272–73; *Eighteenth Annual Report of the Board of Managers of the Massachusetts Colonization Society* (Boston: T. R. Marvin & Son, 1859), 8; Wilson J. Moses, *Alexander Crummell: A Study of Civilization and Discontent* (New York: Oxford University Press, 1989), 128; R. R. Gurley to Joseph Tracy, April 21, 1862, American Colonization Society Papers, Manuscript Division, Library of Congress (hereafter ACS Papers).

12. Moses, *Alexander Crummell*, 11–145.

13. Jonathan W. White, ed., *To Address You as My Friend: African Americans' Letters to Abraham Lincoln* (Chapel Hill: University of North Carolina Press, 2021), 34–35 (hereafter *My Friend*); *Boston Herald*, May 15, 1862; Joseph Tracy to R. R. Gurley, April 18, 1862, and Tracy to William McLain, April 18, 1862, ACS Papers; Moses, *Alexander Crummell*, 135, 141.

14. *Welles Diary*, 60.

15. San Francisco *Pacific Appeal*, September 13, 1862; Kate Masur, "The African American Delegation to Abraham Lincoln: A Reappraisal," *Civil War History* 56 (June 2010): 123–28, 133, 141–43; William Seraille, "Afro-American Emigration to Haiti during the American Civil War," *The Americas* 35 (October 1978): 192–94; *Baltimore Sun*, April 11, 1862; Washington, DC, *National Republican*, April 30, 1862 (hereafter *NR*); *Freedom's Witness*, 50–51.

16. *Freedom's Witness*, 54–55.

17. Pardon Case File A-471, RG 204 (Records of the Office of the Pardon Attorney), Entry 1a (Pardon Case Files, 1853–1946), National Archives at College Park (hereafter NACP); Lincoln remission of prison term of Wormley and Ringgold, May 2, 1863, RG 59 (General Records of the Department of State), Entry 897 (Pardons and Remissions), vol. 7, p. 448, NACP.

18. *Freedom's Witness*, 96; Johnson to Lincoln, March 3, 1863, Johnson to John P. Usher, April 10, 1863, and Johnson to William H. Seward, April 9, 1863, NARA microfilm M160, reel 8.

CHAPTER 3

1. *Welles Diary*, 54.

2. *CWL*, 5:425, 438, 503; *Recollected Words*, 215; Allen C. Guelzo, *Lincoln's Emancipation Proclamation: The End of Slavery in America* (New York: Simon & Schuster, 2004), 139–44.

3. Masur, "African American Delegation," 130–31; Boyd's Washington directories for 1862 and 1864.

4. *Dictionary of American Biography*, vol. 8, pp. 10–11; Norbert Brockman, *An African Biographical Dictionary* (Denver: ABC-CLIO, 1994), 306–7; Henry Louis Gates Jr. and Evelyn Brooks Higginbotham, eds., *African American National Biography*, 8

vols. (New York: Oxford University Press, 2008), 6:621–22; Marie Tyler-McGraw, *An African Republic: Black and White Virginians in the Making of Liberia* (Chapel Hill: University of North Carolina Press, 2007), 71, 152–75.

5. *CWL*, 5:373; William McLain to R. R. Gurley, August 26, 1862, ACS Papers.

6. *CWL*, 5:370–75; Elizabeth Dowling Taylor, *A Slave in the White House: Paul Jennings and the Madisons* (New York: Palgrave Macmillan, 2012), 201–2, 206, 213–15.

7. Camden *West Jersey Press*, August 20, 1862; *New York Sun*, quoted in Indianapolis *Daily Sentinel*, August 21, 1862; *Barre* (MA) *Gazette*, August 22, 1862.

8. Philadelphia *Press* and *Syracuse Journal*, quoted in *Douglass' Monthly*, September 1862; *Springfield* (MA) *Republican*, August 16, 1862; *Liberator*, August 29, 1862; Columbus (OH) *Crisis*, September 3, 1862.

9. *My Friend*, 38–39; Jacob R. S. Van Vleet to Lincoln, August 17, 1862, Lincoln Papers.

10. *Douglass Speeches*, 510–13.

11. New York *National Anti-Slavery Standard*, October 11, 1862; *New York Times*, October 3, 1862 (hereafter *NYT*); *Liberator*, August 29, 1862; Wilbur Diary, August 21, 1862.

12. *Liberator*, August 22, 1862.

13. James Oakes, *Freedom National: The Destruction of Slavery in the United States, 1861–1865* (New York: W.W. Norton, 2013), 308–10; James Oakes, *The Radical and the Republican: Frederick Douglass, Abraham Lincoln, and the Triumph of Antislavery Politics* (New York: W. W. Norton, 2007), 190–94; Holzer, *Emancipating Lincoln*, 41, 44.

14. New York *Caucasian*, quoted in Leonardtown (MD) *St. Mary's Beacon*, September 4, 1862.

15. *Letters of Major Jack Downing of the Downingville Militia* (New York: Bromley, 1864), 135–36.

16. *Freedom's Witness*, 69–70.

17. *Liberator*, September 12, 1862.

CHAPTER 4

1. *NYT*, November 2, 1862.

2. *Boston Traveler*, February 9, 1863.

3. *Boston Journal*, January 5, 1892; *Baltimore Sun*, July 18, 1856; *ES*, July 21, 1862; George W. Williams, *History of the Negro Race in America, from 1619 to 1880* (New York: G. P. Putnam's Sons, 1885), 192; Thomas S. Malcolm to Edwin M. Stanton, May 18, 1864, and William Coppinger to Daniel L. Collier, March 28, 1864, NARA microfilm M1064 (Letters Received by the Commission Branch of the Adjutant General's Office, 1863–1870), reel 104.

4. Samson to Gurley, November 1, 1862, ACS Papers.

5. Leonard to Gurley, January 28, 1863, William Coppinger to Gurley, November 27, 1863, and Thomas S. Malcolm to James Hall, January 5, 1863, ACS Papers; statement of Malcolm, February 6, 1863, and receipt from Leonard, February 3, 1863, NARA microfilm M160, reel 8.

6. *Boston Traveler*, February 9, 1863.

7. Charles Joyce, "Freedmen Warriors, Civil Rights Fighters," *Military Images* 34 (Autumn 2016): 44.

8. William Coppinger to Gurley, November 27, 1863, Leonard to Thomas S. Malcolm, December 14, 1863, Malcolm to James Hall, January 5, 1863, Coppinger to Hall, January 5, 1864, and Chauncey Leonard to Gurley, January 9, 1864, ACS Papers.

9. *My Friend*, 182–83; John Hay to Edwin M. Stanton, July 27, 1864, NARA microfilm M1064, reel 104.

10. Edwin Bentley to R. O. Abbott, July 15, 1864, NARA microfilm M1064, reel 104.

11. Joyce, "Freedmen Warriors," 42 48; Leonard to C. T. Beach, March 24, 1865 (MSS.4148), University Libraries Special Collections, University of Alabama, Tuscaloosa; Leonard to Lorenzo Thomas, September 30, 1864, October 31, 1864, November 1, 1864, November 30, 1864, December 31, 1864, April 30, 1865, May 31, 1865, NARA microfilm M619 (Letters Received by the Office of the Adjutant General [Main Series], 1861–1870), reels 273, 374; Leonard to Mrs. Williams, May, 4, 1865, Elias Williams Pension (28th USCT), RG 15 (Records of the Department of Veterans Affairs), NARA (hereafter Pension).

12. Leonard Pension.

13. Leonard Pension; *Springfield* (MA) *Republican*, November 28, 1879; *Boston Globe*, July 7, 1890; *Boston Journal*, January 5, 1892. Leonard appears to have been arrested several times after the war. See "Meetings," 30.

14. *Freedom's Witness*, 70–71; "Meetings," 44–45; *ES*, June 10, 1863. Turner asked James Mitchell to set up a meeting to discuss the $600,000 colonization fund with the president. It is known for certain that Turner had private audiences with members of Lincoln's Cabinet, including Salmon P. Chase.

15. *Freedom's Witness*, 71.

16. *LATN*, 191–94; *CWL*, 6:365; *Hay Diary*, 217.

17. R. J. M. Blackett, *The Captive's Quest for Freedom: Fugitive Slaves, the 1850 Fugitive Slave Act, and the Politics of Slavery* (New York: Cambridge University Press, 2018), 115–23; Rochester *North Star*, June, 13, October 24, 1850, April 10, 1851; Washington, DC, *Daily National Intelligencer*, December 5, 1851; *Baltimore Sun*, August 25, 1853; Philadelphia *North American and United States Gazette*, August 24, 1853; Montpelier *Vermont Patriot and State Gazette*, November 24, 1853; Rochester *Frederick Douglass' Paper*, December 16, 1853; New Orleans *Daily Picayune*, August 12, 1854; *New York Herald*, July 30, 1856, March 25, 28, 1858; Bellows Falls *Vermont Chronicle*, March 6, 1860.

18. *CWL*, 7:295.

INTERLUDE 2

1. *CWL*, 5:39.
2. *Congressional Globe*, 37th Cong., 2nd sess., p. 1806.
3. *Congressional Globe*, 37th Cong., 2nd sess., pp. 2502-3.
4. Tunkhannock (PA) *Wyoming Democrat*, March 4, 1863.
5. *Springfield* (MA) *Republican*, June 27, 1862; *LATN*, 100-101. Lincoln may have said this because James Redpath, a white man, was "fishing" for the position himself. See *Douglass' Monthly*, September 1862.
6. *LATN*, 100-101; *Negro's Civil War*, 305.
7. William H. Seward to Ernest Roumain, March 2, 1863, and Fabre Geffrard to Ernest Roumain, April 7, 1863, Eugene Maximilien Haitian Collection, Schomburg Center for Research in Black Culture, microfilm reel 37; *Lowell Daily Citizen*, March 20, 1863; "An Iowa Woman in Washington, DC, 1861-1865," *Iowa Journal of History* 52 (January 1954): 77-78; *Burlington* (IA) *Weekly Hawk-Eye*, May 9, 1863.
8. *Douglass' Monthly*, March 1863.
9. *NYAA*, December 12, 1863.

CHAPTER 5

1. *CWL*, 6:28-31.
2. *CWL*, 5:356-57; *AL-AL*, 2:463-67.
3. *An Act for the Benefit of Robert Small* [*sic*], *and others*, act of May 30, 1862, 12 Stat. 904.
4. *Congressional Record*, 49th Cong., 1st sess., vol. 17, appendix, p.320; *Freedom's Witness*, 60-61.
5. Avis Thomas-Lester, "Civil War hero Robert Smalls seized the opportunity to be free," *Washington Post*, March 2, 2012.
6. *CWL*, 6:149-50; Arthur J. Larsen, ed., *Crusader and Feminist: Letters of Jane Grey Swisshelm, 1858-1865* (Saint Paul: Minnesota Historical Society, 1934), 220.
7. *NYAA*, May 23, 1863.
8. Margaret Leech, *Reveille in Washington, 1860-1865* (New York: Harper & Brothers, 1941), 307-10; *NR*, April 25, May 8, 11, 1863; *ES*, May 19, 1863; *NYAA*, May 23, July 4, 1863.
9. E. R. Carter, *The Black Slide* (Atlanta, 1894), 160.
10. *NR*, March 18, 1863; Milwaukee *Sentinel*, April 13, 1863; *CR*, March 28, 1863; Douglas R. Egerton, "The Slaves' Election: Fremont, Freedom, and the Slave Conspiracies of 1856," *Civil War History* 61 (March 2015): 35-63; *My Friend*, 66-67.
11. *Chicago Evening Journal*, April 4, 1863.
12. *CR*, April 25, 1863.
13. *NYAA*, May 9, 1863.

14. George E. H. Day to Ira Harris, August 12, 1863, James Morrison MacKaye Papers, LC; *New-York Tribune*, June 1, 1863; *NR*, June 2, 1863; *NYT*, June 12, 1863; *CR*, March 28, 1863; *New Bedford Evening Standard*, April 22, 1863; both leaflets are in Lincoln Papers; *CWL*, 6:239, 242–44.

15. Cleveland *Plain Dealer*, April 22, 1863; New York *Principia*, April 23, 1863; *Indiana State Sentinel*, April 29, 1863; St. Paul *Pioneer and Democrat*, April 16, 1863.

16. *NYT*, July 22, 1863.

17. *Buffalo Courier*, July 23, 1863; *Buffalo Weekly Express*, July 28, October 10, 1863; *Liberator*, September 4, 1863. About this time, Lincoln told a white delegation that there was no open position for Fremont in the Army at this time. See *CWL*, 6:239, 242–44; *NYT*, June 12, 1863; *Baltimore Sun*, June 13, 1863.

18. *CWL*, 7:450.

19. *CWL*, 6:409–10.

20. Herman Belz, *Abraham Lincoln, Constitutionalism, and Equal Rights in the Civil War Era* (New York: Fordham University Press, 1998), 110 21; Edwin S. Redkey, *A Grand Army of Black Men: Letters from African-American Soldiers in the Union Army, 1861–1865* (New York: Cambridge University Press, 1992), 237; Donald Yacovone, ed., *A Voice of Thunder: The Civil War Letters of George E. Stephens* (Urbana: University of Illinois Press, 1997), 319–21.

CHAPTER 6

1. *Douglass Speeches*, 414, 433, 435; *NYAA*, April 5, 1862.

2. *Douglass Speeches*, 524; Frederick Douglass, *The Life and Times of Frederick Douglass* (Boston: De Wolfe, Fiske, & Co., 1895), 414–16 (hereafter *Life and Times*); David W. Blight, *Frederick Douglass: Prophet of Freedom* (New York: Simon & Schuster, 2018), 391 (hereafter *FD*).

3. *FD*, 391–406; Oakes, *Radical and the Republican*, 206–8.

4. *CWL*, 6:357; *Douglass Speeches*, 538–43.

5. *Life and Times*, 417–25; *Liberator*, January 29, 1864.

6. Roy P. Basler, ed., *The Collected Works of Abraham Lincoln: Supplement, 1832–1865* (Westport, CT: Greenwood Press, 1974), 198; *FD*, 406–12. Ironically, Martin Luther King Jr. would also call Lincoln "vacillating" in the last public speech he ever gave.

7. *Liberator*, January 29, 1864.

8. *NYT*, January 14, 1864.

9. *An Act making Appropriations for the Support of the Army for the Year ending the thirtieth June, eighteen hundred and sixty-five, and for other Purposes*, act of June 15, 1864, in 13 Stat. 126–30; Belz, *Lincoln, Constitutionalism, and Equal Rights*, 119–37.

CHAPTER 7

1. *NR*, January 1, 1864.

2. *NR*, December 31, 1863, January 1, 1864; *ES*, January 1, 1864.

3. Quoted in "Color Was a Bar," 6; *LATN*, 233.

4. *NYAA*, January 23, 1864.

5. Wilbur Diary, January 3, 1864; *National Anti-Slavery Standard*, January 23, 1864; *ES*, January 6, 1864; *NYAA*, February 13, May 14, 1864.

6. Quoted in *NYAA*, January 23, 1864; *McArthur Democrat* (OH), January 7, 1864; "Color Was a Bar," 9; "Receptions," 54.

7. William Kauffman, ed., *The Diary of Edmund Ruffin*, 3 vols. (Baton Rouge: Louisiana State University Press, 1972–1989), 3:307.

8. Gerald S. Henig, "The Indomitable Dr. Augusta: The First Black Physician in the US Army," *Army History* 87 (Spring 2013): 23–24; George Hendrick and Willene Hendrick, *Black Refugees in Canada: Accounts of Escape during the Era of Slavery* (Jefferson, NC: McFarland, 2010), 107; Richard M. Reid, *African Canadians in Union Blue* (Vancouver: University of British Columbia Press, 2014), 146–76.

9. Augusta to Lincoln, January 7, 1863, and Augusta to Stanton, January 7, 1863, both in Augusta Combined Military Service Records (hereafter CMSR), RG 94 (Records of the Adjutant General's Office), Entry 519 (Records of the Record and Pension Office, Carded Military Service Records, 1784–1903), NARA.

10. Augusta CMSR; *Cleveland Daily Leader*, May 8, 1863; Jacqueline Tobin with Hettie Jones, *From Midnight to Dawn: The Last Tracks of the Underground Railroad* (New York: Doubleday, 2007), 231.

11. *NYAA*, September 26, 1863.

12. *Baltimore Sun*, April 18, 1863; *ES*, April 17, 1863; *Davenport Daily Gazette*, April 28, 1863; Augusta CMSR. Menard also said, "Of all the Presidents, the name of Abraham Lincoln would be heard in thunder-tones in ages yet to come!"

13. C. Peter Ripley et al., eds., *The Black Abolitionist Papers*, 5 vols. (Chapel Hill: University of North Carolina Press, 1985–1992), 5:205–11; Columbus (OH) *Crisis*, May 13, 1863; Harrisburg *Patriot and Union*, May 14, 1863; *Liberator*, May 8, 1863; Concord (NH) *Independent Democrat*, May 7, 1863; Freehold (NJ) *Monmouth Democrat*, May 14, 1863.

14. *NYAA*, June 20, September 5, 19, 1863.

15. Court-Martial Case File OO-116, RG 153 (Records of the Office of the Judge Advocate General [Army]), NARA; Augusta CMSR; Taylor CMSR and Pension. Andrew Johnson remitted Taylor's sentence and released him from prison in July 1865.

16. Sen. Rep. Com. No. 17, 38th Cong., 1st sess.; *Congressional Globe*, 38th Cong., 1st sess., pp. 553–55, 816–18; *Syracuse Daily Courier and Union*, February 15, 1864; Howard K. Beale, ed., *The Diary of Edward Bates, 1859–1866* (Washington, DC: Government Printing Office, 1933), 331–32; *NYAA*, February 13, 20, April 2, 1864.

17. *Detroit Free Press*, February 27, 1864.

18. *Urbana* (OH) *Union*, February 10, 1864.

19. Abbott Pension.

20. Washington, DC, *Daily National Intelligencer*, February 24, 1864; *NR*, February 24, 1864; *ES*, February 24, 1864.

21. Anderson R. Abbott Papers, Toronto Public Library (scan of memoir provided by Jill Newmark of the National Library of Medicine).

22. *Stoddard*, 172; William M. Thayer, *The Character and Public Services of Abraham Lincoln, President of the United States* (Boston: Dinsmoor, 1864), 22; *Detroit Free Press*, March 4, 1864.

23. J. B. McPherson and others to Lincoln, n.d. [February 1864], RG 94 (Records of the Adjutant General's Office), Entry 360 (Colored Troops Division, 1863–1889, Letters Received), NARA; Joel Morse to John Sherman, May 14, 1864, Augusta CMSR.

24. Wilbur Diary, October 11, 1863. This entry had to do with when he was relieved from being surgeon in charge at the contraband camp.

25. Honig, "Augusta," 20 30; Ripley, *Black Abolitionist Papers*, 5:205 11; Reid, *African Canadians*, 153; John Sherman and others to Ulysses S. Grant, February 22, 1871, NARA microfilm M968 (Letters of Application and Recommendation During the Administration of Ulysses S. Grant, 1869–1877), reel 2.

INTERLUDE 3

1. Keyssar, *Right to Vote*, 316.

2. *CWL*, 1:48. Curiously, Lincoln's proposal was also a restriction on suffrage as white men were not required to pay taxes or serve in the military to vote in Illinois at this time.

3. *AL-AL*, 1:103–4, 108–11, 154–55. Lincoln's public opposition to black suffrage was a political trap for his political rival Stephen Douglas. See Douglas L. Wilson, *Honor's Voice: The Political Transformation of Abraham Lincoln* (New York: Alfred A. Knopf, 1998), 204–5.

4. *CWL*, 2:265–66.

5. *CWL*, 3:145–46.

6. *CWL*, 2:256.

7. *CWL*, 2:9–10; *LATN*, 39.

8. Morel, "America Wasn't Founded on White Supremacy."

CHAPTER 8

1. David C. Rankin, "The Origins of Negro Leadership in New Orleans during Reconstruction," in Howard Rabinowitz, ed., *Southern Black Leaders of the Reconstruction Era* (Urbana: University of Illinois Press, 1982), 155–73.

2. Petition to Shepley, n.d., George F. Shepley Papers, Maine Historical Society; Buffalo *Evening Courier and Republic*, November 25, 1863; *AL-AL*, 2:582–591; *Negro's Civil War*, 277.

3. *Janesville* (WI) *Daily Gazette*, March 22, 1864; *My Friend*, 171–74.

4. *Recollected Words*, 14.

5. John Niven, ed., *The Salmon P. Chase Papers*, 5 vols. (Kent, OH: Kent State University Press, 1997), 4:321.

6. *My Friend*, 174–76; *Congressional Globe*, 38th Cong., 1st sess., p. 1107.

7. Francis B. Carpenter, *Six Months at the White House with Abraham Lincoln* (New York: Hurd and Houghton, 1866), 267–68 (hereafter *Six Months*); *Liberator*, April 15, 1864; Rankin, "Origins of Negro Leadership," 155–73.

8. *CWL*, 7:243.

9. Matthew D. Norman, "'Our Beloved Father Abraham': African American Civil War Veterans and Abraham Lincoln in War and Memory," in Brian Matthew Jordan and Evan Rothera, eds., *The War Went On: Reconsidering the Lives of Civil War Veterans* (Baton Rouge: Louisiana State University Press, 2020), 219; *LATN*, 228, 246; *NYT*, June 23, 1865.

10. William Still, *The Underground Rail Road* (Philadelphia: Porter & Coates, 1872), 150–52.

11. David S. Cecelski, *The Fire of Freedom: Abraham Galloway and the Slaves' Civil War* (Chapel Hill: University of North Carolina Press, 2012); Catherine W. Bishir, *Crafting Lives: African American Artisans in New Bern, North Carolina, 1770–1900* (Chapel Hill: University of North Carolina Press, 2013), 167–71.

12. *NYAA*, May 14, July 2, 1864; New Berne *North Carolina Times*, May 21, 1864; Cecelski, *Fire of Freedom*, 115–27.

13. *NYAA*, March 11, 1865.

14. *NYAA*, April 30, 1864.

15. H. C. Percy, "Father Parker," *American Missionary* 12 (August 1868): 169–72; John W. Blassingame, ed., *Slave Testimony: Two Centuries of Letters, Speeches, Interviews, and Autobiographies* (Baton Rouge: Louisiana State University Press, 1977), 465. According to his obituary, Parker began attending the AME's annual conference in Baltimore in 1863. This meeting probably took place in May 1864. See *CR*, June 27, 1878.

16. *CWL*, 7:281–82.

17. *AL-AL*, 2:635.

18. *Liberator*, June 3, 1864.

19. Beverly Wilson Palmer, ed., *The Selected Letters of Charles Sumner*, 2 vols. (Boston: Northeastern University Press, 1990), 2: 273, 279.

20. *CWL* 7:101; *Recollected Words*, 427. Some scholars have questioned the authenticity of these quotations. The original Wadsworth letter has never been found, and it was first published in the newspapers shortly after Lincoln died. The words spoken to Stoddard were recorded many years later. However, considerable evidence exists that

Lincoln was privately pushing black suffrage with many political leaders. See *AL-AL*, 2:772–77.

21. *AL-AL*, 2:802–3.

CHAPTER 9

1. *Men of Mark*, 291–95, 662–65.

2. Grimes and others to Lincoln, August 21, 1863, and Kelly to Lincoln, August 21, 1863, Lincoln Papers; LeRoy P. Graf, ed., *The Papers of Andrew Johnson, Volume 7: 1864–1865* (Knoxville: University of Tennessee Press, 1986), 422–23. The *NYAA* of September 5, 1863, lists several other members of the committee.

3. *Chicago Tribune*, August 29, 1863.

4. *CWL*, 6:401; *Report of the Twenty-Fifth Anniversary of the American Baptist Missionary Convention: Held at the Meeting House of the First Colored Baptist Church, Alexandria, Va. from Friday, August 18th, to Sunday, August 27th, 1865* (New Bedford, MA: E. Anthony & Sons, 1865), 10–12, 21; Lewis G. Jordan, *Negro Baptist History, USA, 1750–1930* (Nashville: Sunday School Publishing Board, 1930), 83, 293–94; Grimes to Simeon S. Jocelyn, October 9, 1863, American Missionary Association Collection, Amistad Research Center, Tulane University, New Orleans, LA (hereafter AMA Collection).

5. *ES*, October 9, 1863; *Baltimore Sun*, October 10, 1863; *NR*, October 6, 1863; *CR*, October 3, 17, 1863; *NYAA*, October 3, 1863; *My Friend*, 188–89.

6. *NYAA*, October 17, 24, 31, November 7, 1863; *ES*, October 9, 1863; *Alexandria Gazette*, October 6, 10, 1863; *Baltimore Sun*, October 10, 1863; New York *World*, October 10, 1863; *Springfield* (MA) *Republican*, October 10, 1863; *Lowell Daily Citizen and News*, October 12, 1863; Newark (NJ) *Centinel of Freedom*, October 13, 1863; *Letter from Washington*, 35.

7. *An Act to incorporate the "African Civilization Society,"* act of May 5, 1863, in *Laws of the State of New York Passed at the Eighty-Sixth Session of the Legislature* (Albany: Weed, Parsons & Company, 1863), 758–59; James Mitchell to Lincoln, November 5, 1863, Lincoln Papers; *My Friend*, 190–92; *LATN*, 121.

8. Edwin S. Redkey, "Black Chaplains in the Union Army," *Civil War History* 33 (December 1987): 349; Marine Christopher, *America's Black Congressmen* (New York: Thomas Y. Crowell, 1971), 87–88; Edythe Ann Quinn, *Freedom Journey: Black Civil War Soldiers and the Hills Community, Westchester County, New York* (Albany: State University of New York Press, 2015), 94–95; Ripley, *Black Abolitionist Papers*, 1:504; *Men of Mark*, 866–67; Edwin G. Burrows and Mike Wallace, *Gotham: A History of New York City to 1898* (New York: Oxford University Press, 1999), 857.

9. *CR*, January 9, 1864; *My Friend*, 190–92.

10. James Mitchell to John P. Usher, November 5, 1863, Lincoln Papers; Washington, DC, *Daily National Intelligencer*, November 16, 1863; Mitchell to H. M. Wilson,

October 5, 1863 (newspaper clipping), enclosed in Mitchell to Lincoln, November 5, 1863.

11. *My Friend*, 190–93.

12. *Lowell Daily Citizen and News*, November 16, 1863.

13. *NYAA*, December 19, 1863.

14. LeVere CMSR; Redkey, "Black Chaplains," 349; Edythe Ann Quinn, *Freedom Journey: Black Civil War Soldiers and The Hills Community, Westchester County, New York* (Albany: SUNY Press, 2015), 94–95; Eric Foner, *Freedom's Lawmakers: A Directory of Black Officeholders during Reconstruction* (New York: Oxford University Press, 1993), 35–36; Christopher, *America's Black Congressmen*, 87–96.

15. Records of the Board of Commissioners for the Emancipation of Slaves in the District of Columbia, 1862–1863, NARA microfilm M520; *ES*, June 27, 1862; *Congressional Serial Set*, 38th Cong., 1st sess., House Exec. Doc. No. 42.

16. D. I. Murphy, "Lincoln, Foe of Bigotry," *America* 38 (February 11, 1928): 432–33.

17. Philadelphia *Inquirer*, July 5, 1864.

18. *Hay Diary*, 220.

19. *Six Months*, 196; Murphy, "Lincoln, Foe of Bigotry," 433.

20. *Letter from Washington*, 171.

21. Ruth Edmonds Hill, ed., *The Black Women Oral History Project*, 10 vols. (Westport, CT: Meckler, 1991), 6:46–48.

22. *My Friend*, 196.

23. *ES*, August 3, 1864.

24. *CWL*, 7:431–32; *Welles Diary*, 462; Beale, *Diary of Edward Bates*, 393.

25. *ES*, August 5, 1864; Washington, DC, *Weekly National Intelligencer*, August 11, 1864.

26. Wilson and Davis, *Herndon's Informants*, 602. This reminiscence, which was recorded in 1887, dated this event as August 1862, but it was almost certainly 1864.

27. *ES*, August 5, 1864, April 13, 1870, July 5, 1872; Washington, DC, *Weekly National Intelligencer*, August 11, 1864.

28. *Daily Milwaukee News*, August 14, 1864.

29. Diary entry for August 6, 1864, Beale, *Diary of Bates*, 395.

30. Opening statement of George W. Madison, June 5, 2009.

CHAPTER 10

1. James B. Conroy, *Jefferson's White House: Monticello on the Potomac* (Lanham, MD: Rowman & Littlefield, 2019), 104–6, 158–59; Robert V. Remini, *Andrew Jackson* (New York: Harper & Row, 1966), 170.

2. *CWL*, 5:125–26; Donald, *Lincoln at Home*, 32.

3. *CWL*, 7:389.

4. Virginia Walcott Beauchamp, ed., *A Private War: The Letters and Diaries of Madge Preston, 1862-1867* (New Brunswick, NJ: Rutgers University Press, 1987), 30; *My Friend*, 24, 42, 66, 85, 98, 112, 127, 169, 190, 226, 228, 230-33; Booker T. Washington, "Speech Draft RE: Influence of Lincoln, Given at New York Republican Club of NYC," February 12, 1909 (GLC07232), Gilder-Lehrman Institute of American History, New York.

5. *My Friend*, 229-32. The poem originally appeared as "The Flag of the Union" in *Harper's Weekly*, February 20, 1864.

6. E. G. Trask to Lincoln, November 9, 1864, RG 107 (Records of the Office of the Secretary of War), Entry 18 (Letters Received [Main Series], 1801-1889), NARA.

7. *Chicago Tribune*, December 23, 1864.

8. Griffin Lee [Paschal B. Randolph], *Pre-Adamite Man: The Story of the Human Race, from 35,000 to 100,000 Years Ago!* 2nd ed. (New York: Sinclair Tousey, 1863); *My Friend*, 71-73; *NR*, July 28, 1866.

9. *NR*, October 6, 1863; *NYAA*, September 12, October 10, 24, 1863; "Artists of Abraham Lincoln Portraits: David B. Bowser" file, Lincoln Financial Foundation Collection, Fort Wayne, Indiana; Richard A. Sauers, *Advance the Colors: Pennsylvania Civil War Battle Flags*, 2 vols. (Harrisburg: Capitol Preservation Committee, 1987), 1:46-47.

10. Philadelphia *Press*, March 9, 1864; *Liberator*, July 1, 1864.

11. *New York Herald*, December 18, 1861; Michael Burlingame, ed., *An Oral History of Abraham Lincoln: John G. Nicolay's Interviews and Essays* (Carbondale: Southern Illinois University Press, 1996), 130; *Lincoln's White House*, 37-38, 84-85, 87; Louis A. Warren, "The Lincoln's [*sic*] Executive Mansion Library," *Lincoln Lore* no. 1079 (December 12, 1949); Julia Taft Bayne, *Tad Lincoln's Father* (Boston: Little, Brown and Co., 1931), 11, 32-33, 108-10, 158-59, 162-65, 192-93; *Stoddard*, 145.

12. Newark *Advertiser*, quoted in *The Liberator*, July 1, 1864; *Six Months*, 200-201; *CR*, April 16, 1864.

13. Donald B. Cole and John J. McDonough, eds., *Witness to the Young Republic: A Yankee's Journal, 1828-1870* (London: University Press of New England, 1989), 448.

14. Justin G. Turner and Linda Levitt Turner, eds., *Mary Todd Lincoln: Her Life and Letters* (New York: Alfred A. Knopf, 1987), 174.

15. Boston *Congregationalist*, July 18, 1872.

16. *CWL*, 5:403-4.

17. *CWL*, 7:282. In some cases, African Americans also pointed out that Lincoln's actions were subject to the will of God. See *NYAA*, August 6, 1864.

18. Ronald C. White Jr., *Lincoln's Greatest Speech: The Second Inaugural* (New York: Simon & Schuster, 2002), 111-12.

19. *Wheeling Daily Intelligencer*, July 10, 1864; *Baltimore Sun*, July 22, 1864; *NYAA*, August 6, 1864.

20. R. Stockett Matthews to Lincoln, July 6, 1864, and August 31, 1864, and James W. Tyson to Lincoln, August 26, 1864, Lincoln Papers.

21. *ES*, September 7, 1864; *CWL*, 7:542-43; *Baltimore Sun*, April 1, 1867.

22. *Six Months*, 199; *CR*, October 15, 1864; *CWL*, 1:382.

23. Lincoln Bible File, Special Collections and Archives, Fisk University, Nashville, TN.

24. *ES*, September 7, 1864; *CR*, October 15, 1864; *Baltimore American*, quoted in Akron (OH) *Summit County Beacon*, July 28, 1864; *LATN*, 207.

25. *Six Months*, 197.

26. William H. Gilbert, diary entry for November 14, 1864, William H. Gilbert Diaries, Huntington Library, San Marino, CA (hereafter HL); A. M. Jenkins to Lincoln, September 9, 1864, Lincoln Papers.

27. Correspondence and speech, Lincoln Bible File.

28. "Editorials," *Fisk University News* 6 (May 1916): 1–2, 5–6; Lenida Crosthwait, "Statement Relative to Lincoln Bible," and Arthur A. Schomburg, "The Lincoln Bible," Lincoln Bible File.

29. "Lessons from the Life of Lincoln Given at Fisk on Emancipation Day," *Fisk University News* 9 (November 1919): 1–6.

30. Lincoln Bible File.

31. Julie Zauzmer, "The New Museum of the Bible Confronts the Challenge of Presenting Slavery and the Confederacy," *Washington Post* (November 16, 2017).

INTERLUDE 4

1. Horace Porter, *Campaigning with Grant* (New York: Century, 1897), 216–20; *NR*, June 24, 1864; *LATN*, 182; Carl J. Guarneri, *Lincoln's Informer: Charles A. Dana and the Inside Story of the Union War* (Lawrence: University Press of Kansas, 2019), 279.

2. *Hay Diary*, 210; *Welles Diary*, 431.

3. Christopher Phillips, "Race, Class, and Copperheadism: The Localist Foundations of Dissent in the Civil War's Middle Border," in Stewart L. Winger and Jonathan W. White, eds., *Ex parte Milligan Reconsidered: Race and Civil Liberties from the Lincoln Administration to the War on Terror* (Lawrence: University Press of Kansas, 2020), 122.

CHAPTER 11

1. *They Knew Lincoln*, 160–67; Sen. Doc. 53, 58th Cong., 3rd sess. (1904); diary of Michael Shiner, entries for July 10–12, 1864, Naval History and Heritage Command, Washington, DC. This line by Elizabeth Thomas has been attributed to others as well.

2. Michael Vorenberg, "'The Deformed Child': Slavery and the Election of 1864," *Civil War History* 47 (September 2001): 240–57; *CWL*, 7:451, 499–502; *AL-AL*, 2:676–77.

3. John Eaton, *Grant, Lincoln and the Freedmen: Reminiscences of the Civil War* (New York: Longmans, Green, & Co., 1907), 168–74; *FD*, 435.

4. *CWL*, 7:508.

5. *Douglass Speeches*, 571–72.

6. *Life and Times*, 434–36; *Recollected Words*, 145; *CWL*, 5:388.

7. Harold Holzer, ed., *President Lincoln Assassinated!!: The Firsthand Story of the Murder, Manhunt, Trial, and Mourning* (New York: Library of America, 2015), 323–24.

8. Eaton, *Grant, Lincoln and the Freedmen*, 175–76; Columbus *Daily Ohio States-man*, November 1, 1865; John H. Rapier Jr. to James P. Thomas, August 19, 1864, in Deborah Willis, *The Black Civil War Soldier: A Visual History of Conflict and Citizen-ship* (New York: New York University Press, 2021), 146.

9. *My Friend*, 79–82. Ironically, Douglass had rejected John Brown's entreaties to join his original plan in 1859.

10. Mark E. Neely Jr., "Lincoln and the Theory of Self-Emancipation," in John Y. Simon and Barbara Hughett, eds., *The Continuing Civil War: Essays in Honor of the Civil War Round Table of Chicago* (Dayton, OH: Morningside, 1992), 58.

11. *CWL*, 7:507.

12. *CWL*, 7:251.

13. *CWL*, 8:41–42.

14. William Blair Lord and Henry M. Parkhurst, eds., *The Debates of the Constitu-tional Convention of the State of Maryland*, 3 vols. (Annapolis: Richard P. Bayly, 1864), 3:1925–26.

15. *LATN*, 219.

16. *ES*, November 2, 1864; *Baltimore Sun*, November 3, 1864; *Liberator*, Decem-ber 23, 1864.

17. Michael Burlingame, ed., *Lincoln Observed: Civil War Dispatches of Noah Brooks* (Baltimore: Johns Hopkins University Press, 1998), 141–42.

18. *Douglass Speeches*, 542, 572; Foner, *Life and Writings of Frederick Douglass*, 3:43, 404.

19. Redkey, *Grand Army of Black Men*, 212–13.

20. Foner, *Life and Writings of Frederick Douglass*, 3:424.

21. *Miscegenation Indorsed by the Republican Party* (Campaign Document, No. 11), 7; Lancaster (PA) *Intelligencer Journal*, December 1, 1863; January 5, September 24, 29, 1864; Oakes, *Radical and the Republican*, xxi, 229.

22. *Plymouth Weekly Democrat* (IN), October 6, 1864.

23. *AL-AL*, 2:695.

24. Foner, *Life and Writings*, 3:424.

25. Yacovone, *Freedom's Journey*, 59–66; *My Friend*, 235.

26. *Negro's Civil War*, 304–5.

27. Noah Andre Trudeau, ed., *Voices of the 55th: Letters from the 55th Massachusetts Volunteers, 1861–1865* (Dayton, OH: Morningside House, 1996), 241.

28. *Proceedings of the National Convention of Colored Men, Held in the City of Syracuse, N.Y., October 4, 5, 6, and 7, 1864, with the Bill of Wrongs and Rights, and the Address to the American People* (Boston: J. S. Rock and Geo. L. Ruffin, 1864), 24–25.

29. *NYAA*, January 23, 1864.

30. *My Friend*, 129–30.

31. *Boston Daily Advertiser*, June 29, 1864; New York *World*, May 12, 1864.

32. New York *Anti-Slavery Standard*, November 9, 1864.

33. *LATN*, 217; Herbert Aptheker, ed., *A Documentary History of the Negro People in the United States* (New York: Citadel Press, 1951), 530.

34. *CWL*, 8:113.

CHAPTER 12

1. Nell Irvin Painter, *Sojourner Truth: A Life, A Symbol* (New York: W. W. Norton, 1996), 3, 7, 11–15, 19–20 (hereafter *Sojourner Truth*).

2. *Narrative of Sojourner Truth; A Bondswoman of Olden Times* (Battle Creek, MI: Review and Herald, 1884), 39–54; *Sojourner Truth*, 32–35.

3. *Sojourner Truth*, 3–37, 73–76, 121–31, 138–42, 160–63; *FD*, 197–98.

4. *Liverpool Mercury*, March 22, 1865.

5. *West Eau Claire Argus*, December 14, 1865; *Liverpool Mercury*, March 22, 1865; *NR*, September 22, 1865; Wilmington (NC) *Daily Journal*, December 23, 1866; *Narrative of Sojourner Truth*, 130.

6. Fred Tomkins, *Jewels in Ebony* (London: S. W. Partridge, 1869), 4.

7. Leslie J. Pollard, "Aging and Slavery: A Gerontological Perspective," *Journal of Negro History* 66 (Autumn 1981): 228–34.

8. *Narrative of Sojourner Truth*, 174–75.

9. *Sojourner Truth*, 200; *Narrative of Sojourner Truth*, 174–76; *Negro's Civil War*, 43; Earl Conrad, *Harriet Tubman: Negro Soldier and Abolitionist* (New York: International Publishers, 1942), 41; *NYAA*, August 6, 1864.

10. Boston *Congregationalist*, March 30, 1866.

11. Carleton Mabee, "Sojourner Truth and President Lincoln," *New England Quarterly* 61 (December 1988): 520; *Sojourner Truth*, 200–204.

12. *Liberator*, December 23, 1864; *NYAA*, December 24, 1864; *Narrative of Sojourner Truth*, 176–82; *Sojourner Truth*, 206; Mabee, "Sojourner Truth," 521–27. The later edition of *Narrative* changed "this cause" to "his cause."

13. Conrad, *Harriet Tubman*, 41.

14. *Topeka Tribune*, November 9, 1866; *Narrative of Sojourner Truth*, 181–83, 200; Tomkins, *Jewels in Ebony*, 1; Portland (ME) *Daily Mirror*, December 27, 1864; *Sojourner Truth*, 213–19.

15. Tomkins, *Jewels in Ebony*, 1–2; Wilbur Diary, February 25, 1865.

16. Lucy N. Colman, *Reminiscences* (Buffalo: H. L. Green, 1891), 51–52; Tomkins, *Jewels in Ebony*, 2.

17. *Liverpool Mercury*, March 22, 1865.

18. Tomkins, *Jewels in Ebony*, 2.

19. *Rev. Calvin Fairbank: During Slavery Times: How He 'Fought the Good Fight' to Prepare 'The Way'* (Chicago: R. R. McCabe, 1890), 177–78.

20. Colman, *Reminiscences*, 66–68.

21. *Liberator*, November 25, 1864.

22. *Sojourner Truth*, 206; Mabee, "Sojourner Truth," 520; Henry Chase, "Memorable Meetings: Classic White House Encounters," *American Visions* 10 (February–March 1995): 31; "Color Was a Bar"; Colman, *Reminiscences*, 52.

23. Colman, *Reminiscences*, 67.

24. Erlene Stetson and Linda David, *Glorying in Tribulation: The Life Work of Sojourner Truth* (East Lansing: Michigan State University Press, 1994), 145–46.

25. Margaret Washington, *Sojourner Truth's America* (Urbana: University of Illinois Press, 2009), 315.

26. Wilbur Diary, April 28, 1866.

27. Stetson and David, *Glorying in Tribulation*, 145.

28. *Liberator*, December 23, 1864.

CHAPTER 13

1. *Letter from Washington*, 223; "Color Was a Bar," 11.

2. *Stoddard*, 214–15; Boston *Traveler*, January 14, 1865; *Boston Recorder*, February 24, 1865; Wilbur Diary, January 2, 1865; Cleveland *Plain Dealer*, January 13, 1865; *Daily Milwaukee News*, January 16, 1865; Marc Newman, ed., *Potomac Diary: A Soldier's Account of the Capital in Crisis, 1864–1865* (Charleston, SC: Arcadia, 2000), 48.

3. *Liberator*, January 20, 1865.

4. *AL-AL*, 2:769; Missouri *Republican*, quoted in Cleveland *Plain Dealer*, January 13, 1865; "Receptions," 59.

5. "Color Was a Bar," 11; "Receptions," 63.

INTERLUDE 5

1. *LATN*, 223.

2. Joel Schor, *Henry Highland Garnet: A Voice of Black Radicalism in the Nineteenth Century* (Westport, CT: Greenwood Press, 1977), 205–9; *NYAA*, February 25, 1865.

3. *Letter from Washington*, 232–34.

CHAPTER 14

1. Frank A. Rollin, *Life and Public Services of Martin R. Delany* (Boston: Lee & Shepard, 1886); Robert S. Levine, ed., *Martin R. Delany: A Documentary Reader* (Chapel Hill: University of North Carolina Press, 2003), 1–2, 377–84.

2. Charles V. Dyer to Lincoln, April 26, 1863, and Peter Page to Lincoln, May 1, 1863, Lincoln Papers; Ripley, *Black Abolitionist Papers*, 5:261–62; Robert Ewell Greene, *Swamp Angels: A Biographical Study of the 54th Massachusetts Regiment* (Madison, FL: BoMark/Greene Publishing Group, 1990), 80–82.

3. *ES*, February 20, 21, 22, 1865.

4. Victor Ullman, *Martin R. Delany: The Beginnings of Black Nationalism* (Boston: Beacon, 1971), 302; *LATN*, 160.

5. Rollin, *Life of Delany*, 162–71. Lincoln's note to Stanton is dated February 8, 1865, in Rollin's *Life of Delany*, but that date cannot be correct, as, by Delany's own account, the men did not meet until February 9. The original letter was possibly destroyed on the night of April 14, 1865, when an arsonist burned Wilberforce University. Delany was keeping his "valuables" at the college, including his correspondence "with distinguished Americans." See Rollin, *Life of Delany*, 309. However, there is no doubt that Delany met with Lincoln. A brief contemporary account of the meeting is in the *NYAA*, March 11, 1865. In this account, Lincoln tells Delany "Your views seem to me very feasible." When this book went to press, a copy of Lincoln's note appeared for sale on the website of the 19th Century Rare Book and Photograph Shop. It is dated February 21.

CHAPTER 15

1. WPA interviews of "Parson" Williams, September 27, 1937, and Dennis Simms, September 28, 1937; *Letter from Washington*, 242–44; White, *Lincoln's Greatest Speech*, 32, 182; "Iowa Woman in Washington, DC," 90.

2. *CWL*, 8:332–33; Lucas Morel, "Of Justice and Mercy in Abraham Lincoln's Second Inaugural Address," *American Political Thought* 4 (Summer 2015): 455–66.

3. White, *Lincoln's Greatest Speech*, 32, 182.

4. *Life and Times*, 443–45; *FD*, 457.

5. *Behind the Scenes*, 156–57.

6. *Life and Times*, 443–45; *FD*, 457–60; *Behind the Scenes*, 158–59; Wilbur Diary, March 5, 1865; *LATN*, 235; "Receptions," 49–50.

7. *Behind the Scenes*, 158–61.

8. "Color Was a Bar," 1–2, 14–18.

9. *Life and Times*, 437.

10. *Life and Times*, 436.

11. *Douglass Speeches*, 622.

CHAPTER 16

1. *Letter from Washington*, 239, 253; *FD*, 418; Masur, *Example for All the Land*, chap. 1; *Behind the Scenes*, 111–16.

2. *They Knew Lincoln*, 124–25.

3. *CWL*, 6:380; Paul N. Herbert, *God Knows All Your Names: Stories in American History* (Bloomington, IN: AuthorHouse, 2009), 233.

4. *They Knew Lincoln*, 77–78.

5. *LATN*, 204.

6. *AL-AL*, 2:24, 252, 278, 570, 578–79, 691, 825; *Lincoln's White House*, 10, 29–30, 189–91; *Recollected Words*, 13; *Chicago Tribune*, January 19, 1864; Eric Foner, *The Fiery Trial: Abraham Lincoln and American Slavery* (New York: W.W. Norton, 2010), 258; *They Knew Lincoln*, 127–34.

7. *CWL*, 8:354; *They Knew Lincoln*, 135–41.

8. David J. Gerleman, "A Good Boy Generally," *Lincoln Editor* 9 (July–September 2009): 4–5.

9. It should be noted that there are some instances in which Lincoln used the term "boy" to refer to adult white males. See, for example, *AL-AL*, 1:346, 2:425, 797.

10. George Harrington to R. B. Coleman, November 16, 1864, Solomon James Johnson Papers, Moreland-Spingarn Research Center, Howard University, Washington, DC; *They Knew Lincoln*, 132.

11. For an argument that this headstone may not belong to Lincoln's servant, see Phillip W. Magness and Sebastian Page, "Mr. Lincoln and Mr. Johnson," *NYT* (February 1, 2012).

12. *They Knew Lincoln*, 105–17; Sweet, "Representative 'of Our People,'" 21–41.

13. Anna L. Boyden, *Echoes from Hospital and White House: A Record from Mrs. Rebecca R. Pomroy's Experience in War-Times* (Boston: D. Lothrop, 1884), 96–97; *LATN*, 199.

14. Noah Brooks, *Washington in Lincoln's Time* (New York: Century, 1895), 56.

15. Rachel G. C. Patten to Simeon S. Jocelyn, January 21, 1863, AMA Collection.

16. *They Knew Lincoln*, 81–88.

17. *Stoddard*, 89–90.

18. *CWL*, 2:405.

19. *Letter from Washington*, 253.

20. Esther May Carter, *She Knew Lincoln* (Cuyahoga Falls, OH: privately printed, 1930), 5–18. This story appeared in newspapers as early as 1901. See "Reminiscences about Abraham Lincoln, Bu-By" file, Lincoln Financial Foundation Collection, Fort Wayne, Indiana.

INTERLUDE 6

1. J. J. Hill, *A Sketch of the 29th Regiment of Connecticut Colored Troops* (Baltimore: Daugherty, Maguire, & Co., 1867), 26–27; R. J. M. Blackett, ed., *Thomas Morris Chester, Black Civil War Correspondent: His Dispatches from the Virginia Front* (Baton Rouge: Louisiana State University Press, 1989), 294–97; *AL-AL*, 2:789–90.

2. *Liberator*, June 9, 1865.

3. *AL-AL*, 2:789–92; Margaret Washington Creel, *"A Peculiar People": Slave Religion and Community-Culture Among the Gullahs* (New York: New York University Press, 1988), 261–62; Redkey, *Grand Army of Black Men*, 177; Hill, *Sketch of the 29th Regiment of Connecticut*, 27; *Liberator*, June 9, 1865.

4. Alexander H. Newton, *Out of the Briars: An Autobiography and Sketch of the Twenty-Ninth Regiment Connecticut Volunteers* (Philadelphia: A.M.E. Book Concern, 1910), 66–67; *AL-AL*, 2:788–95.

5. Blackett, *Thomas Morris Chester*, 297; *AL-AL*, 2:796; *Behind the Scenes*, 167–69.

6. Gerald Schwartz, ed., *A Woman Doctor's Civil War: Esther Hill Hawk's Diary* (Columbia: University of South Carolina Press, 1984), 132.

CHAPTER 17

1. *CWL*, 8:403.

2. *Behind the Scenes*, 176–78.

3. *CWL*, 8:403; George Alfred Townsend, *Katy of Catoctin, or, The Chain-Breakers: A National Romance* (New York: D. Appleton, 1886), 490; Terry Alford, "What Did Booth Say at Lincoln's April 11, 1865, Speech?" *For the People: Newsletter of the Abraham Lincoln Association* 21 (Spring 2019): 4.

4. Benjamin F. Morris, ed., *Memorial Record of the Nation's Tribute to Abraham Lincoln* (Washington, DC: W. H. & O. H. Morrison, 1865), 117.

5. Newton, *Out of the Briars*, 67–68.

6. *Welles Diary*, 628–32.

7. Larsen, *Crusader and Feminist*, 287–88.

8. Anderson R. Abbott, "Some Recollections of Lincoln's Assassination," *Anglo-American Magazine* 5 (May 1901): 401; Wilbur Diary, April 16, 17, 1865; *Letter from Washington*, 256; Larsen, *Crusader and Feminist*, 287–88.

9. Chauncey Leonard to Lorenzo Thomas, April 30, 1865, NARA microfilm M619, reel 374; Wilbur Diary, April 16, 1865.

10. Margaret Washington, *Sojourner Truth's America* (Urbana: University of Illinois Press, 2009), 322.

11. *LATN*, 241, 248.

12. *Letter from Washington*, 259.

13. William T. Coggeshall, *Lincoln Memorial: The Journeys of Abraham Lincoln: From Springfield to Washington, 1861, as President Elect; and from Washington to Springfield, 1865, as President Martyred* (Columbus: Ohio State Journal, 1865), 110–11.

14. "George W. Julian's Journal—The Assassination of Lincoln," *Indiana Magazine of History* 11 (December 1915): 337.

15. Wilbur Diary, April 18, 1865.

16. Amherst (NH) *Farmer's Cabinet*, May 4, 1865.

17. Abbott, "Some Recollections," 401; Blassingame, *Slave Testimony*, 466.

18. Wilbur Diary, April 20, 1865.

19. *LATN*, foreword.

20. Smith, *Lincoln and the US Colored Troops*, 97–98; Levi S. Graybill, diary entry for April 18, 1865, Levi S. Graybill Papers, HL.

21. *LATN*, 242.

22. *AL-AL*, 2:820; *Welles Diary*, 632.

23. Robert M. Reed, *Lincoln's Funeral Train: The Epic Journey from Washington to Springfield* (Atglen, PA: Schiffer, 2014), 31.

24. Drew Gilpin Faust, *This Republic of Suffering: Death and the American Civil War* (New York: Knopf, 2006), 157; *AL-AL*, 2:823–24; *LATN*, 243; Emilie Davis Diaries, entries for April 22–24, 1865, Historical Society of Pennsylvania, Philadelphia, PA; *NYAA*, May 6, 1865.

25. *Man and Martyr*, 36; *AL-AL*, 2:824; Holzer, *President Lincoln Assassinated*, 310; Martha Hodes, *Mourning Lincoln* (New Haven, CT: Yale University Press, 2015), 164; Allen C. Guelzo, "How Abe Lincoln Lost the Black Vote: Lincoln and Emancipation in the African American Mind," *Journal of the Abraham Lincoln Association* 25 (Winter 2004): 5, 11.

26. Coggeshall, *Lincoln Memorial*, 222, 264–65; Jackson, "Story of Mattie J. Jackson," 265–66.

27. *AL-AL*, 2:825; *LATN*, 244.

28. Court-Martial Case File OO-934, RG 153.

29. Hodes, *Mourning Lincoln*, 99, 112, 140, 244.

30. Guelzo, "How Abe Lost," 5; *New Orleans Tribune*, May 7, 1865; *AL-AL*, 2:820.

31. Smith, *Lincoln and the US Colored Troops*, 99.

32. David Hackett Fischer, *Liberty and Freedom: A Visual History of America's Founding Ideas* (New York: Oxford University Press, 2005), 327; Schwartz, *Woman Doctor's Civil War*, 133–34, 139; James Robert Hester, ed., *A Yankee Scholar in Coastal South Carolina: William Francis Allen's Civil War Journals* (Columbia: University of South Carolina Press, 2015), 189.

33. *LATN*, 245.

34. Aptheker, *Documentary History of the Negro People*, 538.

35. Redkey, *Grand Army of Black Men*, 278–79.

EPILOGUE

1. Holzer, *Lincoln Assassinated*, 309–12, 323–24.

2. Philadelphia *Press*, August 10, 1868.

3. *Philadelphia Inquirer*, September 8, 1866.

4. Holzer, *Emancipating Lincoln*, 154; *They Knew Lincoln*, 149.

5. Thomas Eakins, *The Dancing Lesson* (1878), The Metropolitan Museum of Art, New York City.

6. R. Swinburne Clymer, *The Rose Cross Order* (Allentown, PA: Philosophical Publishing Co., 1916), 52.

7. Jonathan W. White, ed., *A Philadelphia Perspective: The Civil War Diary of Sidney George Fisher* (New York: Fordham University Press, 2007), 261.

8. James T. Stratton to Isaac Goodnow, July 4, 1865, HL.

9. *New-York Tribune*, June 17, 1865; *Celebration by the Colored People's Educational Monument Association in Memory of Abraham Lincoln on the Fourth of July, 1865, in the Presidential Grounds, Washington, DC* (Washington, DC: McGill & Witherow, 1865); *Letter from Washington*, 275–76.

10. Amherst (NH) *Farmer's Cabinet*, May 4, 1865.

11. *NYAA*, May 6, 1865; Wilbur diary, October 10, 1865.

12. *National Anti-Slavery Standard*, April 29, 1865; Jordan, *Negro Baptist History*, 63–65; *Report of the Twenty-Fifth Anniversary of the American Baptist Missionary Convention*, 15–16, 23–24.

13. "Reception," 51–52.

14. Oakes, *Radical and the Republican*, 247–55, 265; Paul H. Bergeron, ed., *The Papers of Andrew Johnson, Volume 10: February–July, 1866* (Knoxville: University of Tennessee Press, 1992), 41–48; John W. Blassingame and John R. McKivigan, eds., *The Frederick Douglass Papers, Series 1: Speeches, Debates, and Interviews, Volume 4: 1864–1880* (New Haven, CT: Yale University Press, 1991), 111; *Sojourner Truth*, 208; *CR*, February 17, 1866.

15. *Springfield* (MA) *Republican*, July 24, 1866; Boston *Congregationalist*, July 27, 1866.

16. Ronald C. White, *American Ulysses: A Life of Ulysses S. Grant* (New York: Random House, 2016), 537; John Y. Simon, ed., *The Personal Memoirs of Julia Dent Grant (Mrs. Ulysses S. Grant): 45th Anniversary Edition* (Carbondale: Southern Illinois University Press, 2020), 175; Seale, *President's House*, 1:455–56.

17. *CR*, February 3, 1881.

18. Knoxville *Sentinel*, October 21, 1901; *Baltimore Sun*, October 20, 1901; Raleigh *Morning Post*, October 20, 1901; New Orleans *Times-Picayune*, October 19, 1901; *Trenton Evening Times*, October 19, 1901; Cleveland *Plain Dealer*, October 20, 1901; *Topeka Daily Herald*, October 23, 1901.

19. Springfield *Daily Illinois State Journal*, October 16, 1874.

20. Ronald E. Butchart, *Schooling the Freed People: Teaching, Learning, and the Struggle for Black Freedom, 1861–1876* (Chapel Hill: University of North Carolina Press, 2010), 27; Smith, *Lincoln and the US Colored Troops*, 100; Heather Andrea Williams, *Self-Taught: African American Education in Slavery and Freedom* (University of North Carolina Press, 2007), 72; *P. B. Randolph the "Learned Pundit" and "Man with Two Souls": His Curious Life, Works, and Career, the Great Free-Love Trial, Randolph's Grand Defence, His Address to the Jury, and Mankind, the Verdict* (Boston: Randolph, 1872), 15–19; Hodes, *Mourning Lincoln*, 261–62; John McKee Barr, *Loathing Lincoln: An American Tradition from the Civil War to the Present* (Baton Rouge: Louisiana State University Press, 2014), 97; Joseph S. Caulk to Andrew Johnson and Edwin M. Stanton, January 31, 1866, NARA microfilm M494 (Letters Received by the Secretary of War From the President, Executive Departments, and War Department Bureaus, 1862–1870), reel 84. (I thank Sean Scott for making me aware of the Caulk letter.)

21. Redkey, *Grand Army of Black Men*, 222; San Francisco *Elevator*, July 28, 1865; Louis A. Warren, "A Negro Artist's Oil Painting of Lincoln," *Lincoln Lore* 1297 (February 15, 1954).

22. Kirk Savage, *Standing Soldiers, Kneeling Slaves: Race, War, and Monument in Nineteenth-Century America* (Princeton: Princeton University Press, 1997), 89–92, 233; F. Lauriston Bullard, *Lincoln in Marble and Bronze* (New Brunswick, NJ: Rutgers University Press, 1952), 64–72; Louis A. Warren, "A Negro Artist's Oil Painting of Lincoln," *Lincoln Lore* 1297 (February 15, 1954).

23. *ES*, February 19, 1876; *LATN*, 7–8; Hollis Robbins and Henry Louis Gates Jr., eds., *The Portable Nineteenth-Century African American Women Writers* (New York: Penguin, 2017), 349–52; Alexandria, VA, *People's Advocate*, June 10, 1876 (thanks to Matthew Bowdish for making me aware of this source).

24. *Douglass Speeches*, 615–24.

25. Chris Myers Asch and George Derek Musgrove, "A Monument to Black Resistance and Strength: Considering Washington, DC's Emancipation Memorial," historians.org (August 5, 2020); *Washington Bee*, May 16, 1891.

26. Washington *Evening Star*, January 26, 1891.

27. *Cleveland Gazette*, October 7, 1893.

28. *Washington Bee*, January 23, 1892, February 14, 1914.

29. Henry Burke, "The Mason-Dixon Line, Part XVII: A Friend of Lincoln's," http://henryrburke.blogspot.com/ (posted May 26, 2011; accessed January 15, 2021).

APPENDIX

1. For de Fleurville's letter to Lincoln, see *My Friend*, xv–xix.

2. "Life of Henry McNeil [*sic*] Turner" (p. 12), Henry McNeal Turner Papers, Moorland-Spingarn Research Center, Howard University.

3. *Men of Mark*, 763; Pinchback to Nathaniel P. Banks, September 10, 1863, Pinchback CMSR; Pinchback Pension; James Haskins, *Pinckney Benton Stewart Pinchback* (New York: Macmillan, 1973), 1–33.

4. "Meetings," 45.

SELECTED BIBLIOGRAPHY

Abbreviations for frequently cited sources are in brackets.

PRIMARY SOURCES

Manuscripts

Haverford, PA
    Haverford College, Quaker and Special Collections.
        Julia Wilbur Diary (transcriptions by Alexandria Archaeology) [Wilbur Diary].

Washington, DC
    Library of Congress, Manuscript Division.
        Abraham Lincoln Papers [Lincoln Papers].
        American Colonization Society Papers [ACS Papers].
    National Archives and Records Administration [NARA].
        Compiled Military Service Records, RG 94 (Records of the Office of the Adjutant General), Entry 519 (Records of the Record and Pension Office) [CMSR].
        Records of the Office of the Secretary of the Interior Relating to the Suppression of the African Slave Trade and Negro Colonization, 1854–1872, National Archives microfilm M160.
        Pension Records, RG 15 (Records of the Department of Veterans Affairs) [Pension].

Newspapers

New York *Anglo-African* [*NYAA*].
New York Times [*NYT*].
Philadelphia *Christian Recorder* [*CR*].
Washington, DC, *Evening Star* [ES].
Washington, DC, *National Republican* [*NR*].

Published Primary Sources

Basler, Roy P., ed. *The Collected Works of Abraham Lincoln: Supplement, 1832–1865.* Westport, CT: Greenwood Press, 1974.

Basler, Roy P. et al., eds. *The Collected Works of Abraham Lincoln.* 9 vols. New Brunswick, NJ: Rutgers University Press, 1953–1955 [*CWL*].

Beale, Howard K., ed. *The Diary of Edward Bates, 1859-1866.* Washington, DC: Government Printing Office, 1933.

Burlingame, Michael, ed. *Inside the White House in War Times: Memoirs and Reports of Lincoln's Secretary, William O. Stoddard.* Lincoln: University of Nebraska Press, 2000 [*Stoddard*].

Burlingame, Michael, and Ettlinger, John R. Turner., eds. *Inside Lincoln's White House: The Complete Civil War Diary of John Hay.* Carbondale: Southern Illinois University Press, 1997 [*Hay Diary*].

Carpenter, Francis B. *Six Months at the White House with Abraham Lincoln.* New York: Hurd and Houghton, 1866.

Cole, Jean Lee, ed. *Freedom's Witness: The Civil War Correspondence of Henry McNeal Turner.* Morgantown: West Virginia University Press, 2013.

Douglass, Frederick. *The Life and Times of Frederick Douglass, from 1817 to 1882, Written by Himself.* London: Christian Age, 1882 [*Life and Times*].

Fehrenbacher, Don E., and Virginia Fehrenbacher, eds. *Recollected Words of Abraham Lincoln.* Stanford: Stanford University Press, 1996.

Foner, Philip S., and Yuval Taylor, eds. *Frederick Douglass: Selected Speeches and Writings.* Chicago: Lawrence Hill Books, 1999 [*Douglass Speeches*].

Gienapp William E., and Erica L. Gienapp, eds. *The Civil War Diary of Gideon Welles, Lincoln's Secretary of the Navy: The Original Manuscript Edition.* Urbana: University of Illinois Press, 2014 [*Welles Diary*].

Graf, Leroy P., et al., eds. *The Papers of Andrew Johnson*, 16 vols. Knoxville: University of Tennessee Press, 1967–2000.

Holzer, Harold, ed. *President Lincoln Assassinated!!: The Firsthand Story of the Murder, Manhunt, Trial, and Mourning.* New York: Library of America, 2015.

Keckley, Elizabeth. *Behind the Scenes: Thirty Years a Slave and Four Years in the Lincoln White House.* New York: G. W. Carleton, 1868.

Leasher, Evelyn. ed. *Letter from Washington, 1863–1865.* Detroit: Wayne State University Press, 1999.

McPherson, James M., ed. *The Negro's Civil War: How American Negroes Felt and Acted During the War for the Union.* New York: Pantheon, 1965.

White, Jonathan W., ed., *To Address You as My Friend: African Americans' Letters to Abraham Lincoln.* Chapel Hill: University of North Carolina Press, 2021 [*My Friend*].

Yacovone, Donald, ed. *Freedom's Journey: African American Voices of the Civil War.* Chicago: Lawrence Hill Books, 2004.

SECONDARY SOURCES

Blight, David W. *Frederick Douglass: Prophet of Freedom.* New York: Simon & Schuster, 2018 [*FD*].

Burlingame, Michael. *Abraham Lincoln: A Life.* 2 vols. Baltimore: Johns Hopkins University Press, 2008 [*AL-AL*].

——. "African Americans at White House Receptions during Lincoln's Administration," *Journal of the Abraham Lincoln Association* 41 (Summer 2020): 47–64 ["Receptions"].

——. "President Lincoln's Meetings with African Americans," *Journal of the Abraham Lincoln Association* 41 (Winter 2021): 27–54 ["Meetings"].

Cecelski, David S. *The Fire of Freedom: Abraham Galloway and the Slaves' Civil War.* Chapel Hill: University of North Carolina Press, 2012.

Conroy, James B. *Lincoln's White House: The People's House in Wartime.* Lanham, MD: Rowman & Littlefield, 2016.

Foner, Eric. *The Fiery Trial: Abraham Lincoln and American Slavery.* New York: W. W. Norton, 2010.

Franklin, John Hope. *The Emancipation Proclamation.* New York: Doubleday, 1963.

Guelzo, Allen C. *Lincoln's Emancipation Proclamation: The End of Slavery in America.* New York: Simon & Schuster, 2004.

Holzer, Harold. *Emancipating Lincoln: The Proclamation in Text, Context, and Memory.* Cambridge, MA: Harvard University Press, 2012.

Horton, James Oliver, and Lois E. Horton. *The Man and the Martyr: Abraham Lincoln in African American History and Memory.* Gettysburg, PA: Gettysburg College, 2006.

Masur, Kate. *An Example for All the Land: Emancipation and the Struggle over Equality in Washington, DC.* Chapel Hill: University of North Carolina Press, 2010.

——. "The African American Delegation to Abraham Lincoln: A Reappraisal." *Civil War History* 56 (June 2010): 117–44.

——. "Color Was a Bar to the Entrance: African American Activism and the Question of Social Equality in Lincoln's White House." *American Quarterly* 69 (March 2017): 1–22.

Oakes, James. *The Radical and the Republican: Frederick Douglass, Abraham Lincoln, and the Triumph of Antislavery Politics.* New York: W. W. Norton, 2007.

Quarles, Benjamin. *Lincoln and the Negro.* New York: Oxford University Press, 1962. [*LATN*]

——. *The Negro in the Civil War.* Boston: Little, Brown and Co., 1953.

Rollin, Frank A. *Life and Public Services of Martin R. Delany.* Boston: Lee & Shepard, 1868.

Simmons, William J. *Men of Mark: Eminent, Progressive and Rising.* Cleveland: Geo. M. Rewell, 1887.

Smith, John David. *Lincoln and the US Colored Troops.* Carbondale: Southern Illinois University Press, 2013.

Sweet, Natalie. "A Representative 'of Our People': The Agency of William Slade, Leader in the African American Community and Usher to Abraham Lincoln." *Journal of the Abraham Lincoln Association* 34 (Summer 2013): 21–41.

Painter, Nell Irvin. *Sojourner Truth. A Life, A Symbol.* New York: W. W. Norton, 1996.

Washington, John E. *They Knew Lincoln.* New York: E. P. Dutton, 1942.

ACKNOWLEDGMENTS

M any friends and colleagues have made this book possible. I thank Christopher Newport University's Department of Leadership and American
Studies, Provost David Doughty, and the faculty senate for support of my
research through professional development funds and a Faculty Development
Grant. David Salomon has generously provided me with research assistance
each year through CNU's Summer Scholar program. CNU's Center for American Studies, co-directed by Nathan and Elizabeth Busch, has been an incredible
place to work for the last decade and a staunch supporter of my scholarship.
My Center for American Studies junior fellows, Taylor Bagwell, Hannah
Broughton, Maggie Byers, Daniel Glenn, and Michael Sparks, did fantastic
work digging up sources for me for this and other projects. Chloe Baker, Reagan
Connelly, Kailey Ritchie, and Michael Sparks helped me proofread the page
proofs. I also thank my American Studies students from our senior seminar in
Spring 2019 for helping me think through the ideas in this book. Robert Colby,
Jim Conroy, and Sean Scott all read the manuscript and offered helpful advice,
for which I am grateful. My agent, Mary Evans, who I met through my friend
Ron White, has been an ardent proponent of this project and helped me rethink
the framing of the book. Kate Jenkins suggested the title. DeLisa Harris of Fisk
University showed me the Baltimore Bible, which was an incredible experience.
I thank Jon Sisk, Elaine McGarraugh, and the team at Rowman & Littlefield for
carefully guiding this book to publication. Finally, I thank my family for their
untiring support. My parents, Bill and Eileen White, inspired me to love both
history and teaching. I wouldn't be a college professor today without their love
and guidance. While writing this book I often thought back to when Lauren and

I lived in Washington, DC—the times, before kids, we spent walking the city, near the White House or through Lincoln Park. I cherish every moment with her, Charlotte, and Clara, and appreciate their willingness to stop at historic sites on nearly every trip we take.

INDEX

ABOUT THE AUTHOR

Jonathan W. White is associate professor of American Studies at Christopher Newport University. He is the author of ten books and over one hundred articles, essays, and reviews on Lincoln and the Civil War. His writing has appeared in *Smithsonian*, *Time*, the *New York Times*, and the *Washington Post*. He lives in Newport News, Virginia.